FAMILY AND HUMAN DEVELOPMENT ACROSS CULTURES

A View From the Other Side

FAMILY AND HUMAN DEVELOPMENT ACROSS CULTURES

A View From the Other Side

Çiğdem Kağıtçıbaşı
Koc University

LAWRENCE ERLBAUM ASSOCIATES, PUBLISHERS
1996   Mahwah, New Jersey

Lawrence Erlbaum Associates, Inc., Publishers
10 Industrial Avenue
Mahwah, New Jersey 07430

Library of Congress Cataloging-in-Publication Data

Kâğıtçıbaşı, Çiğdem
    Family and human development across cultures : a view from the other side /
Çiğdem Kâğıtçıbaşı.
        p.   cm.
    Includes bibliographical references and indexes.
    ISBN 0-8058-2076-0 (cloth). — ISBN 0-8058-2077-9 (pbk.)
    1. Socialization—Cross-cultural studies.   2. Family—Psychological aspects—Cross-cultural
studies.   3. Developmental psychology—Cross-cultural studies.   4. Cultural relativism.
    5. Ethnopsychology.   I. Title.
    HQ783.K34   1996
    303.3′2—dc20   95-47534
                                                                                                              CIP

Books published by Lawrence Erlbaum Associates are printed on acid-free paper,
and their bindings are chosen for strength and durability.

Printed in the United States of America
10 9 8 7 6 5 4

To the memory of my mother

Contents

Foreword

M. Brewster Smith
University of California, Santa Cruz

This is an extraordinary book by an author who needs no introduction in the world of international psychology. Çiğdem Kağıtçıbaşı (ğ is silent in Turkish, lengthening the preceding vowel; ç has the value of *ch*, ş of *sh*), who is professor of psychology at Koc University in Istanbul and past president of the Turkish Psychological Association, is also former president of the International Association of Cross-Cultural Psychology and two-term member of the executive committee of the International Union of Scientific Psychology. In 1993 she received the American Psychological Association's award for Distinguished Contributions to the International Advancement of Psychology. This volume represents the culmination of a distinguished career, which I have been privileged to follow with admiration ever since her graduate study at the University of California, Berkeley, some three decades ago. In that sense, as her preface attests, it is a very personal book.

But it is also an exemplary, up-to-the-moment exposition of a view of human and social development "from the other side"—from the perspective of what Kağıtçıbaşı aptly calls the Majority World (no longer sensibly labeled Third World) of countries that do not participate fully in the benefits and problems of the industrial and postindustrial West. Further, it is an authoritative presentation of the cross-cultural perspective, as an essential corrective to the unthinking culture-boundedness of much Euro-American psychology. It is a searching analysis of perspectives on human development that escape the pitfalls of extreme relativism to which advocates of a culturally contextual approach are vulnerable, in terms of criteria of cognitive competence and of developing selfhood in which autonomy and relatedness are in balance. It is an original contribution to the theory of family change, opposing the expectation of modernization theory that families in the developing world will converge on the Western individualistic model. It is a wise and constructive analysis of the role of psychology in inducing social change, focused on problems of the Majority World but just as relevant to the Euro-American context. And it is a critical review of research and theory on early childhood care and education (ECCE) in the United States and in the Majority World; ECCE is the particular mode of intervention, in the family context, with which she has been involved. In each of these widely dispersed topical areas, the breadth and depth of her command of the specialized literature is amazing. Readers who are already well acquainted with some of them (who else will be familiar with them all?) will respect her guidance to the very extensive bibliography in their own areas of competence and welcome it in the areas new to them.

All of the foregoing comes to concrete focus in her account of the Turkish Early Enrichment Project. This Lewin-style action-research, which Kağıtçıbaşı conceived and directed in the shantytowns of Istanbul, is exemplary in a number of respects. It was planned with sensitivity to the Turkish cultural context, but with nonrelativistic standards of cognitive and social competence in child development in mind. The intervention focused on the family, specifically the mother, as the primary context of socialization in the preschool years. The research design permitted appropriately controlled comparisons, with multiple outcome measures. Strikingly positive short-term results were obtained, expecially on cognitive and school-related measures, for the effects of training the mothers and of educational day-care centers. In the almost unprecedented 10-year follow-up, major effects of mother training persisted (including empowering benefits to the mothers themselves), whereas the advantages of day-care center experience dissipated with time. The findings make sense in terms of Kağıtçıbaşı's interpretation that intervention with the mothers reoriented the functioning of the family systems of participants in ways that were self-sustaining. She then draws the book together, making explicit how her project, which has had substantial impact on Turkish programming for early childhood enrichment, suggests useful ways in which psychology in the Majority World can become engaged with national and pan-human objectives of global human development.

I would like to highlight several respects in which Kağıtçıbaşı provides intellectual leadership that is much needed by psychology in the Euro-American and Majority Worlds alike. These are contributions of the book that I enthusiastically applaud.

For one, I am delighted with the way that she has enlarged on the recent critique of the individualism of Euro-American culture. Many voices in psychology and the social sciences, including feminists but not restricted to them, would give higher priority to values of relatedness, as complementing the individualistic values of agency or autonomy. From her Majority World perspective and her command of the large recent literature documenting the prevalence of "collectivist" values outside Euro-American cultural precincts, she challenges modernization theory when it predicts the supplanting of relatedness values in the less developed world by Western individualism. True, economic development with its accompanying urbanization is a strong corrosive for many aspects of traditional cultures. But the example of Japan and other East Asian "success stories" indicates that relatedness values can survive economic development. Addressing her colleagues in the Majority World, she calls for new goals of personal autonomy in a context that preserves the values of relatedness distinctive of non-Western cultures. Her mother-training ECCE project demonstrates that it is possible to apply psychology toward realizing this objective, which she sees as humanly desirable for the Have-Nots as it is for the Haves.

Recently, a polarity has become salient contrasting the cross-cultural psychology of Triandis, Berry, Bond, and others with the cultural psychology of Cole, Rogoff, Shweder, and their associates. The former is charged by its critics with continuing the outmoded positivist tradition, employing imposed "etic" dimensions of comparison drawn inappropriately from individualistic Western culture; the latter is committed to contextual, "emic" treatment of experience and behavior in each culture's own terms, but is vulnerable to sometimes nihilistic relativism. Kağıtçıbaşı comes from the cross-cultural tradition, of which she is an acknowledged leader, but she insists, articulately and persuasively, that cultural and cross-cultural approaches are complementary, not competing; she believes psychology can give proper attention to cultural context without giving up its strategies of comparison or its aims to discover principles that transcend history and culture. (Rogoff, on her part, also does not see the approaches in opposition to one another.)

Her integrative approach comes to a focus in her insistence on the relevance of standards of human development that apply across nations and cultures and across the barrier between Haves and Have-Nots in Euro-American societies. This attempt to combine cultural contextualism with universalistic standards is a complex, difficult intellectual maneuver, not an easy political compromise. I think it is the right choice. It has become politically incorrect to regard school-related cognitive competences as more "developed" than the less abstractive competencies of children in premodern rural societies or streetwise culture; the presently indispensable value of formal schooling is even disparaged. Kağıt-çıbaşı reminds us that in the Majority World, universal schooling and literacy is a consensual/objective engraved in the Universal Declaration of Human Rights and the Convention on Rights of the Child but only very partially attained, expecially for girls and women. "Middle-class" cognitive competencies are very much needed to cope with the complexities of the contemporary world, whether on the part of disadvantaged minorities in the United States or the hordes of rural immigrants to the exploding cities of the Majority World. As she observes, it is only a step from the extreme relativism of some postmodern admirers of traditional culture to implicit advocacy of a double standard: first-class preschools and elementary schools for *our* children to prepare them for *our* world, but, for instance, rote learning in Koranic schools (or *no* schools, for girls) as preserving the valued culture of Those Others. The ethical/political issues are difficult, but Kağıtçıbaşı's position is courageous and clear.

Those who disagree in principle with her stance that calls for contextualism without complete relativism will not only have to contend with her argument; they will also have to come to terms with the implications of her intervention research on early childhood enrichment and mother empowerment. I have recently been involved in the armchair defense of scientific empiricism in psychology from postmodernist assault, trying to sustain the human effort to approach truth and goodness in formulations that transcend the particular historicocultural contexts from which they are derived. I am impressed that Kağıtçıbaşı's demonstration of the effectiveness of her mother-training intervention in a Majority World setting is a much stronger answer to the extreme cultural relativists than any philosophical metatheoretical argument. The concrete example is persuasive: relevant culturally contextual scientific research *can* be done and it is useful and influential on public policy. Articulate elites in the developing countries will want to support interventions such as she exemplified; so will the participants themselves as they encounter such programs. This is the way to go!

This volume will immediately become obligatory reading and a valuable resource to the band of cultural and cross-cultural psychologists, still too few, who are committed to reshaping mainstream Euro-American psychology so as to make it more truly universal, less unwittingly culturebound. It should have equal immediate interest to psychologists in the Majority World and Euro-American psychologists who want to collaborate with them in challenging enterprise of applying psychology to the problems of societal development. But the appropriate audience for this book as textbook and resource is much broader. Kağıtçıbaşı's view of family and human development "from the other side" is very relevant to the concerns of mainstream psychologists on "this" side of the great divide between Have and Have-Not societies. We Euro-Americans have parallel problems in relating to internal Have-Not minorities. In our current well-motivated wave of political correctness, we may be bemused by similar qualms of relativism concerning the relevance of "middle-class" cognitive standards to children and adults who have been systematically excluded from middle-class opportunities and benefits. The wave of support for early intervention projects peaked with President Johnson's Great Society programs, and these projects mostly neglected the family context of early child development. Perhaps Kağıtçıbaşı's hope-inspiring example from Istanbul may stimulate blasé American psychologists to take heart, and once more seriously address the problem of bringing excluded minorities into full citizenship. Certainly, she has given professors and students of developmental psychology and of family relations much to ponder.

Preface

A PERSONAL ACCOUNT

Interpersonal Relations

A few years ago I was invited to participate in a symposium at an international congress of cross-cultural psychology. I was asked to present a personal account of how I became a cross-cultural psychologist, mainly in terms of how I came to be involved in cross-cultural research. That task helped me look back and delve into the background of my present academic interests. It was a process of reconstruction. As I tried to pinpoint the beginning of my academic interest in cross-cultural or cultural psychology, I found myself going back further and further. So, an attempted academic reconstruction turned into an autobiographical reconstruction. Obviously, everyone's work must reflect personal experience, though this is rarely made explicit. I would like to start this book by making this personal experience explicit. This is because I believe this exercise might help put what I have to say into some perspective—an international perspective at that.

I was a graduate student in the social psychology program at the University of California, Berkeley during the 1960s. I was well versed in the social psychological literature of the 1950s and 1960s. But, what intrigued me more than the highly popular cognitive dissonance theory and the lure of the experimental laboratory was the social, political, and psychological implications of the then-no-longer-in-vogue authoritarian personality theory (Adorno, Frenkel-Brunswick, Levinson, & Sanford; 1950). This was despite the influential methodological critique of Christie and Jahoda (1954). So, against my supervisor and mentor M. Brewster Smith's good advice, I undertook a cross-cultural comparative study, instead of a clean laboratory experiment, for my doctoral research to test the cross-cultural generality of the authoritarian personality theory. Although I called myself a social psychologist, I was in fact a cross-cultural psychologist at heart at a time when nobody I knew was doing "cross-cultural psychology."

Yet, this was only a "natural" development given the fact that I was a foreign student in the United States and was using, almost automatically, a cultural filter in my reading. Thus, my study emerged out of the realization when I read the *Authoritarian Personality* (Adorno et al., 1950) that some of the characteristics of the so-called authoritarian *personality* were in fact *social norms* in Turkey. The following is the opening paragraph of the resultant publication, which describes the general view underlying the study.

> Some findings of social psychology may refer to general panhuman relationships, others to relationships that hold only within specific sociocultural settings. Only systematic cross-cultural comparison can separate these or identify the limits within which particular generalizations hold. An example of findings that seem likely to be culturally specific are those in support of a general syndrome of "authoritarianism." In cultures in which social norms bear differentially on the components of this syndrome, one should expect different patterns of relationship to obtain. Such contrasts were anticipated between the United States and Turkey. This study examines the assumed inherent dynamic organization of personality attributes and attitudinal variables underlying "authoritarianism" in the light of a cross-cultural comparison. (Kağıtçıbaşı, 1970, p. 444).

I maintain the above view in a general sense some 25 years later. I believe it forms a raison d'etre of cross-cultural psychology, which sheds important light on human behavior.

This early realization of cross-cultural variability in some "basic" personality characteristics, assumed to be universal, had something to do with my own early experiences in culture contact, in addition to being a foreign student at Berkeley. When they occurred, they were simple events; only much later have I been able to put them into perspective, attributing to them a culturally situated meaning. I want to relate some of these experiences, going further back in time.

As a teenager I was a boarding student at an American school for girls in Istanbul, Turkey. There was much physical contact among girls (kissing on both cheeks, embracing, walking arm in arm in the corridors, in the garden, courtyard, etc.) as a natural part of interpersonal affection and warm peer relations.[1] We used to get a kick out of the shocked glances of the new American teachers (mostly young women) before they got acculturated to "the ways of the natives."

---

[1]There is still much more physical contact among same-sex friends and kin in "contact" cultures such as Turkey than in "noncontact" Western cultures. However, the absolute amount of physical contact is probably less today than before, especially among the educated middle-class groups in those societies due to "cultural diffusion," especially through the media, of the Western models.

Some mischievous girls used to overdo the show of affection for its shock value in the presence of these teachers.

After I graduated from the American school in Istanbul and was accepted at Wellesley College (in Massachusetts, USA), an important part of my self-induced preparation/orientation to life in the United States was to restrain myself from showing physical affection.

During my last years at the American school in Istanbul I studied British and American literature and 20th-century philosophy, which focused on phenomenology and existentialism. Apart from scholarly work by Kierkegaard, Jaspers, Husserl, Heidegger, and Sartre, I also read some plays by Sartre. These were my earliest scholarly contacts with the pervasive individualistic perspective in Western philosophy and literary tradition. The closing words of Sartre's *No Exit*, "Hell is other people" were stamped in my memory. This statement intrigued me in its utmost strangeness. Today I see it as a reflection of extreme individualism.

My first impression of "suburban America" (Newton Center, Massachusetts), where I stayed with an American family, was beautiful homes, spacious gardens with lovely trees and flowers, clean streets, and no people. I often wondered where the people were. Not once did I meet any neighbors or see my host family visiting them.

I had a close friend at Wellesley, whom I visited and stayed with at her family's home during some short vacations. One day when she was very sad, I asked her what was wrong. She said, "It is a personal matter." I was shattered. This was clearly a rejection for me; obviously she did not consider me very close if she could not confide in me. In my understanding there could not be anything that I would withhold from my best friend; I would at least let her know the nature of the problem even if I did not reveal the details. What for her was a simple assertion of her privacy was for me a declaration of rejection. The memory is still vivid after more than 30 years.

These everyday events and experiences have all had to do with what I consider today a basic aspect of interpersonal relations showing cross-cultural variation, that is, interpersonal connectedness (relatedness) or separateness. From another perspective, they have to do with the self, again in terms of its level of individuation (separateness, boundedness) or connectedness with others. Obviously, there were many other experiences involving misunderstanding or readjustment during my student years in the United States, and there have been others since then in my international contacts. However, I find it important that most of the episodes I remember, like those I have mentioned, have to do with the connectedness-separateness dimension of interpersonal relations.

Some episodes may be eye opening even if one is no longer a "naive student." Consider a conversation I had a few years ago with a well-known North American cross-cultural psychologist friend and his wife. When I asked after their son, who was about 21 years old at the time, my friend said he was staying with them in their home, but they were not charging him rent. I couldn't believe what I heard and wondered if he was joking; he was not.[2]

Yet another episode occured while I was on a sabbatical leave at Harvard University and Radcliffe College (Bunting Institute) some ten years ago. I became acquainted with a renowned anthropologist, several years my senior. One day when we were getting into the back seat of a car I attempted to help her in first. My behavior offended her; she said she was not old enough to need help getting into a car. My behavior was a reflection of my respect and appreciation for her age and accomplishments. She took it as an insult to her independence and autonomy. The interesting point here is that I, the cross-cultural psychologist, let my old country values take precedence over my knowledge of American values, and she, the highly experienced anthropologist, did not recognize that.

Experiences like these remind one of the cross-cultural diversity in the interpersonal relations sphere that goes deep into cultural meaning systems and conventions. This diversity exists side by side with a remarkable commonality, deriving from our common biologically based human nature and our immense intercultural-international communication systems, including similar educational experiences, working as strong converging and unifying forces. If even among educated people, culturally sensitive and internationally minded social scientists at that, there could be such differences in understanding, there would naturally be greater differences among common people immersed in their own cultures.

The aforementioned experiential examples demonstrate how living in another cultural context or acculturation through early exposure to another culture sensitizes one to *culture*, as such. It is very much like "the fish in water"; you "see" culture when you get out of it. What is probably even more important, however, is that once you become conscious of it, you cannot ignore it. This is probably the summary of my first involvement with cultural and cross-cultural psychology. It has important implications for the kind of psychology I practice and that I think should be pursued.

Of particular significance to me is to understand the underlying dimensions of interpersonal relations, their variation across cultures, and their antecedents. The interpersonal connectedness-separateness dimension, as reflected in the previous personal episodes, signals a clue to an understanding of the self and its development in context. This context is the family and, moving out from it, the sociocultural environment. The observed variations in self-construals and self–other relations appear to be deeply rooted in the cross-cultural diversities in contexts (Kağıtçıbaşı, 1990; Markus & Kitayama, 1991). How and why these variations come about is, for me, the key question to understanding an important aspect of human reality.

---

[2]Another North American colleague interpreted this episode to mean that I was surprised my friend *was not* charging rent to his son! In case other Western readers also misinterpret what I have written, let me explain: I was surprised that it would even occur to my friend to charge rent to his own son.

Social Relevance

Another thread of influence running through both my personal life and professional career is a deep concern for and a commitment to social well-being. The roots of this commitment go back to my early socialization in family and school, which for me coincided. Both my parents were teachers with a mission to contribute to the education and development of a modern secular society out of the ashes of an old one based on tradition and religion.[3] They started their own private school with very limited funds. At age 2 I found myself in school and I have been there all my life. I was brought up with the ideal of "doing something worthwhile for society," an idea nourished especially by my mother.

In retrospect, such ideals were taken seriously by many young people of my generation, especially among the children of the educated teachers and civil servants who carried considerable responsibility for "building a modern nation." Indeed, early studies conducted in the post-World War II period among youth in developing countries point to much higher "patriotism" and reveal a great value for "doing something good for one's family and country," as compared with American youth. For example, Gillespie and Allport (1955) talked about the strong national loyalties of youth in newly emergent nations in the process of nation building.

The historical context of nation building probably did make the loyalty felt to the nation more salient in young persons' values. However, as evidenced by a great deal of subsequent research and current work, this is not the whole story. For example, in my 1966 comparative study of Turkish and American adolescents, I found the same high level of national loyalty among the Turkish sample, for whom nation building was not relevant. In contrast, American adolescents valued personal achievement and happiness (Kağıtçıbaşı, 1970). Furthermore, in a later study with Turkish adolescents (Kağıtçıbaşı, 1973), I found patriotism (loyalty to the country) to fit into a "modern" outlook and to be associated with belief in internal control of reinforcement, optimism, and achievement motivation. It was negatively associated with a more traditional outlook, characterized by religiosity, authoritarianism, and belief in external control of reinforcement.

Even when achievement motivation is studied, which is often assumed to focus on the self, the same loyalty to society can be seen. Thus Phalet and Claeys (1993) found Turkish adolescents (both in Turkey and in Belgium) to combine individual and group loyalties (Kağıtçıbaşı, 1987b) into a "social achievement motivation," contrasted with the individualistic achievement motivation of the Belgian youth. Similar findings of socially oriented achievement motivation have been reported for the Japanese (DeVos, 1968), the Indians (Agarwal & Misra,

---

[3]The republican secularist reforms were in full swing. They had been started by Atatürk and the founders of the Turkish Republic after the war for independence was won in early 1920s, following the collapse of the Ottoman Empire after World War I. The ties with the six centuries of Ottoman past were severed and by 1940s the reforms were consolidated.

1986; Misra & Agarwal, 1985), and the Chinese (Bond, 1986, p. 36; K-S. Yang, 1986, pp. 113,114).

The previous examples point to the continuing pervasiveness of the loyalty and commitment to entities transcending the self in the so-called collectivistic cultures. In the individualistic culture, however, it has been claimed that "the primary loyalty is to the self—its values, autonomy, pleasure, virtue and actualization" (Kagan, 1984). I do not mean to infer here value judgments about what is good and what is bad, but rather to point to differences in emphasis in focusing on the self or on the larger collectivity in which the self is embedded. As becomes apparent in the following chapters, this is one of the central themes in the book.

There has been some recent questioning of the vulnerability of "lives organized around self-actualization and the pursuit of gratification" and a recognition of the fact that "human lives seem most meaningful and satisfying when they are devoted to projects and guided by values that transcend the self" (M. B. Smith, 1994, p.407). Other critics have also expressed their concerns with too much individualism, especially in the United States (e.g., Bellah, Madsen, Sullivan, Swidler, & Tipton, 1985; Cushman, 1990; Lasch, 1979, 1984; Sampson, 1987; Schwartz, 1986; Taylor, 1989). There have been pleas for a greater commitment to society (Etzioni, 1993; Sarason, 1981, 1988; M. A. Wallach & L. Wallach, 1983, 1990).

To some extent these recent developments have had an effect in making my own commitments more salient for me, which I have expressed here. The difference between the individualistic and the collectivistic concerns appears to be continuing. It is understandable, therefore, that much of Western academic psychology is still somewhat oblivious of societal problems,[4] but in contrast there is a loud cry from the collectivistic Majority World[5] for a more socially relevant psychology that assumes responsibility for societal development (e.g., Kağıtçıbaşı, 1991d, 1994b; Nsamenang, 1992; D. Sinha, 1983; D. Sinha & Kao, 1988). Some Western cross-cultural psychologists have also joined in, as in an early call by Jahoda (1975).

The stress on the social relevance and applied significance of psychology is a key to my general orientation to it. This orientation is deep seated in both my personal and academic background and cultural context. Thus I see psychological inquiry not only as an important tool in understanding behavior but also in changing it, at a macrolevel, to improve the human condition. This may be seen

---

[4]There are some signs that this may be changing. See note 23 below.

[5]I am using the "Majority World," instead of "Developing Countries" or the "Third World." The developing countries are not getting any closer to the developed countries (if anything, the gap is widening), and with the collapse of the "Second World," the "Third" does not make much sense. Majority World, referring in fact to the majority of the world's population, emerges as a preferable term.

as an overly ambitious or presumptuous view of the field, if not also a naive one. Even though I am well aware of some truth in such an objection, as well as of the multiple causation of human phenomena, including to a large extent non-psychological causes, I am, nevertheless, of the opinion that psychology does have the potential to contribute to the improvement of the human condition.

My work during the last 15 years has involved research along two different but related paths. One of these has been theoretical in orientation, whereas the other has been more problem oriented with an applied emphasis. These seemingly disparate research interests have been quite integrated in my own thinking, and I hope to reflect this integration in this book.

Thus, on the one hand, I study self–family–culture interfaces and their modifications across time and space and, on the other hand, I study planned change through an applied intervention project. This project, which is "action research" in the Lewinian tradition, is presented here both in its own right and as a case study demonstrating the applied significance and policy relevance of psychology.

ACKNOWLEDGMENTS

This book was written during a sabbatical leave in the 1993–1994 academic year at the Netherlands Institute for Advanced Study (NIAS). I appreciate this leave granted to me by Bogazici University. I am truly grateful for the perfect atmosphere and the superb support at NIAS, which contributed greatly to my work. Pilar van Breda-Burgueno of NIAS ably typed several revisions of the manuscript.

Ype Poortinga read the first version of the manuscript and gave me much valuable feedback. I also benefited from the comments of John Berry, Pierre Dasen, Patricia Greenfield, and anonymous reviewers, as well as the support of Walt Lonner. I am thankful to Marc Bornstein for taking the initiative to contact Lawrence Erlbaum for me, acting as a liaison. I appreciate the assistance of Judith Amsel and Sondra Guideman of Lawrence Erlbaum Associates with the editing and the production of the book.

My students Asli Carkoglu, Nurcan Karamolla, Didem Gurbey, Ayse Uskul, Sahika Ayhan, Ozge Koca, and Esin Uzun helped in various ways. Throughout my work on the manuscript, my husband, Oguz Kağıtçıbaşı, provided me with invaluable moral support and encouragement, without which I could not have finished this demanding task. I am indebted to all. Thanks also to my colleagues and students at Bogazici University who have considerably influenced my thinking on human development, the family, and cross-cultural psychology. Many years were spent at Bogazici before my recent move to Koc University. I feel a deep sense of gratitude to Bogazici.

Çiğdem Kağıtçıbaşı

1 Introduction

ABOUT THIS VOLUME

This volume is, on the one hand, about the psychology of human development and human relations within the cultural context. The development of human relations and the self is situated within the family and society. In my thinking, the links between the person, family, and society are crucial for an understanding of global human psychology. On the other hand, this volume is also about the integration of theory and practice. Specifically, I make an attempt to find out whether a culturally sensitive conceptualization of individual–family–culture links has any relevance for applications and policies designed to promote human well-being. Clearly, there are two types of linkages that need clarification. The first one has to do with some of the intersections between the levels of analysis— the individual (self), the group (family), and the larger context in which both exist (culture and society). The second one relates theory and application.

Linking Self, Family, Society

My purpose here is to look into some limited aspects of family dynamics and family socialization within varying sociocultural contexts with a view to discover their functional (or causal) links with human development. Thus, a contextual– developmental–functional approach is undertaken here.

The approach is contextual in that the study of the person and human development automatically implicates the family as the context, and thus figures the family explicitly in the conceptualization. Similarly, when the family is under

1

focus, it is automatically situated in its sociocultural environment. This approach is very much in line with the ecological orientation of Bronfenbrenner (1979), with traces of the classical field theory of Lewin (1951), and symbolic interactionism of G. H. Mead (1934), on the one hand, and with the current contextualist models, on the other (e.g., Featherman & R. M. Lerner, 1985; Hurrelmann, 1988; R. M. Lerner, 1983, 1989). Much thinking in cross-cultural psychology is also contextualistic, almost by definition, and the approach here is akin to the current theorizing in this field (e.g., Berry, 1976; Berry, Poortinga, Segall, & Dasen, 1992, p. 12; Eckensberger, 1990; Price-Williams, 1980).

The approach here is also developmental. This is because it is not enough to note or even to establish with some certainty differences across contexts. The way these differences emerge is just as important for psychological inquiry. More and more, the significance of a developmental approach is being recognized, and a developmental orientation is seen as inherently complementing a cross-cultural one (Bornstein, 1984; Bornstein & Bruner, 1989; Eckensberger, 1990; Heron & Kroeger, 1981; Jahoda, 1986; Rogoff, Gauvain, & Ellis, 1984; Rogoff & Morelli, 1989). This is not to say that all cross-cultural work takes cognizance of developmental processes, but that the recognition of the need to do so is increasing. It is interesting to note in this context that in her invited address at the centennial convention of the American Psychological Association, Anastasi (1992) pointed to the recent progress of cross-cultural psychology and life-span developmental psychology as the two most important developments of the last decades.

Finally, the present approach is functional because social and psychological adaptive mechanisms are invoked to explain why a particular type of development occurs. I should note, however, that this functional approach is not deterministic and allows for flexibility and feedback mechanisms. It also tries to stay away from teleological reasoning. Adaptive mechanisms are, rather, used as clues to understand why self–family–culture linkages get established in particular ways, showing variability as well as similarity across cultures. The contextual, developmental, and functional approaches are elaborated on when necessary throughout.

In forming the links among the self, family, and the larger sociocultural environment, I work from a cultural and cross-cultural perspective. A cultural approach is presupposed by contextualism, and a cross-cultural approach is required for the unambiguous interpretation of the observed cultural differences (Van de Vijver & Poortinga, 1990). To understand the functional relations among the society, the family, and the development of the self, the underlying dynamics need to be discovered. A cross-cultural comparative orientation provides the grounds for such an endeavor, as it supplies more variation than can be obtained in a single culture study (Berry et al., 1992; Rogoff et al., 1984; J. W. Whiting & Child, 1953).

Linking Theory and Application

The second basic task I undertake in this volume is to integrate theory and application. By application I do not mean individual-focused psychological practice, which readily comes to mind, but rather the use of psychology in large-scale efforts to improve human well-being and to contribute to societal development. Psychologists' contribution to development efforts focuses on its human aspects; therefore, any applied work would benefit from a knowledge of the cultural context in which human phenomena occur. Intervention attempts in developing countries need to be especially sensitive to the human relations in the "culture of relatedness" (Kağıtçıbaşı, 1985a) prevalent in these societies. Thus, interventions may be expected to work better if they take into consideration and build on the existing human connectedness, as reflected in closely knit family, kinship, and community ties, rather than counteracting them, for example, in building individualistic independence and competition.

The emphasis on applied research occupies a central place in my orientation to psychology (Kağıtçıbaşı, 1994b). Theory that is not put to the test of application has limited utility, and applications not informed by theory tend to be haphazard and expensive "shots in the dark" that can't be afforded, especially in the Majority World (see footnote 5 in Preface) countries with limited resources. In other words, I believe that psychology need not choose between theory and scientific rigor on the one hand and relevance on the other, and it is incumbent on the psychologist, especially on one who lives in the Majority World, to be involved in efforts to uphold human well-being. Culturally sensitive and both "socially and scientifically responsible" (Drenth, 1991) psychological research can go a long way toward contributing to social development efforts.

This book presents, in some detail, an applied research project that I have carried out with my colleagues in Istanbul, Turkey. I believe it deserves attention both for demonstrating the integration of theory and practice on the one hand, and the potential of psychology for contributing to human development on the other. The Turkish Early Enrichment Project and its follow-up study together spanned a 10-year period. I attempt to bridge the gap between theory and application by using this applied research as a case in point.

A CULTURAL AND CROSS-CULTURAL PERSPECTIVE

This topic covers a wide scope and includes extensive research and theory spanning the fields of cultural and cross-cultural psychology, anthropology, and sociology. I would like to give here a rather brief and general overview of the issues involved and examine the relevant concepts. My approach here is basically psychological, though I resort to anthropological and sociological conceptualizations where appropriate.

Recent Developments in Cross-Cultural Perspective

Human development always occurs within culture, but it is rarely studied as such by academic psychology. The issue does not concern only developmental psychology but is true of all psychology whose unit of analysis is typically the individual. This outlook is in line with the goal of discovering universal regularities in psychological processes and behavior, which psychology inherited from physics. Accordingly, a physical science model adhering to a positivistic philosophy of science is typically adopted. This implies a methodological orientation isolating the behavior from its natural context to control for "unwanted" variation. Thus, social and cultural factors are often absent in analyses.

This is noticeable from a cursory glance at popular developmental psychology textbooks. They tend not to include cultural differences, or they treat them as extraneous variables (noise), and they view the individualistic trajectory as the normal way of developing. These textbooks influence how development is viewed in American psychology and abroad.

This state of affairs has been noted by critics both within and outside psychology. For example, focusing on human development, T. Schwartz (1981) stated: "Developmental psychology has largely missed the opportunity to consider the child in the cultural milieu, which is the *sine qua non* of the developmental completion of a human nature" (p. 4). Similarly, Jahoda and Dasen (1986), in their introduction to the special issue of the *International Journal of Behavioral Development*, called for a "Cross-cultural developmental psychology . . . [which] is not just comparative [but] essentially is an outlook that takes culture seriously" and deplored the fact that "theories and findings in developmental psychology originating in the First world tend to be disseminated to the Third World as gospel truth" (p. 413).

In his influential work on the ecology of human development, Bronfenbrenner (1979) complained about the "marked asymmetry: a hypertrophy of theory and research focusing on the properties of the person and only the most rudimentary conception and characterization of the environment in which the person is found" (p. 16), and claimed that "developmental psychology . . . is the science of the strange behavior of children in strange situations with strange adults for the briefest possible periods of time" (p. 19).

These views are echoed by those who believe that a noncontextual approach to behavior in general and to human development in particular is inadequate (e.g., Bornstein, 1991; Bronfenbrenner, 1986; Dasen, 1984; Jahoda, 1986; Kağıtçıbaşı, 1984, 1992b; R. M. Lerner, 1989; MacDonald, 1986; Pepitone, 1987; Price-Williams, 1980; Rogoff et al., 1984; Rogoff & Morelli, 1989; Shweder & Bourne, 1984; Tajfel, 1972; Triandis, 1972; Tyler, 1989).

The extensive criticism, substantiated by insightful research, has aimed to be a corrective to the "narrow" focus of psychology. It has been an outcry, loud and clear, serving as the basis for the advancement of a wide range of disciplines and critical views spanning cross-cultural and cultural psychology, on the one hand, and social constructionism and indigenous psychology, on the other. Most research in mainstream psychology is still going about its usual business. Nevertheless, the developments in cultural and cross-cultural psychology over the past 25 years are substantial, and they do challenge the established scientific traditions of psychological research though probably not yet strongly enough to shake them (Bond, 1988; Lonner, 1989). As a crude indicator of the notable growth of the field, several publications and textbooks could be cited. A number of journals are devoted to cross-cultural psychological research, among them are the *Journal of Cross-Cultural Psychology*, *International Journal of Psychology*, *International Journal of Intercultural Relations*, *International Journal of Behavioral Development*, and *Psychology and Developing Societies*. Some others have an international cross-cultural outlook: for example, *Journal of Social Psychology*, *Inter-American Journal of Psychology*, *European Journal of Social Psychology*. To date, there have been four reviews of cross-cultural psychology in the *Annual Review of Psychology* (Brislin, 1983; Kağıtçıbaşı & Berry, 1989; Segall, 1986; Triandis, Malpass, & Davidson, 1973) and one of cultural psychology (Shweder & Sullivan, 1993). The six-volume *Handbook of Cross-Cultural Psychology* appeared in 1980. A second edition of the *Handbook* is currently in preparation.

A great number of books, written or edited by cross-cultural psychologists have been published in the series on *Cross-Cultural Research and Methodology* and in the selected volumes from the conferences of the International Association for Cross-Cultural Psychology. There are also numerous publications that provide overviews of the field, including the annual *Nebraska Symposium on Motivation* (Berman, 1990) and some textbooks of cross-cultural psychology (Berry et al., 1992; Segall, Dasen, Berry, & Poortinga, 1990); cross-cultural social psychology (Moghaddam, Taylor, & Wright, 1993; P. B. Smith & Bond, 1993; Triandis 1994), and psychology in cultural context (Brislin, 1993; Lonner & Malpass, 1994; Matsumoto, 1994). All this activity points to a growing cross-cultural psychology.

Particularly in the cross-cultural study of human development the affinity to an anthropological approach emphasizing the specific cultural context is notable. Starting with the pioneering work of the Whitings and their associates on child rearing in six cultures (Minturn & Lambert, 1964; B. B. Whiting, 1963; B. B. Whiting & J. W. Whiting, 1975), much work has been conducted by psychologists and anthropologists at times working together. Several books on cross-cultural child development, including a handbook (R. L. Munroe, R. H. Munroe, & B. B. Whiting, 1981) provide overviews of this work (e.g., Bornstein, 1991; Greenfield & Cocking, 1994; R. L. Munroe & R. H. Munroe, 1975; Stigler, Shweder, & Herdt, 1990; Valsiner, 1989; Wagner, 1983; Wagner & Stevenson, 1982; Werner, 1979).

Research and conceptualization regarding the importance of the cultural context for psychology have also been emerging from the non-Western world. This is significant when we consider the fact that psychology has traditionally been a Western, and to a large extent, American preoccupation. The rest of the world has typically followed suit, demonstrating a remarkable degree of "traditional acquiescence" (Kağıtçıbaşı, 1994a, 1994b). More recently, however, the progress of cross-cultural psychology has benefited from scholarship in non-Western countries, particularly in Asia. In addition to a growing number of contributions to journals and books containing cross-cultural psychological work from non-Western psychologists, some volumes have come out dealing specifically with psychology and human development in the Majority World (e.g., Curran, 1984; Nsamenang, 1992; Ohuche & Otaala, 1981; Oppong, 1980; Pandey, 1988; Saraswathi & Dutta, 1987; Saraswathi & Kaur, 1993; D. Sinha, 1981; D. Sinha & Kao, 1988; Suvannathat, Bhanthumnavin, Bhuapirom, & Keats, 1985).

A new development emerging mainly from non-Western contexts is the so-called indigenous psychology (Adair, 1992; Bond, 1986; G. E. Enriquez, 1990; Heelas & Locke, 1981; Kağıtçıbaşı & Berry, 1989; Kim & Berry, 1993; D. Sinha, 1986, 1992). It purports that each culture should be studied within itself, as it forms the all-important context of psychological phenomena. In this approach "from within," the historical-cultural characteristics, symbols and artifacts are used as materials to construct a meaningful portrait of a people. "Natural," rather than "imposed," categories are utilized, reminiscent of the typically "emic" approach of anthropologists.

"Indigenization," or indigenous psychology, has been proposed to be an antithesis of the universalist orientation, typical of much of cross-cultural psychology. However I believe they are complementary approaches (Kağıtçıbaşı, 1992a), each providing feedback for the other. If indigenization is seen as an approach, rather than a goal in and of itself, then it is likely to be followed by a comparative approach. And when commonalities emerge out of such comparison among different indigenous realities, we begin to approach universality (Berry, 1989). This point is discussed further later.

Benefits of the Cross-Cultural Perspective

The greatly increasing volume of cross-cultural research is a clear indication of the growing appreciation of the value of a cross-cultural perspective. The advantages involved have been repeatedly voiced by those conducting such research. The following are some of the oft-quoted benefits within a developmental perspective.

A cross-cultural developmental approach uncovers a greater range of variation than any single culture study. With a more comprehensive coverage of diversity, a wider perspective emerges according to which what is typical and what is atypical may need to be redefined (Bornstein, 1984).

With increased coverage of variation, it also becomes more possible to distinguish between biological and environmental influences. That is, the greater the commonality found in a developmental sequence or psychological process over highly varied cultural contexts, the greater the likelihood of its biological roots, though shared social structures may also be a cause. With a finding of increased diversity in a psychological phenomenon across cultures, environmental causation is implicated.

In view of the aforementioned two points regarding increased degree of variability in cross-cultural study, theories based on research with more limited samples may need to be revised if they are to hold up to their claims of universality.

The theory-testing potential of cross-cultural research is thus very important. Any psychological theory claiming universality, as they all do, must be demonstrated to hold cross-culturally. Obviously, a theory can never be proven in absolute terms, as there is always the likelihood of one disconfirming case. Nevertheless, if a theory finds supportive evidence in highly diverse cultural contexts, its claim to "external validity" and universality would be a lot stronger than if it is tested in only a single cultural context. The more a theory receives cross-cultural confirmation, the more closely it approximates universal generality. Indeed, most cross-cultural research in human development has had such a theory-testing goal. This research has served theory very well; for example, Piagetian and Vygotskian theories have enjoyed cross-cultural extensions.

Such testing also helps refine theory. For example, as cross-cultural research showed that the "formal operations" stage of Piaget was very rare among illiterate adults, he changed his orientation and accepted that formal operations may not be a universal stage but may occur only in specific familiar domains. This reformulation was subsequently supported by research conducted in the United States (D. Kuhn & Brannock, 1977; reported in Rogoff et al., 1984). Cross-cultural developmental research, which has contributed significantly to theoretical advancement, cannot boast the same degree of success in serving the well-being of the world's children (Dasen & Jahoda, 1986; Kağıtçıbaşı, 1991a; 1992b; Wagner, 1983) for that has not been its intention. Much work needs to be done which is both informed by culturally relevant theory *and* is problem oriented in order to promote children's well-being. This is a basic theme in this volume.

Another advantage of cross-cultural comparative research is the possibility of disentangling some variables highly associated in one culture by going to another society where this is less so. This allows for refined analysis by unconfounding variables. For example, it is difficult to study separately the effects of age (maturation) and the experience of schooling in Western contexts because these two variables are highly confounded (all children are at school). By conducting studies in cultures where this is not the case, the effects of maturation, as separate from schooling, can be studied (Rogoff, 1981; Rogoff et al., 1984).

As in the previous example, cross-cultural research has the potential to study naturally occurring cause–effect relations that cannot be manipulated experimentally, by utilizing natural quasi-experimental studies. To follow-up the previous example, it is not possible to deprive some children of schooling in order to study the effects of age on cognitive development independently of schooling. However, if such is naturally the case, cause–effect relations can be pursued accordingly.

Cross-cultural study can also provide comprehensive descriptions of psychological phenomena. With increased range of variation covered—for example, in age-specific human development—we can get a fuller spectrum of development, which is a prerequisite for explanation (Bornstein, 1984). Especially in the hands of anthropologists, who have contributed greatly to the study of cross-cultural human development, rich description can be a valuable source of knowledge and understanding.

Such comparative description and cross-cultural work, in general, provide insight into human adaptation (Rogoff et al., 1984). It brings into focus variation in ecological/environmental factors and how they are experienced by the people being studied. Functional relations among the ecological, economic, and sociopolitical contextual variables and the psychological behavioral characteristics of people reflect biological/cultural adaptations (Berry, 1976; Berry et al., 1992).

Cross-cultural psychological study also works as a corrective for the researcher's ethnocentrism. This is mainly because it sensitizes researchers to the cultural basis of their own beliefs. Cross-cultural psychologists are likely to realize that psychology, as it has been constructed historically, is indeed an indigenous psychology of the Western world. It needs to be tried out for validity in the non-Western world if its claim to universality is to be substantiated by evidence. A lot of psychological theories are cultural constructions, reflecting a particular orientation to and interpretation of "reality."

There are important implications of this view in both the explanation of human phenomena and in applications across cultures. For example, the way sex roles or human competence are conceptualized within the prevalent folk theories of a people may be quite different from those of the psychologist armed with Western theory. It takes much sensitivity to work out differences in interpretation and to avoid blunders in applied work that may entail interventions to change behaviors. Here a psychologist with a cross-cultural orientation and experience would have a definite advantage over the one with a unicultural background.

Apart from these substantive contributions of the cross-cultural approach to improve theory and understanding, it has also had a different type of impact on mainstream thinking in psychology in general, and developmental psychology in particular. This has had to do with the potential of some cross-cultural research to unravel socioeconomic development and culture.

A great deal of earlier cross-cultural research was conducted in preindustrial and some in preliterate societies, or using the Human Relations Area Files, which consist of anthropological information on the same types of societies. As

Azuma (1986) noted, "A limitation of such studies is that cultural variables covary with the degree of industrialization of the society" (p. 3). This confounding of socioeconomic structural factors (such as education, standard of living, etc.)—that is, level of societal development—with cultural beliefs and values blurs interpretation. Also as these societies are often remote and very different from contemporary societies, findings from them tend to be ignored by mainstream psychologists as irrelevant (obscure anthropological description), though the cognitive area may be an exception.

More recently, with the increased volume of comparative research emerging from contemporary nation states, it has been possible to keep socioeconomic level characteristics rather similar in cross-cultural comparison and to focus on other cultural differences. It is more difficult to ignore this type of research, for it often involves socioeconomically similar samples, such as urban educated groups, university students, and so on, with nevertheless different cultural orientations. For example, with the recent economic growth in the "Pacific Rim" and the high mathematics-science achievement levels of Japanese and Chinese children (both in their own countries and in the United States), the West has become interested in Eastern and especially the Japanese culture (Japanese management, Japanese childrearing, Japanese education, etc.). Such interest leads to a greater appreciation of cross-cultural research.

Some significant social problems that require solutions are amenable to cross-cultural study. Among these, ethnic issues and global development efforts currently have high priority. Thus, with the need to improve ethnic relations and to contribute to the human aspects of global development, there is increasing allocation of resources for applied intervention research both in the Majority World and also involving ethnic minorities in the Western world. This attracts the attention of mainstream psychologists to ethnic and cross-cultural research as well.

Finally, and as related to all of the previous points, probably a most important benefit that cross-cultural orientation is providing to general psychology is a "sensitization to culture." In a way, one could say that it has taken the demonstration of cultural differences in comparative research to get the psychologists to take culture seriously. Both cross-cultural and ethnic psychological research has played an important role here (Berry, 1985). The integration of culture into psychological analysis promises to widen the scope of our understanding; it can be a breakthrough for psychology.

The Culture Concept

Anthropologists have been studying culture from the very beginning. It is often noted that there are some 164 definitions of culture (Kroeber & Kluckhohn, 1952). Obviously there are different views about how best to conceptualize culture and what aspects to emphasize. There appears to be agreement, however, regarding its comprehensive nature. Thus, the following characterizations, and others, have been proposed: "traditional ideas and especially their attached values," "the mass of learned behaviour passing through generations," "shared symbols and meanings," "different experiences of groups that lead to predictable and significant differences in behavior," "a 'gestalt' of ideas, practices, norms and meanings that organize behavior as a system," "a superordinate organizer with a pervasive influence on its constituent elements," "a system, a set of interrelated and inextricably linked elements," "mental programming or software."

Psychologists tend to adopt Herskovits' (1948) all-inclusive definition of culture as "the man-made part of the environment" (Segall et al., 1990), including both "physical culture" and "subjective culture" (subjective responses to what is man made) (Triandis, 1972). Various cultural conceptions have been elaborately discussed recently (e.g., Berry et al., 1992; Van de Vijver & Hutschemaekers, 1990).

The important point here is situating the psychological phenomenon in its cultural context. This appears as "obvious" because we know that "it is rare (perhaps even impossible) for any human being ever to behave without responding to some aspect of culture" (Segall et al., 1990, p. 5). Nevertheless, what appears obvious turns out to be less so when an attempt is made to integrate culture into psychological analysis (Van de Vijver & Hutschemaekers, 1990).

First of all, the diffuse, all-inclusive nature of culture presents a problem in research. As a superordinate entity, it cannot serve as an explanation or an independent variable (Segall, 1983). Such explanations can turn into empty tautologies, such as "Chinese are this way because of their culture." Thus, attempts are made by psychologists to define culture in less molar and more molecular ways or to operationalize it (Poortinga, Van de Vijver, Joe, & Van de Koppel, 1987; Segall, 1984; B. B. Whiting, 1976). In this more molecular conceptualization, culture is treated as a "set of conditions" (Segall, 1984) that is quite different from culture as a system (Rohner, 1984). It is also conceptualized as "shared constraints that limit the behavior repertoire available to members of a certain socio-cultural group" (Poortinga, 1992, p. 10).

Second, and as related to the previous issue of definition, a perennial methodological problem and a long-standing issue is how to study behavior in culture. The two basic approaches here, having traditional counterparts in psychology and sociology, are those that prescribe studying the phenomenon either from within or from without. This distinction has been the basis of "cultural" and "cross-cultural" psychology, where the former studies human phenomena from within and the latter from without. It has also formed a current debate on the issue of cultural versus cross-cultural psychology, which is discussed later. The two views have been expressed in different labels in different disciplines and orientations, but the basic similarities among them prompt me to group them together. The views from within and from without have their parallels in the idiographic and nomothetic approaches in psychology, going back to Cronbach's characterization of "the two disciplines of scientific psychology" (1957), and before him to Allport (1937), who ascribed the distinction to the German philosopher Windelband. They also found parallels in the qualitative and quantitative research traditions in sociology and the hermeneutic versus positivistic approaches in anthropology. In cross-cultural psychology the emic–etic debate and the indigenous (or relativist) versus universalist orientations (Berry et al., 1992), respectively, appear analogous. Finally, the current debate between cultural and cross-cultural psychology reflects the same basic distinction.

① What is common in the idiographic, hermeneutic, emic, indigenous, relativist, cultural approaches is an emphasis on the uniqueness of concepts in each cultural context, because they derive their meanings from these contexts. There is also a stress on the variability and the uniqueness of the individual case (person, culture, etc.) that requires its study from within and in its own right, defying comparison. In contrast ② the nomothetic, positivist, etic, universalist, cross-cultural approaches study the "typical," not the unique, which can be compared using a common standard or measure. The emphasis is on the underlying similarities that render comparison possible. There appears to be a basic conflict between the emic and the etic, if accepted as exclusive orientations, because being stuck in one would negate the other (Kağıtçıbaşı, 1992a).

As psychology ventures into integrating culture into its analyses and strives to account for cultural diversity while claiming generality (Dasen & Jahoda, 1986, p. 413), it is bound to "move out" from individuals into their interaction with the environment. Yet, this is where this basic conflict comes in. It is between what Lightfoot and Valsiner (1992, p. 394) called "the need to conceptualize 'context dependency' of psychological phenomena and the 'context-eliminating' theoretical traditions of psychology." It can be resolved if there is a genuine understanding that eliminating the context or abstracting behavior from its environment is not the only route toward reaching generality. Indeed, it may be a route that does not lead to real generality but to pseudo-generality. This type of generality is assumed but not empirically demonstrated. The assumption is that the causal relation that is found in the behavior abstracted from the environment in the pure controlled laboratory condition holds across cultures or environments because it is independent of the latter. Yet, even the most ardent experimentalist knows that complete abstraction from the environment is impossible in research with human beings who bring their "culture" into the laboratory, in the form of expectations, habits, values, and so on.

The other, and surer, route toward generality, though laborious, is integrating context into psychological study and examining its impact. When this type of context-dependent study, uncovering causal relations, is conducted in other contexts also, the obtained similarities and differences can weave the path toward generalities.

The recent debate about whether cultural or cross-cultural psychology provides the better conceptual scheme for studying human phenomena (Markus & Kitayama, 1992; Shweder, 1990, 1991; Shweder & Sullivan, 1993; Van de Vijver & Hutschemaekers, 1990) has once again brought the issue to the fore. The discussion revolves about some more basic methodological and conceptual issues such as whether a comparative (decontextualizing) or a wholistic, contextualizing (situated) methodology is to be used in the study of human psychological phenomena and whether universalism or relativism of psychological functioning is to be assumed. It is reminiscent of the earlier etic–emic debate (Berry, 1969, 1989; Jahoda, 1977, 1983) and the current discussion on universalist orientation versus indigenous psychology (Berry et al., 1992; G. E. Enriquez, 1990; Kim & Berry, 1993; D. Sinha, 1989, 1992).

I do not subscribe to the either–or stance of the debate and believe that the two approaches can be, and should be, complementary (Kağıtçıbaşı, 1992a). To my understanding, cultural psychology is psychology within the cultural context, and as such all human psychology should indeed be cultural psychology, as human phenomena always take place within culture. However, as we are far from this ideal, psychological inquiry that takes cognizance of the cultural context can be labeled cultural psychology. If in such inquiry a comparative approach is used and thus at least two cultures are implicated, even if implicitly, we are in the realm of cross-cultural psychology. It is important to note that a comparative approach does not preclude a contextualistic orientation. Indeed, a contextualistic orientation and a comparative orientation are basic to my thinking, as already made clear. In this, I am in agreement with Eckensberger (1990) and with Price-Williams, who observed that "contexts are not necessarily unique; they can be compared" (1980, p. 82). That is why in this book I see myself involved in both cultural and cross-cultural psychology. However, for the sake of simplicity and not to use both terms together, I use "cultural psychology" unless specifically referring to cross-cultural comparison.

Similarities and Differences

This brings me to a consideration of the meaning attributed to similarities and differences obtained in cross-cultural comparisons. It does not make much sense to insist on an either–or position (universalism or relativism) because this is an empirical issue. It is the researcher's task "to know when it makes sense to emphasize likeness, [and when] difference . . ." (to quote a phrase from Shweder, 1984, p. 60 which he later appears to abandon by rejecting likenesses) (Shweder, 1990, 1991; Shweder & Sullivan, 1993). As I mentioned earlier, with the greater comprehensive coverage of variation in cross-cultural study, common and variable characteristics and biological and environmental factors can be distinguished more effectively than when a smaller range of variation is entailed.

However, it should also be noted that similarity across cultures dos not necessarily imply genetic determination. It can be due to some universal (or commonly shared) psychological or structural factors. For example, all societies have developed rules and social control mechanisms for maintaining intragroup harmony, care of the young, and socialization of children. Thus, there are similarities, as well as differences, across cultures. These similarities may be due to analogous functional links among behaviors in different cultures, rather than to biological commonalities (see also Lonner, 1980 and Van de Vijver & Poortinga, 1982).

Yet, when similarities are found between cultures an ethological explanation is commonly invoked (H. Papousek & M. Papousek, 1991; Sigman & Wachs, 1991), and they are attributed to culture only when differences are found. One reason for this is the assumption of the uniqueness of each culture. This is a view derived from descriptive anthropology and is readily accepted by cross-cultural psychologists. It leads to the expectation that cross-cultural comparison should uncover differences in behavior. Thus, cross-cultural research reports are replete with statements such as "the Indian self . . . , the Japanese mother . . . "; or "the Greek philotimo," the "Latin American simpatia," the "Japanese amae" or the "Mexican historic-sociocultural premises." Yet study after study finds similar characteristics among behavior patterns in countries such as India, Korea, Mexico, Greece, Japan, and so forth, which remain implicit. Indeed, Triandis (1989) noted sentiments in other collectivistic cultural groups similar to the "Greek philotimo," and a Turkish researcher (Ayçiçeği, 1993) found the "Mexican historic-sociocultural premises" (Diaz-Guerrero, 1991) regarding sex roles to be typical in Turkey!

There is a need to go beyond the descriptive psychological portrayal of different peoples toward discovering underlying reasons for behavior that may be shared to some extent among them. Thus the current two-way thinking (difference implying cultural, similarity biological causation) needs to be expanded to at least a three-way thinking. When a difference is found in cross-cultural comparison, a contextual (environmental/cultural) interpretation would be implied, except for few known race differences. When a similarity is found, however, there is an ambiguity because either shared biology or shared structure (psychological, ecological, social or cultural) may be the cause. Or, there might even be the further possibility of a combination of the two. The challenge is unraveling these influences.

If we are interested in possible generalization, the comparison of two or more emic portrayals is needed (Berry, 1969, 1989; Triandis, 1978). This is where an etic or cross-cultural comparative approach comes into the picture. It is important to note here that the ultimate aim of this approach should be more the discovery of shared characteristics than of differences, that is, if psychological theory aspires for universality. But interestingly enough, a focus on differences is prevalent here. Of course, there are exceptions, as exemplified in the well-known studies utilizing data from a great number of countries in order to discover patterns of beliefs or values (e.g., Hofstede, 1980; S. H. Schwartz, 1992; S. H. Schwartz & Bilsky, 1987, 1990). However, in these studies structures are typically imposed from outside rather than discovered in cultural (emic) study. What appears to be lacking are studies conducted within the cultural context that reveal functional/adaptive links among phenomena that may, in turn, repeat themselves in different contexts, thus pointing to some fundamental causal relations.

ORGANIZATION OF THE BOOK

This introductory chapter has focused on cultural and cross-cultural perspectives in psychology, which provide a general conceptual framework. Given the benefits of a cross-cultural approach in widening the scope of our understanding, I make frequent use of it in discussions throughout the book. Nevertheless, my main focus is on human development in cultural context, as mediated by the family. I examine it from a functional–contextual perspective and with both a theoretical and applied emphasis. Its coverage here is quite varied and spans wide ground. The different chapters deal with different yet related topics.

The book is composed of two parts. The first part focuses on human development, family, and culture. The chapters in this first part mainly cover theory and research linking phenomena at the individual, group (family), and societal levels of analyses. Human development in cultural context and the more specific process of the development of social/cognitive competence; the relations between culture and self; and family change through social change are examined. Throughout the discussions, a cross-cultural, contextual, functional, and developmental perspective is assumed.

The first part contains four chapters dealing with the central issues discussed in the introduction. Chapter 2 studies "Development in Context." Numerous examples from across cultures and diverse theoretical perspectives point to the necessity of construing human development in context. Though the cultural context is stressed, an ecological perspective to context is used with different layers of embedded environmental influences, ranging from the family to societal values. Context is seen to impart meaning to human experience, as for example in the construal of "childhood" itself.

Chapter 3 examines "Socialization for Competence" and builds upon the previous chapter. Theoretical and cultural conceptions of cognitive competence are reviewed. There is a discussion of cultural variability in the meaning of "competence" and particularly cognitive competence. It deals with difficult issues of relativism versus comparative standards and the danger of double standards in the study of competence across cultures. A basic theme, also discussed in chapter 2 and later in chapter 6, is the culture gap between traditional child-rearing values and the new environmental demands emerging with social change and urban lifestyles, which may result in a disadvantage for the child.

Chapter 4 provides a discussion of the concept of self across cultures and looks into the complex interplay of "Culture and Self." Several theoretical and disciplinary perspectives are examined, including a review of the recent critique of individualism in the Western, particularly in the American, context. A distinction is made between the "relational self" and the "separated self," which is another basic theme throughout the book. It is also conceptualized as a dimension of (inter)dependence–independence in interpersonal relations. Autonomy, control, and achievement, as well as the development of the self, are interpreted within this perspective.

Chapter 5 explores "Family and Family Change." Family is studied as the microcontext of development. Three prototypical family patterns are discussed, and a model of family change is proposed through social change. The commonly accepted modernization view of convergence toward the Western model is questioned, and a shift toward a "model of emotional interdependence" is proposed. This is a family/human model, as the development of the self within the family is also studied. There is a proposed shift toward the development of the "autonomous-relational self" through socioeconomic development within the culture of relatedness (collectivism).

Part II moves from theory to application. It focuses on induced change and the role of psychology both in general terms and also with regard to early enrichment. It examines the applied significance of psychology in promoting healthy human development and analyzes the psychology (social science)–social policy interface.

Chapter 6, "Induced Change: The Role of Psychology," critically appraises the role of psychology in the light of the foregoing discussions and forms a link between the two parts of the book. It asks the question of how psychology can help promote "human development" and assigns a socially, as well as a scientifically, responsible role to psychology. There is a more extensive discussion here of the "political" issues of values, standards, and relativism in the study of human development across cultures. Some controversial topics are confronted, such as schooling, religious education, school readiness, and the nature–nurture underpinnings.

Chapter 7, "Early Childhood Care and Education (ECCE)," narrows down the question to early enrichment. It provides an overview of the early childhood care and education research and applications, both in the Western and the Majority World. This is seen as an area where psychological expertise, especially in the field of developmental psychology, can inform research and applications. Some issues in ECCE are reviewed, such as the relative effectiveness and cost-effectiveness of center-based and home-based approaches.

Chapter 8, "The Turkish Early Enrichment Project," is presented as a case in point. It describes a longitudinal study of early enrichment, coupled with a follow-up, where both the home and preschool environment and mother training are studied in terms of their differential effects on the development of children. Effects of the project intervention on the overall development and school achievement of children as well as on the mothers and the home environment are discussed. The holistic, interactional, contextual orientation of the project is seen as its main strength, leading to gains sustained over time.

Chapter 9, "Search for Integration and Policy Relevance," builds the policy implications of the Turkish Early Enrichment Project and examines the general issue of psychology and social policy. Policy relevance of psychology (and of social science) is discussed with a particular focus on global human development and well-being. An integration of the foregoing topics and discussions is searched here. The development of the self and of human competence in family and culture is viewed again, with an "involved" stance. The socially relevant role of psychology comes to the fore.

All chapters are interrelated, yet each stands on its own. As such, they may be seen as independent topics, and in particular, the first and the second parts differ in theoretical and practical emphasis. Nevertheless, in my thinking, the different parts hang together, and I try to weave them together. Specifically, the theoretical perspectives set out in Part I serve as the theoretical underpinnings of the intervention presented in Part II. Similarly, the call for the greater involvement of psychology in socially relevant research serves as the moral justification for the intervention. Theory, (applied) research, and policy need to be interrelated, and this is what this book is about.

HUMAN DEVELOPMENT, FAMILY, CULTURE

2 Development in Context

Psychological phenomena always occur in context, not in a vacuum; therefore, context always figures in the psychological "reality." This is, of course, stating the obvious. Nevertheless, when it comes to studying human psychological functioning, a contextual-interactionist perspective is not commonly used. I have already pointed to this issue in the introductory chapter and have noted some criticism of traditional noncontextual approaches as well as recent significant attempts at contextual analysis. In this chapter I want to elaborate these trends further, focusing on human development.

Human development is socialization, together with maturation. It encompasses the lifelong process of becoming social, becoming a member of a society. Thus, it involves constant interaction with the sociocultural environment. Any study of human development, therefore, must have contextual and temporal dimensions. Indeed, significant trends in these directions are getting established with the rise of cultural and cross-cultural psychology on the one hand, and lifespan developmental approaches on the other.

In cultural and cross-cultural study, culture is often invoked as the context of psychological functioning, though context can be conceptualized at other levels also (physical, interpersonal, familial, etc.), as is discussed later. One reason underlying the conceptualization of context as culture is the paramount role of culture as an "organizer" of meaning. I want to start the discussion of context, therefore, at the cultural level—that is, context as meaning.

CONTEXT AS MEANING

A contextual approach to the person–environment relations that focuses on culture considers culture as a source of meaning. Indeed, cultural context provides precious meaning to observed behaviors and their causal links, which can further expound the dynamics underlying the behaviors. Thus, the "same" behavior may assume different meanings in different contexts.

 Some examples can demonstrate how this may happen. Azuma (1986) discussed the meaning of a common response of the Japanese mother to her child who refuses to eat a particular vegetable. She would often say, "All right, then, you don't have to eat it. " He reported that his American colleagues interpreted such statements to mean that the mothers did not feel very strongly that the child should eat the vegetable (she could eat something else). Yet, Azuma indicated that it was those mothers, in particular, who felt most strongly about the child eating the vegetable, and that is why they used the strong threat, "You don't have to obey me," which means "We have been close together. But now that you want to have your own way, I will untie the bond between us. I will not care what you do. You are not a part of me any longer" (Azuma, 1986, p. 4).

Clearly, the same words carry different meanings for the Japanese mothers and the American researchers. Do they have correspondingly different meanings for the children in the two cultures? Azuma continued by saying that the Japanese mothers reported this strategy to be most effective in getting their children to cooperate. This is because in the family culture where *amae* (dependence of the child on the mother and mother's complete indulgence in the child) is the key in early socialization, this statement would carry a meaning of rejection for the child. For American children, however, it would carry only the meaning that they are free not to eat the vegetable.

 This simple example shows the importance of socially defined and contextually situated meaning. A research program examining the relations between parental control and children's perception of parental acceptance is another case in point. Research carried out in North America and Germany found parental control to be associated with perceived parental hostility and rejection (R. P. Rohner & E. C. Rohner, 1978; Saavedra, 1980; Trommsdorff, 1985). However, the same behavior of parental control was found to be associated with perceived parental warmth and acceptance in Japan (Kornadt, 1987; Trommsdorff, 1985) and in Korea (R. P. Rohner & Pettengill, 1985).

The reasons that apparently the same behavior is attributed opposite meanings by children and adolescents in different cultural context is an intriguing problem that can only be addressed with a reference to the contextually situated meaning systems that define what is and is not "normal." Specifically, in cultural contexts such as in the United States nonrestrictive discipline is the norm in child socialization stressing autonomy. In this kind of context, strong parental discipline is the exception and is, therefore, more likely to be perceived as "not normal," and thus reflecting hostility or rejection on the parents' part.

From a "social comparison process" perspective (Festinger, 1954; Gerard & Rabbie, 1961), one would expect that the behavior or experience that is different from others' would be interpreted as "not normal." This kind of comparison can only be done by children old enough to perceive the differences between their own situation and that of other children. Such deviant childrearing behavior can even function as pathology, precisely because the children and adolescents exposed to it would interpret it as "not normal" in comparing themselves to other children they know. Taking this reasoning one step further, deviant restrictive parental control can actually reflect parental hostility in such a cultural context.

In a different culture, where childrearing is characterized by strong parental control, as in Japan and Korea, however, the "same" strong parental control has an entirely different meaning. It is "normal" and therefore "good." When the child who is exposed to it compares herself with other children, she finds she is not different from them, i.e. she is not rejected by her parents. Indeed Trommsdorff (1985) notes, "Japanese adolescents even feel *rejected* by their parents when they experience only little parental control and a broader range of autonomy" (p. 238; emphasis in original).

Further refinement is brought into the picture by Lau and his colleagues (Lau & Cheung, 1987; Lau, Lew, Hau, Cheung, & Berndt, 1990), who differentiated between "dominating" and "order keeping" parental control in their work with Chinese adolescents and adults. They found a negative relationship between dominating (restrictive) control and parental warmth, but a positive relationship between "order keeping" (and caring) control and warmth. This is in line with Moos' earlier distinction between dysfunctional and functional controls (R. H. Moos, 1976; R. H. Moos & B. S. Moos, 1981) and parallels Baumrind's (1971, 1980, 1989) conceptualization of authoritarian and authoritative parenting, which is examined further later.

These studies point to the importance of how control is perceived and whether or not it is seen as "normal" and legitimate, an attribution that is, in turn, influenced by social conventions and norms. In general, higher levels of control are common wherever childrearing does not stress the development of individualistic independence in the child. It is demonstrated by much research pointing to conformity oriented child rearing in more closely knit familial and cultural contexts (Barry, Child, & Bacon, 1959; Berry, 1976, 1979; Bond, 1986; Kağıtçıbaşı, 1982a; D. Sinha, 1981). In a comparative study conducted some time ago (Kağıtçıbaşı, 1970), I asked Turkish and American adolescents how much parental control and affection they experienced while growing up. While no cross-cultural difference was obtained in perceived parental affection, Turkish adolescents perceived more parental control than American adolescents. Thus, that study provided evidence for the independence of parental affection and control dimensions of childrearing. It also pointed to the social-normative and cultural basis of parental control, though not of parental affection.

Parental affection may be a candidate for a psychological universal, possibly based on biological/evolutionary processes involving protection and care of the offspring for the continuation of the species (Batson, 1990). Parental control in socialization, on the other hand, is closely related to values and goals of socialization, which show variation across cultures and through time (Peisner, 1989).

As mentioned earlier, a key factor here is the desired level of dependence–independence in child socialization. This is one of the main themes in this book.

These two examples of culturally defined meaning point to the importance of integrating context (culture) into psychological analysis. Indeed, culture forms a significant part of the psychological reality under consideration.

The Increasing Relevance of Context

The view positing the importance of the cultural context as providing meaning is in line with the social constructionist position deriving from Berger and Luckmann (1967), which "is principally concerned with elucidating the processes by which people come to describe, explain, or otherwise account for the world in which they live" (Gergen, 1985, p. 3). Interpretive anthropologists who have a "symbols and meanings" approach to cultural analysis also provide important insights into the cultural construction of "reality" (Kirkpatrick & White, 1985; Marsella, DeVos, & Hsu, 1985; Marsella & White, 1984; Shweder & Bourn, 1984; Shweder & R. LeVine, 1984). The more recent formulations of cultural psychology also stress the "implicit meanings that shape psychological processes" (Shweder & Sullivan, 1993, p. 507; see also Shweder, 1991; Stigler et al., 1990)

Thus, cultural context, as a source of meaning, has been highlighted by social constructionists, interpretive anthropologists, and cultural psychologists alike. Other currents of theory and research have also helped bring context to the fore, both at the cultural level and at other levels. They constitute independent academic traditions, spanning different disciplines. Nevertheless, there have been some points of contact among them, and they have all shared a contextualistic thinking. Several can be mentioned: Systemic models of person–environment interaction (Bertalanffy, 1968); ecological theory (Bronfenbrenner, 1979); ecocultural theory in cross-cultural psychology (Berry, 1976, 1980; Berry et al., 1992; Segall et al., 1990); cross-cultural child development research by anthropologists (Barry et al., 1959; R. A. LeVine, 1974; B. B. Whiting, 1963; J. W. Whiting & Child, 1953; B. B. Whiting & J. W. Whiting, 1975); life-span development theory (Baltes & Brim, 1979; Baltes, Reese, & Lipsitt, 1980) and developmental contextualism (Featherman & R. M. Lerner, 1985; R. M. Lerner, 1983, 1989); "everyday cognition and informal education" approaches of cultural psychologists and anthropologists (Cole, Hood, & McDermott, 1978; Greenfield & Lave, 1982; Nunes, Schliemann, & Carraher, 1993; Rogoff, 1981, 1990; Scribner & Cole, 1981), informed by Vygotsky's sociohistorical school of thought (Vygotsky, 1962, 1978); problem- and policy-oriented family research, informed by ecological theory (Bronfenbrenner & Weiss, 1983; Dym, 1988; Sameroff & Fiese, 1992; Weiss & Jacobs, 1988); and the recent ethnic minority research, again from an ecological perspective (Coll, 1990; Harrison, Wilson, Pine, Chan, & Buriel, 1990; McLoyd, 1990; Szapocznik & Kurtines, 1993).

These theoretical and research endeavors have brought the context of development into focus. They are significant trends, in as much as they prompted R. A. LeVine to ask if will "be a 'cross-cultural revolution' in thinking about child development?" (1989, p. 60), and Gupta (1992) to consider the recognition of the importance of the context of development "a clear and discernible trend" (p. 8). They are reflected in a number of recent publications, all situating human development within its sociohistorical and cross-cultural context (Damon, 1989; R. A. LeVine, 1988; Nsamenang, 1992: Valsiner, 1989; P. Woodhead, Light, & Carr, 1991).

An interest in the context of development actually has a long history in psychology, philosophy, and education that goes back to the enlightenment philosphers John Locke and J.-J. Rousseau, reemerges in the writings of John Dewey, and shows up in the early developmental and comparative psychology (Baldwin, 1895, 1909; Novikoff, 1945; Von Bertalanffy, 1933). However, the prominence of the mechanistic and organismic models in developmental psychology, together with the insistence on studying the individual as the unit of analysis, have worked as deterrents to contextualistic conceptualizations (see Eckensberger, 1979; Hurrelmann, 1988; and Kağıtçıbaşı, 1990 for a review of these models of person–environment relations). The mechanistic model espoused by behaviorism had a limited conceptualization of the environment as proximal stimuli. Though this model has been abandoned to a large extent in favor of cognitive models, its narrow focus on the individual has been maintained, with a shift from individual behavior to individual cognition. Even in social learning theory, cognitive structuring of the environment by the individual has been emphasized (Bandura, 1977, 1986).

The organismic model, in its turn, has emphasized maturation and endogenous development, almost to the exclusion of context. Though in Piagetian theory, for example, interaction with the immediate environment through assimilation and accommodation is recognized, environment as the cultural context is assigned a secondary role. Nevertheless, as pointed out earlier, in the face of cross-cultural evidence questioning the generality of the higher stages of cognitive development (formal operations), some of the theory's claims have had to be modified.

Notwithstanding these strong individualistic traditions in psychology, contextual conceptualization in human development has acquired momentum, especially in the last two decades. Two theoretical developments have been especially important in this general paradigm shift. One of these is ecological theory; the other is life-span development theory. Especially with the impetus provided by Bronfenbrenner's (1979, 1986) conceptualization of environmental systems, all nested within one another like Russian dolls, multilevel bases of human development and functioning, are taken more seriously. Similarly, in cross-cultural psychology, Berry's ecocultural model of cognitive style (1976, 1980) has found acceptance as a general model of person–environment relations (Berry et al.,

1992; Segall et al., 1990). The antecedents of ecological theory can be found in Lewin's (1951) topological psychology and field theory, Brunswik's (1955) "Environment–Organism–Environment Arc," and Barker's (1968) ecological psychology. However it is the more recent theorizing and research that has paved the way for the rise of contextual conceptualization.

Life-span developmental approaches (Baltes, 1987; Baltes & Brim, 1979; Baltes et al., 1980; S. M. Lerner, 1982; R. M. Lerner & Busch-Rossnagel, 1981; R. M. Lerner, Hultsch, & Dixon, 1983) also emphasize multilevel integrative organization of psychological functioning and the connections among levels. There is also an acceptance of change and plasticity of the human development processes (Brim & Kagan, 1980) as the environmental influences acting on these processes interact among themselves and change over time. Thus, there is a dynamic interaction both between the developing person and the environment, as well as among the different levels of influencing factors at the biological, psychological, physical, and sociocultural levels.

With this kind of a holistic approach through time to human development, several types of interactions among different variables become relevant. These may be at the intrapersonal, interpersonal, familial, social, cultural, and historical levels. Thus a great deal of complexity is involved in contextual theory, and integrating frameworks have been proposed to account for biological, psychological, and sociocultural changes in developmental processes (Featherman & R. M. Lerner, 1985; R. M. Lerner, 1989; MacDonald, 1986).

It is not my intention here to discuss the complexities of the theory of contextualism, but rather to stress the value of a contextual approach in general. I have briefly touched on its theoretical background mainly to situate it within psychological thinking. With the recent growth of cultural and cross-cultural psychology, developmental psychology is also becoming more "culture inclusive" (Valsiner, 1989). Thus, culture is figuring as context in a growing body of human development theory and research.

Apart from the theoretical advancement, problem-oriented research has also contributed to the increasing relevance of context in human development. This has taken place quite independently of theory building, though contextual theory has been utilized as general framework. Basically, research aimed at understanding children's sociocultural environments and to design programs to improve children's welfare have singularly focused on context variables. Family interactions, both internal and external, constitute the key contextual influence in this research (Bronfenbrenner, 1979, 1986; Bronfenbrenner & Weiss, 1983; Dym, 1988; Huston, 1991; McLoyd, 1990; Schorr, 1991; Slaughter, 1983, 1988; Szapocznik & Kurtines, 1993; Weiss & Jacobs, 1988). The contextualistic approach has been effectively used in this research mainly in studying child development in adverse environmental conditions, such as poverty.

The main point here is that there are mediating variables (at the levels of the caretaker, family, and community) between the macrolevel adverse conditions (such as poverty) and the growing child. The very existence of mediating variables allows room for action in favor of the growing child. For example, even if poverty cannot be arrested, the mediating family problems such as distress, abuse, and so on, can be reduced by intervention programs providing support to parents. Thus, context, at different levels, assumes a key importance for applied research.

FEATURES OF CONTEXT

The discussion up to now has focused on the academic and theoretical developments that have helped bring context into the foreground of the study of human development, despite strong noncontextual academic traditions in psychology. Let us now consider context in relation to psychological functioning. This discussion focuses on what constitutes context.

The context of human development comprises numerous levels of influences, all interrelated with and embedded in one another. As it is impossible to integrate them all at the same time into a single study, different "components" figure in different approaches. One way of conceptualizing contextual variables is in terms of their degree of comprehensiveness, as encompassing systems. For example, Bronfenbrenner (1979) differentiated among four levels of environmental systems, increasing in complexity and comprehensiveness from micro- to meso- to exo- to macrosystems. They refer to a pattern of experiences by the developing person in a given setting; the interrelations among two or more settings in which the developing person participates; one or more settings that do not involve the developing person but that affect her; and the consistencies among these at the cultural level, respectively. Which one of these different levels of ecological–environmental systems is to be studied at any one time and what variables in it are to be singled out for analysis are empirical and methodological questions. The answer often depends on the researcher's interests and the accessibility of the variable (of the system) to scientific inquiry (see also Berry, 1980, for another example of the "ecological analysis").

This chapter discusses briefly two different contextual features, at different systemic levels, which I consider important and that have been studied extensively: societal values and parental beliefs and values.

Societal Values Regarding Children

Childhood, like any other concept, is socially defined and as such it is a cultural product that shows cross-cultural variation. Obviously, there are also universally shared aspects of the definition of childhood (in terms of young age, small stature, dependence on others, mainly adults; need for care; etc.), mainly based on our common biology.

Childhood has been studied through history and across cultures, and remarkable variation and shifts in its conceptualization have been noted. The historical treatise by Aries (1962) on the discovery and transformation of childhood is well known. It showed that childhood, as a special conceptual entity unto itself, emerged only in late modern history. As Serpell (1993) noted, however, Aries defined childhood in a narrow way, in terms of its representation in Western middle-class society. Nevertheless, other more recent specific studies of changes in the cultural definitions of childhood across time also point to diversities (James & Prout, 1990; Kessen, 1991; R. A. LeVine & White, 1986; Peisner, 1989; M. Woodhead, 1991). The main theme shared in all this work is that social-cultural conceptualizations of childhood, as reflected in social values, are not stable but change over time and space.

This has important implications about children's education, what is expected of them, and how they are treated—in short, their total lives. Examples of diversity in cultural conceptions of childhood and the corresponding social values abound in the literature. I briefly discuss *child work* as a case in point.

B. B. Whiting and J. W. Whiting (1975) and R. L. Munroe, R. H. Munroe, and Shimmin (1984) studied children's work in different cultural contexts. Their findings show, in general, that from an early age in agrarian societies children are expected to do some household chores. The complexity and amount of work increase with the child's age. Thus, in middle childhood a large portion of a child's waking hours are taken up by some sort of work. This is in sharp contrast, for example, to the lifestyles of children in Western urban middle-class contexts, which are characterized by a preponderance of play. For example, B. B. Whiting and J. W. Whiting (1975) reported that 41% of the Nyansongo (Kenya) children's time was devoted to work, compared with only 2% of U. S. children in Orchard Town, New England.

Nsamenang (1992) gave examples of children's work from West Africa. They start with small errands around the house from the time they begin to walk. Child work constitutes an important contribution to the household economy. It is also "an indigenous mechanism for social integration and the core process by which children learn roles and skills" (Nsamenang, 1992, p. 156). Other research from Africa (Dasen, 1988a; Harkness & Super, 1992) presents a similar picture. Indeed, it is a familiar picture in many rural societies and even in urban contexts, where economic hardship prevails, and where children's material contribution (in household chores or economically productive work) can make a difference in family well-being.

A nine-country comparative study on the value of children for parents (Fawcett, 1983; L. W. Hoffman, 1987; Kağıtçıbaşı, 1982a, 1982c) provides further evidence of the salience of children's work in agrarian economies. Children's material contribution (including help with household chores) was considered important by parents in less developed countries and among rural respondents, whereas less value was assigned to this in developed countries and urban settings. The findings of this study are discussed further later on. The point to be made here is that in socioeconomic contexts where children's material contribution to the family is substantial, a utilitarian value is attributed to children and their work is seen as important.

With changing lifestyles, especially with urbanization and increased parental education, child work loses importance. This change is seen in both less actual child work and also in less importance attributed to it by parents. Thus, in the Value of Children study (VOC study) conducted in Turkey, I found that children's "help with household chores" lost salience for parents with increased parent education (28% at no education level; 22% at primary school level; 11% at high school level; and 0% at university level). Similarly, children's "material help" (i.e., contributing to family economy at young age by working in the field/family business/marginal economy, etc.) also lost salience with parent's education (56% at no education level; 54% at primary; 15% at high school; and 20% at university levels) (Kağıtçıbaşı, 1982a). Thus, values attributed to children and their place in family and society show variation. A most important dimension of variation is along rural-urban and socioeconomic status (SES) differences, in short, level of development (in societal and socioeconomic terms).

The cultural conception of childhood obviously differs between contexts where childhood is, in fact, very different. Thus in socio-cultural domains where children, as well as other family members, carry heavy responsibilities, childhood may not be seen as a special, distinctive entity onto itself. In contrast, where children are in school and are an economic cost rather than an asset, child work (even in household chores) is negligible. It is in this context that childhood is given a special, distinctive status and may even turn into a subject of "sentimental idealization" (Kessen, 1991; R. A. LeVine & White, 1991, p. 21; Zelizer, 1981).

When these two socioeconomic cultural contexts are compared, the main difference appears to be a shift from an emphasis on the materialy value of the child for the family (and the parent) to an emphasis on the needs of the child (M. Woodhead, 1991) (that is, from a parent–family-centered to a child-centered outlook). It is also a shift from the utilitarian (economic) to the psychological value of the child (discussed further later). These shifts in societal values take place both through time, as seen in the Western modern history (Aries, 1962; R. A. LeVine & White, 1991), and across space, through socioeconomic/rural–urban variations.

This example of child work shows a general correspondence between a society's conception of childhood and children's actual lifestyles. Indeed, societies set up environments that are conducive to particular types of child behavior, reflecting parental–societal expectations from children, and by and large most children are socialized into those prescribed roles. Whether this fit between societal values and children's "developmental trajectories" (Nunes, 1992) is optimal for all involved (the children, families or the changing society) is a key question asked in this volume.

It refers to the problem of gaps (cultural lags) between societal values reflecting traditions that may no longer be adaptive to changing socioeconomic conditions and the demands of new lifestyles. For example, Boyden (1990) noted that the dowry system in India has led to the widespread abortion of female fetuses (with modern technology providing the information about the sex of the fetus) (p. 202). With the continuing custom of providing a substantial dowry for the daughter at marriage, daughters are seen to be very costly. This appears to be a major reason for the abortion of female fetuses (also confirmed by many colleagues and health professionals from India, personal communication during a month's stay in India in early 1995).

Thus, what is functional at one point in time may not continue to be functional at a later point in time due to changed circumstances; it may even become dysfunctional. This issue has important policy implications, and it is a central theme of this book. All societies undergo social change; for many Majority World societies, the changes in lifestyles reach drastic proportions, especially with large-scale migration from rural villages into urban areas. When studying psychological phenomena, therefore, this change and the possible gaps it creates need to be taken into consideration, rather than assuming stable environmental conditions. This topic is taken up again in more specific terms.

A related issue is when child work is a part of the common process of socialization for adult roles, as for example described by Nsamenang (1992), and when it turns into child abuse. In the previous pages I gave some examples of variations in child work, its extent, and conceptualization in different societies. Particularly with the declaration of the Rights of the Child, there is a debate about the definition of child work and the borderline between child work and child abuse. This is a complex issue that is laden with value judgments. Boyden (1990) attempted an analysis by differentiating "child work" from "child labor."

Parental Goals, Beliefs, and Values

Parental goals, beliefs, and values regarding children reflect societal values, but the latter cannot be subsumed under the former. First of all, there may be differences between the two value systems at different levels, depending especially on the social class status of the parents. Second, parental values have a more direct impact on the child, through parental behavior, than societal values. Thus, parental orientations constitute an important aspect of the context of development. Nevertheless, it is also true that parental beliefs are cultural constructions. For example, Goodnow (1984, 1985, 1988, p. 297) found greater between-group differences than within-group differences in parental beliefs across social class, ethnic, and cultural comparisons. Cross-cultural differences in parental values reflect more general cross-cultural differences in societal values (D. Sinha & Kao, 1988).

Although it may appear obvious that parents hold beliefs about children and childhood and that these have an impact on the child, systematic study of these topics is rather recent in developmental psychology (S. A. Miller, 1988). The research examining parental orientations (beliefs, values, and behavior) has been conducted in different academic traditions that are quite independent of one another (Maccoby, 1992).

For example, research has been carried out by Educational Testing Service (ETS) researchers and others with mainly African-, Anglo-, and Hispanic-American parents in the United States, pointing to complex belief systems about how children develop (Laosa & Sigel, 1982; Mc Gillicuddy-De Lisi, 1982; Mc Gillicuddy-De Lisi, Sigel, & Johnson, 1982; Sigel, 1985; Sigel, Mc Gillicuddy-De Lisi, & Goodnow, 1992). Both ethnic and social class differences emerged in this research, with beliefs held by higher socioeconomic status groups being more adaptive for the child's development on theoretical grounds (S. A. Miller, 1988, p. 273).

Cashmore and Goodnow (1986) noted the importance of social class standing in Australia. When this variable was controlled, the originally emerging "ethnic" differences in parental beliefs and attitudes disappeared. Similar findings were obtained by Lambert (1987) in a cross-national study, by Podmore and St. George (1986) comparing New Zealand Maori and European mothers, and by Laosa (1978, 1980) comparing Anglo- and Hispanic-American mothers in the United States. These are important findings pointing to a common methodological problem of confounding ethnicity and social class standing. Because ethnic minorities often have lower socioeconomic status than the majority population, the obtained differences are difficult to interpret. These findings call for more care in situating the subjects of a study in socioeconomic terms.

Anthropological research studying parental beliefs about child development has stressed the importance of "ethnotheories" (Super & Harkness, 1986), "indigenous theories" (Chamoux, 1986), or "naive theories" (Sabatier, 1986). Super and Harkness (1986; Harkness, 1992; Harkness & Super, 1993) considered the "psychology of the caretaker" as one of the three components of the "developmental niche," with the others being the physical and social setting, and child care and childrearing. This is a conceptualization of the context of development with cross-cultural relevance. From such a perspective, for example, Dasen (1984) showed that the Baoule of Africa stress social skills and manual dexterity in their childrearing because they define intelligence primarily in terms of these skills.

R. A. LeVine (1974, 1988) pointed to adaptation to environmental requirements as a basis for parental goals and behaviors. For example, in agrarian societies, with high infant mortality and hazardous environments, parental goals of protection and survival of children lead to conformity-oriented child socialization and high fertility. This is because in hazardous environments, obedience rather than independence of children is more adaptive for safety.

This type of a functional analysis is in line with earlier work by Kohn (1969), who analyzed parental values and goals for children in terms of "anticipatory socialization" into social class-based work roles. Kohn showed that individual autonomy was encouraged in middle-class child socialization because in middle-class jobs individual decision making is required; working-class parents valued obedience and conformity in children, on the other hand, as these characteristics are more functional in working-class jobs. The Value of Children study referred to earlier also used a similar functional approach in explaining parental values of children across different contexts characterized by different levels of socio-economic development.

In all the aforementioned research, there is a common emphasis on the importance of parental belief systems both for parental behavior and for developmental outcomes. There is a growing confidence about connections, if not correspondence, between parental beliefs and behavior (D'Andrade & Strauss, 1992; S. A. Miller, 1988; Sigel, 1992) and their stability (McNally, Eisenberg & Harris, 1991) which provides further impetus for studying beliefs. There is also a recognition of the need to situate parental beliefs, values, and behavior into their socioeconomic, social–structural contexts. This is especially important in understanding why certain belief systems show systematic variation across different parental groups. The answer often lies in underlying functional relations.

Parental orientations thus constitute an important feature of the developmental context. Recent research shows that parenting does have a demonstrable effect on diverse developmental outcomes across cultures. For example, Bornstein and his collaborators found significant cross-cultural differences in modes of parent–child interaction even in infancy, where typically substantial cross-cultural commonality obtains, interpreted as "intuitive parenting programs" (Keller, Schölmerich, & Eibl-Eibesfeldt, 1988). Furthermore, these variations in parental orientations are found to have consequences for children's cognitive development (Bornstein, 1989; Bornstein, Tal, & Tamis-Le Monda, 1991; Bornstein et al., 1992) and even for their physical/motor development (Bornstein, 1984, p. 245). Similarly, Roopnarine and Talukder (1990) noted cultural specificity of certain parent–infant activities in research in India. Working with Québécois, Vietnamese and Haitian cultural groups in Montréal, Canada, Pomerlau, Malcuit, and Sabatier (1991) identified differences among beliefs about babies in these groups, controlling for SES differences and noted variations in the social and physical environments that distinguish immigrants and natives. Thus, cultural differences appear to exist in childrearing environments from very early on.

Much research into parenting has investigated the relations between characteristics of parenting and the development of the child's cognitive and social competence, especially the former. I discuss the specific issues involved in the next two chapters.

Another aspect of parental beliefs has to do with the definition of parenting itself, as well as in its conceptualization over time. For example, whether a mother defines her role only in terms of loving and caring for the child or also in terms of preparing the child for school and future school achievement appears to have a crucial significance both for her everyday behavior and for child outcomes (Coll, 1990).

Systematic social class, ethnic, and cross-cultural differences have been found in research on just such self-role definitions. For example, educated middle-class Anglo-American mothers are found to consider it important to provide early stimulation to children, even during pregnancy, whereas lower-class Black mothers think it is the school's job to "teach children." Similarly, Mexican-American mothers do not see themselves as "teachers," but Chinese and Japanese mothers coach and give specific instructions regarding school work (Chao, 1994; Coll, 1990; Jarrett, 1993; Laosa, 1980; R. A. LeVine & White, 1986; Sameroff & Fiese, 1992). Similarly, an increasing number of educated middle-class Turkish mothers give endless drills to their children to prepare them for competitive examinations to enter better schools, but low SES Turkish mothers do not because they believe they "don't know enough to help their children."

This is not to say that coaching children is good. Indeed, it can involve too much pressure for both the child and the mother, when taken to an extreme. This is only an example of a class-related parental role definition and behavior. In effect, the middle-class pattern is more conducive to school achievement.

Finally, the general view of the parental role and self-definitions of it have implications for parent–child relationships extending in time through the life cycle. For example, cross-cultural comparisons of Japanese and American mothers' maternal role perceptions show differences in definitions of responsibilities and in time perspectives (Shand, 1985). The American mothers' definition of maternal responsibility is relatively short-term, until children reach adolescence, and involves physical care (with the husband's help) and love with no duties toward the patrilineage. The Japanese mother's self-definition of the maternal responsibility, on the other hand, is lifelong and is embedded in the husband's patrilineal (corporate) structure where she is responsible for bringing up a respectful, cooperative, and highly achievement-oriented child. Studies conducted in other cultures (in "cultures of relatedness"; Kağıtçıbaşı, 1985a) find certain similarities to the Japanese pattern. For example, C. F. Yang (1988), in describing the close networks among the elderly and their offspring, as shown in recent surveys in China, noted that "they are indicative of the traditional parental protection of children until [parents'] death" (p. 109).

In general, lifelong conceptualizations of parental responsibilities go hand in hand with socialization values of interdependence, rather than independence. The latter, in contrast, implies an expectation of the self-sufficiency of the offspring, especially in adolescence, made possible by a stress on autonomy in childrearing.

RELATING DEVELOPMENT TO CONTEXT

In this chapter I have been discussing the context of development, with some examples of that context, that is, societal values regarding children and parental goals, beliefs, and values. There are many other features of the context of development, of course, which are referred to whenever relevant throughout the book. This section concludes the discussion of the developmental context with a consideration of how to relate children's developmental outcomes to context.

As the context of development is a multilayered, multifaceted, and complex system of interacting influences, its conceptualization has emphasized its complexity (Bronfenbrenner, 1979, 1986; Featherman & R. M. Lerner, 1985; Gupta, 1992; R. M. Lerner, 1989). How this complex whole is to be related conceptually and in operational terms to developmental outcomes is a tough question, and some models have been developed to deal with it.

These models typically attempt to delineate mediating factors between the macrolevel influences and the developing person. They also try to explain how these variables mediate, that is, to identify the processes involved. They are helpful in singling out which variables are important and what effects they may be expected to have. So they work as guidelines in applied research in pointing to ways in which interventions may be expected to make optimal effects. I refer to some models relating developmental context to developmental outcomes as examples. They apply mainly to contextual variables associated with the development of low levels of cognitive and socioemotional competence in children.

Sameroff proposed a model of risk factors stressing their number rather than their nature (Sameroff & Fiese, 1992; Sameroff, Seifer, Barocas, Zax, & Greenspan, 1987). Using the data of the Rochester Longitudinal Study in the United States, the researchers delineated 10 risk factors including mother's (low level) education, mother's anxiety, (marginalized) minority status, unskilled occupation of household head, maternal mental illness, low level of mother–infant interaction, and so forth. A number of these factors are more common in lower SES groups, thus social class is found to be associated with developmental risk. However, the presence of multiple risk factors negatively affected child's competence in all social classes; the higher the number of the risk factors, the more deleterious the effect. In terms of preschool intelligence, for example, "children with no environmental risks scored more than 30 points higher than children with 8 or 9 risk factors" (Sameroff & Fiese, 1992, p. 349). Thus, the number of risk factors work in an additive, not a multiplicative, fashion. For example, when two or more stresses occurred together, the chance of a damaging outcome went up at least fourfold, and when four risks were present, the chances of later damage increased tenfold (Sameroff & Fiese, 1992).

This model is similar to other risk models that are in common use in intervention programs in the Majority World. For example, in screening for children at risk and detecting potential risk cases, the number of existing risk factors can provide clues to health workers, and others involved in intervention programs. In these programs, the conceptualization of developmental risk is commonly concentrated on health and nutrition status. However, there are attempts to expand its coverage to include psychological factors (Kağıtçıbaşı, 1991a; Landers & Kağıtçıbaşı, 1990).

Patterson and Dishion (1988) used a multilevel family process model to explain the development of the antisocial problem child from mainly a clinical perspective based on research in the United States. At the family level the relevant process is that depressed parents are more irritable in their discipline confrontations with their children. Irritable discipline is, in turn, causally related to antisocial traits in the child. This process, with parental discipline as the mediator, is found to repeat itself across generations (Belsky & Pensky, 1988; Huesmann, Eron, Lefkowitz, & Walder, 1983; Patterson & Dishion, 1988; Simons, Whitbeck, Conger, & Chyi, 1991; Trickett & Susman, 1988). Furthermore, lower income and socially disadvantaged position aggravate this process through the mediation of increased stress, which in turn serves as an amplifier for the parental antisocial trait. Social disadvantage (low education, low income, low employment levels or unemployment) is additionally associated with lack of opportunity for developing effective social skills and parenting skills, which also serve as a negative mediator. Thus different contextual levels, through time, are used to explain, in interaction, a developmental outcome.

A similar complex multilevel process model is used by McLoyd (1990; McLoyd & Wilson, 1990) to explain how poverty and family income loss affect Black children in the United States. In a review of research, poverty and economic loss are found to diminish the capacity for supportive, consistent, and involved parenting, with psychological distress as the major mediator variable. Negative life events, including disruption of marital bonds and economic hardship, affect children's socioemotional functioning through their negative impact on the parent's behavior toward the child. Parents' social networks are found to reduce emotional strain, decrease the tendency toward punitive parenting, and in this way foster positive socioemotional development in children.

The positive role of mothers' social support networks and informational support in promoting more effective parenting is noted in much research carried out with families, especially in disadvantaged socioeconomic conditions often including father absence (e.g., Coll, 1990; Cotterell, 1986; Garbarino, 1990; Harrison et al., 1990; Slaughter, 1988; Stevens, 1988). This points to the value of family support programs (Weiss & Jacobs, 1988).

These models all recognize different levels of contextual variables that affect the growing child. In addition they make specific predictions (and formulate hypotheses) regarding the processes that mediate the effects of macrosystem level contextual variables and developmental outcome. This has direct implications for applied work and interventions.

Intervention is possible because socioeconomic conditions at the macrosystem level (social class status, poverty etc.) affect the child through the mediation of parental behavior. It may be difficult to change the socioeconomic circumstances of a family, though every effort should be made toward this end. Nevertheless, even if change at this level is limited, parental distress may be ameliorated, and more effective parenting may be fostered through support programs for parents. Such intervention, if successful, would have a direct positive impact on children. Such support programs may build on the existing resources of the family, promote social networks, provide information and emotional support, build up parental skills, and so on.

This is a key theme in this book. Chapter 8 presents such an intervention focused on the parent (mother). Parental behavior, mediating between the macrosystem variables and the child is targeted in this intervention project on early enrichment and parent support for the promotion of the child's overall development.

This chapter has examined, in general terms, development in context, with examples of contextual factors. The family as the main microsystem (Bronfenbrenner, 1979) of developmental context has figured importantly in this discussion. It is considered as the key aspect of context throughout this book. In chapter 5 it will be studied more systematically, as it changes through social change and development. The following two chapters examine more thoroughly two important spheres of development in context: cognitive competence and the self.

3 Socialization for Competence

Socialization is for competence. Childrearing is goal oriented, though the goal is often not explicit and may not be consciously formulated. The long-range goal of socialization, by definition, is becoming a competent member of a society, so socialization is designed to accomplish whatever it takes to ensure this goal. This view probably carries a too rational and goal-directed stance in view of the apparently haphazard everyday childrearing behavior of many parents and child caregivers. It is not meant to characterize all parenting behavior in a rational and purposeful (or teleological) framework, but rather to put it into a general perspective over time. Competence in this perspective refers to what is culturally valued and therefore shows variation across cultures.

The concept of socialization, once central, has fallen into some disrepute as implying a unidirectional process of causation molding a passive child. It should be noted from the outset that socialization, as construed here, does not imply a unidirectional causation with a passive child, but is an active interaction between the caretaker(s) and the child. A similar view was put forward earlier by M. B. Smith (1968). In this interactional perspective the concept of socialization has reassumed a central importance in the cultural and cross-cultural study of human development.

In the psychological study of human development, cognitive and social competence are differentiated and are conceived as positive developmental outcomes. This chapter focuses mainly on the development of cognitive competence. However, as the meaning of competence shows variation across cultures and developmental contexts, what I undertake to examine in this chapter expands beyond the conceptualization of cognitive competence in academic psychology. Furthermore, I examine socialization for competence not only from the point of view of the child developing cognitive skills but in terms of the total interactive process of teaching and learning in context and the meaning attributed to it by all involved. Finally, I want to focus on socialization for competence in highly different socioeconomic–ecological contexts and examine its implications in the more general framework of social change in the world.

It may be informative to review first some examples of socialization for competence outside of Western middle-class family or school contexts, drawn from observations and research reports. They should provide us with some clues into the diverse processes involved in and the meanings attached to socialization for competence in different sociocultural–economic contexts.

In an early anthropological study in a Turkish village, Helling (1966) noted the prevalence of a parental teaching style based on demonstration, imitation, and motor learning rather than verbal explanation and reasoning. As a husband–wife team they observed informal teaching–learning activities and reported, for example, the case of a father "teaching" his son how to cut wood by just doing it (expecting him to imitate) with no explanation. The Hellings went back to the same village 20 years later and did not observe any appreciable change in this nonverbal orientation to "teaching by doing" (Helling, 1986, personal communication). I commonly tell my students at a Turkish university about this case and ask them whether it sounds familiar. They come up with more examples, usually not from their own lives but from what they have observed among "peasants" or "ex-peasants," now urban shantytown dwellers.

Similar descriptions of "teaching and learning" abound in anthropological reports from many cultures, especially among rural populations. For example, early research points to similar patterns in Africa (Gay & Cole, 1967; R. A. LeVine & B. LeVine, 1966), and recently it has been noted among the Australian aborigines (G. R. Teasdale & J. I. Teasdale, 1992). These patterns are clearly widespread, and they work. Children learn to cut wood or develop manual skills with time to produce exquisite handicrafts, mainly through imitation and commonly without verbal instruction or positive reinforcement (R. A. LeVine, 1989). In Western urban contexts, similar nonverbal and less praising parental teaching styles are also noted among, for example, Hispanic minorities in the United States (Laosa, 1980) and Turkish minorities in the Netherlands (Leseman, 1993).

Whether there is extensive verbalization with the child may also have something to do with some general cultural conceptions of childhood. Specifically, whether or not caregivers see themselves in an active, child development-oriented, consciously goal-directed "childrearing" role appears to be important. This type of self-role definition is common among educated middle-class (especially Western and particularly American) parents (Coll, 1990; Goodnow, 1988; Laosa, 1980). In contrast, Kakar (1978) noted that Indian caregivers emphasize pleasure between adult and child and experience little pressure to mold the child in a given direction. Similarly, many less-educated, traditional Turkish mothers, talk about the child growing-up (*büyür*), rather than being brought up (*yetiştirilir*). If they mention childrearing, it is more in the sense of enabling the physical growth of the child (*büyütmek*) (the root verb *büyü*-mek means literally "to get bigger").

Learning by observation and imitation obviously occurs in all contexts and throughout the life span. It forms the basis of "social learning theory" where role learning from models is considered very important (Bandura, 1962; Zimmerman & Rosenthal, 1974). Children also learn effectively by observing each other's behavior (Azmitia, 1988). However, there are limitations to observational learning. For example, it is not effective for transfer to new tasks (Greenfield & Lave, 1982; Laboratory of Comparative Human Cognition, 1993; Segall et al., 1990). Also, observational learning is only one type of learning, and at least some other types involve verbal reasoning. If verbalization with the child, especially verbal communication involving adult reasoning and decontextualized language is lacking or infrequent, there may be serious developmental implications. I elaborate this point later on.

A second example of socialization for competence and adult roles comes from Anandalakshmy and Bajaj' (1981) study of childhood in the weavers' community in Varanasi, India. Describing girlhood, for example, the authors noted that

> most of the girls by the time they are six years old are adept at sweeping, cleaning and washing dishes and looking after siblings. . . . As soon as a girl reaches the age of nine, she is subject to clearly defined restrictions on dress and movement, and is strictly forbidden from loitering in the streets unaccompanied. . . . Living in a fairly enclosed and restricted environment with nothing else to do, the girls imbibe the craft skills of filling spools for weaving by observing their mothers at work. . . . Young, unmarried girls, by and large, lead a life of domesticity unhampered by school routines or tasks. . . . The day's routine runs an uninterrupted course of spooling, interspersed with domestic chores, the care of younger siblings and gossiping and giggling to the background noise of film music on [the] radio. . . . For girls, formal education was not deemed essential at all since all that they had to do was to manage the household. In fact, the adults said that there was the danger of the girls becoming clever and non-conforming as a result of education, and that was why they were not even sent to the *madarsa* to learn the basics in reading and writing. According to their interpretation of the strictures in the Koran, education was proscribed for girls. . . . The competence of parents to prepare their children for adult roles was only partially a function of their economic status. The weavers of higher and lower economic levels did not vary in the socialization practices as much as the other occupational groups which were part of the larger study. (pp. 34–35, 37–38)

In this rich description there is evidence of a great deal of socialization for competence into socially prescribed roles. Indeed, there is no question that most children learn the roles and skills necessary to live as competent adults in this apparently self-sufficient community. Some questions come to mind, of course, such as the implications of this type of socialization for the cognitive competence of the girl child (boys are described to enjoy greater freedom of action and some schooling). Another question is what happens when changes in economic conditions endanger the self-sufficiency of the community and push young people out to look for other types of employment. This would more likely be the case for the poorer wage earners who do not have their own entrepreneurial weaving materials.

Rural to urban mobility in the Majority World is of immense proportions, also feeding into international migration. This is mainly because traditional rural agrarian and other economic activities prove no longer viable for the livelihood of increasing populations. This is the type of global, social–structural change going on in the world that needs to be taken into consideration when studying human conditions.

THEORETICAL CONCEPTIONS
OF COGNITIVE COMPETENCE

The examples I have given of everyday teaching and learning, mainly through observation and imitation, are similar to a great deal of cross-cultural description looking into the development of cognitive competence in preindustrial societies. It is not my intention here to summarize this growing body of knowledge. Excellent reviews are available, some of which I have referred to earlier (Berry, 1984; Berry & Dasen, 1974; Laboratory of Comparative Human Cognition (LCHC), 1983; Rogoff, 1990; Rogoff et al., 1984; Segall et al., 1990; Werner, 1979; Wober, 1974). The development of cognitive anthropology, also called ethnoscience, has drawn attention to indigenous knowledge systems. The corresponding interest in psychology has focused on cognitive systems (Berry, Irvine, & Hunt, 1988).

The roots of some of the present-day debates in the cross-cultural study of competence go back to the 19th- and early 20th-century views of cultural evolution, on the one hand, and the contrasting views of Levy-Bruhl (1910, 1922) and Boas (1911), on the other. Early claims of qualitative differences between logical (Western) and "prelogical" (primitive) thinking versus "psychic unity" of humankind, espoused respectively by Levy-Bruhl and Boas, still have their counterparts. However, this debate has somewhat subsided in importance today, to be replaced by another that partly overlaps with it. This is whether competence (intelligence) is a central process that shows consistency, generalizibility, and transfer over different conditions, or whether it is context-specific learning and represents an adaptation to specific environmental requirements. It is possible to trace the influence of Spearman's g in psychology and of Boas' "psychic unity" view in anthropology in the central process model that has been more dominant in cross-cultural psychology. Levy-Bruhl's legacy, on the other hand, is acknowledged (Shweder, 1990) in the cultural psychology framework, stressing the contextual specificity of each cognition (learning) and therefore claiming it to be qualitatively different from and not comparable to others.

(A) The central processor model is the traditional view of academic psychology, as seen in learning theory, differential psychology, and cognitive psychology. It considers cognitive competence (intelligence) as a basic psychological process that can act on different events (stimuli) in the same way, thus enabling transfer of learning from one situation to another. In cross-cultural psychology this view underlies, for example, Piagetian approaches to cognitive development and the research on cognitive style or psychological differentiation. Thus Piaget's cognitive developmental stages (and the operation they involve) are expected to manifest themselves similarly in different situations (tasks). Similarly, field dependent–independent cognitive styles are assumed to emerge in the same way with different tasks used to test them. Thus comparisons across cultural contexts are possible.

(B) The central processor model has come under attack from an anthropological perspective—that is, "the specific learning model"—that considers context as crucial and studies the functional relations between learning experience and the cognitive skills (T. N. Carraher, Schliemann, & D. W. Carraher, 1988; Childs & Greenfield, 1982; Dasen, 1984; Lave, 1977; LCHC, 1983; Nunes, Schliemann, & D. W. Carraher, 1993; Rogoff, 1990; Rogoff et al., 1984; Rogoff, Mistry, Goencue, & Mosier, 1991; Rogoff & Lave, 1984; Scribner & Cole, 1981; Serpell, 1979; Shweder, 1990; Super, 1981). This perspective is informed by the Vygotskian sociohistorical approach (1978) stressing that behavior is adapted to fit the context, and the context is structured to support the behavior, deriving basically from the adaptation of humans to their environments through cultural history. Thus each learning is adapting to a specific environment and is not transferable to a dissimilar situation (Berry et al., 1992, p. 122).

Research in this tradition has focused on "everyday cognition" through "guided participation" within "the zone of proximal development," where the child's actual level of development is extended upward toward the limits of his potential by the help of adult guidance or that of someone more capable. Thus such tasks as weaving, tailoring, practical categorization, and oral mathematical calculations that children learn in their everyday task-oriented interactions are studied as valuable specific learning experiences. All learning is considered to be context-dependent and "goal-directed action" that is functional for practical problem solving in context. School learning is not considered as superior to or even different from any other type of learning, as it also involves adaptation to school-type tasks, even though its greater generalizability is granted (Segall et al., 1990, p. 203).

This important body of thinking and research has brought in a corrective to traditional work in mainstream developmental psychology that was oblivious of culture. It has also helped to create a recognition of the "indigenous" cognitive competence of people (children and adults alike) who were too readily labeled as lacking in competence because they did not perform well on standard psychometric tests, Piaget tasks, or school-related activities. Finally, it has contributed to a better understanding of the interactive nature of the learning process—a functional, goal-directed activity, which unfolds itself in a systematic way through "teaching" and "learning" by "guided participation," the unit of analysis being the total activity rather than the individual.

Despite the great value of this approach, however, it is not without its problems. The main problem of the "specific learning model" is the lack of transfer to tasks in different situations unless there are similarities in specifics (Berry et al., 1992, p. 122; LCHC, 1983). Nevertheless, there is recent evidence that everyday formal reasoning and mathematical skills transfer (T. N. Carraher et al., 1988; Nunes et al., 1993). It is to be noted, however, that these skills are at higher cognitive levels. Rogoff (1990) also noted that learning for young children involves highly structured specific situations, but this changes with age, with older children having learned much about the process of learning. Guided participation aims to impart this process of learning, which can be expected to generalize.

It appears that learning specific procedural skills (*how* to do something) does not easily transfer to new tasks, but when conceptualization is involved, transfer is seen (Hatano, 1982). Quite a bit of traditional everyday learning is procedural and is thus rather limited. This is especially problematic when social structural changes (rural–urban mobility, shifts in economic activities and job markets) require different types of cognitive skills or competencies. For example, with the introduction of mass production, traditional tailoring skills may lose their economic importance to be replaced by new skills.

Research in Nigeria (Oloko, 1994) found that despite the popular belief that street trading facilitates greater arithmetical skills, nonworking students outperformed working ones most in arithmetic. Similarly, in literacy tests, both in English and in the mother tongue, working children did more poorly than nonworking students. This research points to "street work representing maladaptation to a modernizing economic, social and political environment" (p. 220), as it either interferes with school performance of children or keeps them out of school. Also, school-related cognitive skills and orientations are often required for urban jobs that out-of-school learning may fail to impart.

Finally, there are policy-relevant (and political) implications of conclusions such as "increasingly, school is seen as simply another context for learning, with specific cognitive outcomes" (Segall et al., 1990, p. 203, referring to "everyday cognition" research), or "the apparent superiority of school-based performances is to some extent an artifact of cross-cultural experimental design" (Greenfield & Lave, 1982, p. 185, referring to the research of Cole, Sharp, & Lave, 1976). It should be noted that though these views may be true in the context of research conducted, they are also, in effect, referring to situations in countries where significant efforts are being made to institute universal schooling for children, including attempts to persuade parents to send their children, especially their daughters, to school.

Before ending this section, I should also mention that schooling is receiving critical consideration as well. Its negative aspects have been noted, especially in contexts where "colonial" elements in schooling continue, rendering it "foreign" to the society. I cannot deal here with the complexity and the diversity involved in schooling in different societies (for a critical treatment of the topic see Serpell, 1993). This issue is discussed again in chapter 6.

CULTURAL CONCEPTIONS
OF COGNITIVE COMPETENCE

The previous chapter discussed parental goals, beliefs, and values as an important aspect of the developmental context. This section builds on that discussion and also on the theoretical conceptions of cognitive competence to examine cultural conceptions of competence. Some examples may provide insights.

In Turkish the word *uslu* is used particularly as a characteristic of children, meaning a combination of good mannered, obedient, quiet, not naughty, not boisterous. It is a highly valued characteristic, especially of girls, as evidenced in research (Basaran, 1974; Macro, 1993).

The etymology of the word reveals that it is made of the root *us* and the suffix *lu*, referring to belonging, meaning "with 'us'" or "having 'us'." The *us* root, in turn, means "reason." Thus apparently the word *uslu*, meaning "rational" originally, shifted in meaning in its everyday use in childrearing. Probably restrained, quiet, obedient, good-mannered behavior was associated with being reasonable and rational to start out with, and therefore the term for the latter characteristics (*uslu*) was also used to refer to the former characteristics. With time, however, the more concrete behavioral meaning appears to have gained prominence and the original meaning (rational) got lost.

Uslu is a term used for children. For adolescents (and maybe young adults) the combined term *akilli-uslu* is used. Literally and on its own, *akilli* means "intelligent." However, the combined term has similar behavioral connotations for adolescents as *uslu* has for children. Nevertheless, the connotation of *akilli-uslu* also involves an explicit meaning of being "reasonable" and "reliable" in addition to being good-mannered and not impulsive in this older age period.

This very close association in connotative meanings referring to intelligence, reason, reasonableness, and being reliable and good mannered (not impulsive or boisterous) for adolescents and the complete shift in the meaning of *uslu* from rational to good mannered for children are intriguing. These connotations have to do with a social or interpersonal behavioral dimension of cognitive competence. Because these terms are period specific (for childhood and adolescence, particularly), they have to do with childrearing or socialization orientations and values.

In the nine-country Value of Children study (VOC study), childrearing values were studied that throw light on the aforementioned. Among characteristics of children most desired and second most desired, "obeying their parents" was chosen by 60% of the Turkish parents while "being independent and self reliant" was chosen by only 18% (Kağıtçıbaşı, 1982a, 1982c). The responses from Thailand were very similar. The findings from Indonesia and the Philippines showed even higher stress put on obedience, whereas in the fast industrializing countries of Korea and Singapore, the valuing of independence and self-reliance surpassed even that in the United States (Kağıtçıbaşı, 1982a, 1982c, 1990).

Similar findings were obtained in the Turkish Early Enrichment Project (Kağıtçıbaşı, 1991b, 1994a; Kağıtçıbaşı, Sunar, & Bekman, 1988). This research is presented in the second part of the book; one early finding is pertinent at this point. We interviewed mothers with low income and low education levels in Istanbul. In describing a "good child," mothers stressed being polite (37% of the mothers spontaneously mentioned it) and obedient (35%) more than any other characteristic. Being "autonomous and self-sufficient," however, was a negligible response (3.6%). In line with the emphasis put on respect and obedience was the stress on harmonious relations. Among children's behaviors that please mothers most, good relational behavior, such as "being good to mother," was mentioned most frequently. Good social-relational behavior (including being obedient, showing affection, and getting along well with others) accounted for almost 80% of mothers' spontaneously mentioned desired behavior in children. Thus, in general, a positive social orientation and in particular an obedient disposition are highly valued.

Obedience expectations from children show systematic cross-cultural variation. In more traditional family contexts, especially in rural agrarian and low socioeconomic conditions, a high value is put on obedience in childrearing, which is reflected in a cultural conceptualization of cognitive competence that includes a social component. The previous chapter pointed to the functional or adaptive value of conformity orientations inculcated in children for survival (R. A. LeVine, 1974, 1988) or for occupational requirements (Kohn, 1969). With changes in lifestyles, however, this social component decreases in importance or is separated out from the cognitive component (as reflected in the Value of Children study findings from Singapore and Korea).

Commonly I ask my cross-cultural psychology students to ask people they know "what an intelligent child is like." I also ask them to talk about this with people of different levels of (high and low) education and occupation. Typically, they report characterizations, including social skills (such as *uslu*, obedient, etc.), from respondents with low education–occupation status, but not from highly educated ones.

The so-called social definitions of intelligence, as seen in my examples from Turkey, abound in research from Africa (as reviewed by Berry, 1984) and has even been called "African social intelligence" (Mundy-Castle, 1974). As obvious from the previous examples from non-African countries, this is not unique to

Africa but is commonly seen in "traditional" societies, where "socio-affective" aspects of cognitive competence are stressed. For example, Berry and Bennett (1992) noted that among the Cree of northern Canada the cognitive and so-cial/moral aspects of competence are not differentiated. This is in contrast to the purely cognitive conceptualization of intelligence in Western technological soci-eties. Obviously, as intelligence tests are products of the Western technological society, they reflect the latter notions of intelligence.

A study by Serpell (1977) in a Zambian village demonstrates the contrast between the "folk" conceptions of intelligence and what is measured by intel-ligence tests. He asked five adults to rate the 10-year-old village children in terms of which ones they would choose to carry out an important task. He also asked them to rank the children in terms of intelligence, using the local term for it. The children thus rated were given a number of intelligence tests, including three developed for use with nonschooled children in Zambia. The scores the children received from the intelligence tests did not correlate with the adults' ratings. Despite being free of specific school bias, the tests measured pure cognitive skills and not social skill and social responsibility, which the adults used as criteria.

Similar findings emerge from other research in Africa, starting with the pi-oneering work of Irvine (1966, 1970), who first stressed the importance of studying the everyday meaning of "intelligence" for people. This research em-phasized the importance of indigenous values and the adaptive nature of what is valued (Harkness & Super, 1992; LCHC, 1983; Super, 1983; Super & Harkness, 1986; Wober, 1974). Socialization, in turn, aims to develop the valued charac-teristics in children, in this case social skills and social responsibility, rather than, for example, abstract reasoning, which is associated with intelligence by psy-chologists.

For example, Harkness and Super (1992) contrasted the developmental results of differing parental conceptions of cognitive competence (ethnotheories) and their expression in the organization of daily life settings and customs of childrear-ing in Kokwet (Kenya) and in Cambridge (United States). They described life in Kokwet where it is customary for 5-year-old children to take care of infants, for 3-year-old boys to drive cows from the garden, and for 8-year-old girls to cook dinner for the family; children from Cambridge would be unable to perform these tasks. However, children from Kokwet do poorly in simple cognitive tests (in-volving retelling a story), whereas children from Cambridge have no difficulty with this task.

Clearly, children's cognitive competence in culturally valued domains gets promoted, whereas development in other domains lags behind—if it is recog-nized at all. Thus, learning is functional, it is adaptive to environmental de-mands. The main problem emerges, however, when stable functional relations or adaptive mechanisms get challenged by modifications in lifestyles, accompany-ing social–structural and economic changes.

This problem becomes relevant in studies looking into ethnic and social class differences in Western urban contexts. Most ethnic minorities in the indus-trialized countries of Europe, North America, and Australia are rather recent immigrants from less developed countries and especially from their rural areas (Blacks in the United States and native peoples being the main exception). Many of the childrearing patterns of these ethnic minority populations reflect the kinds of parental conceptions of cognitive competence that I have been discussing here. Specifically, a socially rather than a cognitively oriented conception of competence is valued, stressing conformity–obedience goals, and early learning in the family is based mainly on observation and imitation.

Indeed, research with ethnic minority families points to this type of parental conception and finds a misfit between this cultural conception of competence and that of the school culture in the host society. For example, Nunes (1993) noted that immigrant Mexican parents in the United States believe, erroneously, that if their children are quiet and obedient and listen to the teacher, then they will succeed in school. Okagaki and Sternberg (1993) similarly found that for immi-grant parents from Cambodia, Mexico, the Philippines, and Vietnam, noncogni-tive characteristics (i.e., motivation, social skills, and practical school skills) were as important as or more important than cognitive characteristics (problem-solving skills, verbal ability, creative ability) to their conceptions of an "intel-ligent first-grade child"—but not for Anglo-American parents. Furthermore, parents' beliefs about the importance of conformity correlated negatively with children's school performance, and American-born parents favored developing autonomy over conformity.

Such research points to the importance of parental conceptions of cognitive competence and fits in with earlier work on parental beliefs and behavior (Laosa, 1982; Laosa & Sigel, 1982; McGillicuddy-DeLisi, 1982; McGillicuddy-DeLisi et al., 1982; Sigel, 1982, 1985), referred to in the last chapter. Obviously, parental conceptions of cognitive competence are not the only factors affecting school-related developmental outcomes. Numerous influences, including the typical teaching and learning patterns in the early home environment, play a role. In this context the role of social class is receiving more research attention and is figuring more importantly in studies of risk factors in the development of chil-dren's cognitive and social competence (Laosa & Sigel, 1982; McLoyd, 1990; Sameroff & Fiese, 1992; Werner & R. S. Smith, 1982).

DISADVANTAGE

The aforementioned research shows that some cultural conceptions of cognitive competence held by caretakers and their corresponding behaviors can conflict with mainstream (school) conceptions. If school performance is used as a devel-opmental outcome variable, such home orientations may be considered a "disad-vantage." A simple impressionistic example may provide an illustration.

Recently while waiting for luggage at a major European airport, I noticed a young Turkish family consisting of a father, mother, and two little boys. They were obviously living in Western Europe as an ethnic minority family of lower socioeconomic status. The luggage did not get processed for a long while, and I had a chance to do some naturalistic observation. The bigger boy was about 4 to 4½ years old, and the smaller one was about 3. The bigger boy was trying hard to get his father's attention and to engage him in a conversation, as he was repeatedly telling the father some things and asking eagerly, "Isn't it so, daddy?" The father was not responding; he was not even looking at the child. The mother did not intervene or respond in any way either. She, like her husband, was looking aimlessly into space, as if the children were not there. The smaller boy, in turn, was actively searching for the attention of his older brother. After insistent repetitions, the bigger boy gave up on catching the father's attention and turned to his younger brother, and the two of them carried on.

This behavior contrasts with Western (especially American) middle-class parental behavior. The greater verbal responsiveness of American middle-class parents as compared with working-class parents is documented in research (Laosa, 1980; McLoyd, 1990; Sameroff & Fiese, 1992). Again, I have personally experienced this on several occasions. I have felt surprised and even frustrated at not being able to carry on an uninterrupted conversation with an American colleague or friend if a child was around. If the child says something, even while the other person is talking, the parent typically attends to the child, therefore tuning out the other person.

These two vignettes can be considered rather extreme; the difference, however, is unmistakably there. In a recent nationwide study in Turkey where interviews were conducted with more than 6,000 mothers (Macro, 1993),[6] a child behavior that 73% of the mothers reported as "not tolerated" was "the child interrupting adult conversation." A nationally representative sample was used, thus reflecting cultural standards, as discussed in the last chapter. In non-child-centered cultural contexts, where childhood is not considered as special, verbal responsiveness to children may be less. The traditional motto "children are to be seen and not heard" was widespread in the West until recently and it is still there among lower SES groups, but changes over time as well as across cultures have become apparent.

In the Early Enrichment Project (Kağıtçıbaşı, 1991b, 1994b; Kağıtçıbaşı et al., 1988) we interviewed mothers of young children, living in low income areas of Istanbul. To find out the degree of others' involvement/interaction with their 3- to 5-year-old children, we asked them how often they gave their full attention to the child outside of meal times. Those who said, "never" or "almost never" reached 22%. Together with those who said, "seldom," low involvement was found among more than 40% of the mothers. In terms of what they commonly do when they are with their children at home, 90% of the mothers stated they do

---

[6]Macro is a private research center; I supervised this large-scale survey.

household chores (and a small proportion hand work such as knitting, embroidering), with little direct interaction with their children.

When does lack of responsiveness, especially in terms of verbal interaction, become a disadvantage for the child? Again, research provides us with some answers. I have already referred to the misfit between school expectations and childrearing goals among marginal groups. A background of observational learning without verbal reasoning can be a disadvantage in school (Nunes, 1993). Indeed, early verbal interaction with adults appears to be a crucial antecedent of early language development. Language skills are, in turn, indicative of better school performance.

Studies on early language development point to the role of environmental factors. Reviewing some early research, Slobin (1972) noted that compared to Western children in the United States, France, and Russia, non-Western children reach the two-word sequence of linguistic development at a substantially slower pace. He attributed this difference to the lower density of language addressed to young children in non-Western cultures. More recent work on the development of oral language skills and literacy also points to the importance of extensive adult–child verbal interactions, involving reasoning, asking and answering questions, storytelling, bookreading, and discussions of ongoing events (Snow 1991, 1993). A growing body of research in the area of literacy shows that early home experience with oral language skills and the "culture of literacy" (involving familiarity with printed media, world knowledge, vocabulary, etc.) predict advanced literacy achievement. Children who lack such experience would be disadvantaged in school and as adults in literate society.

For example, an earlier study in Istanbul, Turkey, found large differences in vocabulary of middle- and working-class fifth-grade children (Semin, 1975). Yet, vocabulary is found to be the best single predictor of reading success (Anderson & Freebody, 1981). This finding from research conducted in the United States may well have cross-cultural validity. Similarly, Ataman and Epir (1972) in a study in Ankara, Turkey, found that children from low income families formed concepts of lower level of complexity, compared with middle-class children. In later work, Savaşir and Şahin (1988) and Savaşir, Sezgin, and Erol (1992) found persistent social class differences in vocabulary and verbal competence in Turkey. Working with the children of Turkish migrant workers in the Netherlands, Leseman (1993) found lower SES Turkish children of 3 and 3½ years of age to have lower levels of vocabulary and concept formation skills (in Turkish) than Dutch middle- and working-class children (in Dutch). Other studies on larger cohorts of Dutch and different groups of immigrant children in the 3- to 6-year-old age range found similar results (reported by Leseman, 1993).

In a series of studies with Mexican-American mothers and their children, Laosa (1980, 1982, 1984) pointed to the importance of low maternal education, low social class standing, and minority language status as determinants of children's poor cognitive performance. Mothers' teaching strategies and verbal communication with the child were mediating factors. Specifically, less educated Hispanic mothers typically used less verbal interaction with their young children, less praise, and less inquiring, but more modeling, directives, and negative physical control than Anglo mothers. Laosa (1984) found differences between Hispanic and Anglo children's performance (on the McCarthy scales of children's abilities) as early as 2½ years of age, showing the importance of early language development. Similarly, Slaughter (1988) noted the lack of decontextualized communication and play with young children in Black families in the United States. She indicated that this factor explains why Black infants who surpass White infants in early sensory-motor intelligence fall behind in later language-based cognitive performance.

Wachs and Gruen (1982) also pointed out that verbal stimulation becomes important after the first year, and the amount of parent–child interaction after 24 months of age makes an impact on developmental outcomes. The second year appears critical for early syntactic and semantic development, and starting from age 2, amount and complexity of parental verbal communication with the child is consequential for the child's cognitive development. Goodnow (1988) pointed to "parental modernity" as a possible important moderator variable. This is an outlook associated with "stimulating academic behavior," "stimulating language," and "encouraging social maturity." Parents with such an outlook provide a stimulating environment for their young children and actively prepare them for school.

Applegate, Burleson, and Delia (1992), proposed a model of communication development focusing on the complexity dimension. It purports that the complexity of parental social cognition leads to the complexity of parental communication, which in turn leads to the complexity of the child's social cognition and finally to the complexity of the child's communication. The key in this process model is what they call "reflection-enhancing parenting," found to relate positively to mother's social class and social-cognitive development.

The model proposed by Applegate et al. (1992) combines two different lines of thinking and research on parental language and discipline. I have been referring to the language issue in terms of extensive adult verbal communication and verbal reasoning with the child (as studied, for example by Slobin, 1972; Snow, 1991, 1993). This is also in line with Bernstein's (1974) distinction between "elaborated code" and "restricted code," typical of middle-class and working-class home communication, respectively.

As for parental discipline, several conceptualizations have been developed distinguishing between two main orientations, called power assertive (or authoritarian or parent-centered or punishment-oriented) versus inductive (or authoritative or child-centered or reasoning-oriented) (Baumrind 1971, 1980, 1989; M. L. Hoffman, 1977). Whereas power-assertive/authoritarian parenting tries to control the child's behavior using negative reinforcement, inductive/authoritative parenting tries to influence the child's behavior through reasoning, especially by forming causal relations and drawing the children's attention to the consequences of their acts. Thus, Applegate et al.'s (1992) "reflection-enhancing communication" with the child involves both inductive/authoritative reasoning with the child and the complex (elaborated) language necessitated by this orientation. They find reflection-enhancing communication to be associated with social class.

Other research has examined several aspects of parental discipline and related it to child and adolescent development and school performance. Without attempting to summarize this extensive body of theory and research, a few points may be noted. Studies find consistent relations between authoritative parenting and adolescents' academic success and psychosocial competence (Dornbusch, Ritter, Leiderman, Roberts, & Fraleigh, 1987; Lamborn, Mounts, Steinberg, & Dornbusch, 1991; Steinberg, Elmen, & Mounts, 1989). Thus, effects extend beyond childhood into adolescence. Distinction between dominating (restrictive) parental control and an order setting (functional) parental control (Lau & Cheung, 1987; Lau et al., 1990) showed further that the latter has a positive impact on developmental outcomes. This is because organizing (authoritative, as opposed to authoritarian-restrictive control) involves extensive verbal give and take, in a rational, issue-oriented manner (Lau & Cheung, 1987), as distinguished by Baumrind earlier (1971, 1980).

It is exactly this type of parenting that appears to be lacking in lower social class and marginalized immigration contexts where maternal education is limited. For example, Gutierrez, Sameroff, and Karrer (1988) found lower levels of complexity in parental reasoning about child development among lower class and less acculturated Mexican-American mothers compared with more acculturated and middle-class mothers. Research in Turkey (Kağıtçıbaşı et al., 1988; Macro 1993) points to punishment-oriented control strategies among low SES families.

From the foregoing discussion it may appear that I am lumping together different groups and that I am accepting Western middle-class white (school) culture as the mainstream culture. Some clarification may be in order on both points. My intention in the main discussion in this chapter is not to lump ethnic migrants, rural populations, immigrants into urban centers, and socio-economically disadvantaged populations together into any single social entity. Obviously, this would be a fallacious undertaking. What I have been trying to do is to point to certain shared aspects of the family culture that are a potential source of disadvantage for the child. What these groups share within the macro-system is a marginal and less powerful position vis-à-vis the more powerful mainstream. On this point there is probably agreement. It may be less apparent, however, that these groups also share some characteristics at the microsystem level of family and childrearing. It is to these characteristics that I have been referring.

As for what constitutes mainstream, I do not mean to identify it with Western middle-class (school) culture alone. It may seem that way because the preponderance of research is carried out in the West, mainly in the United States.

However, urban–rural differences and social stratification based on SES levels are even more pronounced in less developed non-Western contexts. The same problems of misfit, even in greater proportions, exist there. Indeed, that is why I started this discussion with some examples from Turkey and critically reviewed some of the (policy) implications of the "everyday cognition" research, based mainly in Africa.

What I have been discussing here with regard to verbal communication involving reasoning (causal explanation, inquiry, perspective taking, etc.) fits in with the socialization for cognitive competence, which I examined earlier. Specifically, nonverbal observational learning and noninductive obedience-oriented child socialization appear not to be optimal for the promotion of high levels of cognitive/linguistic complexity in the child. They may be seen to constitute a disadvantage for the child, especially in contexts of social change (such as urban–rural mobility, ethnic migration, etc.) where the child has to adapt to new environmental (e.g., school) demands for linguistic-cognitive competence, individual decision making, initiative, creative problem solving, and so on (Eldering & Kloprogge, 1989).

Note, however, that the causes of problems of low school performance of some ethnic minority and lower SES children are not inherent in the families or individuals concerned, but also in the general circumstances of majority–minority or social class relationships in a society. For example, pervasive prejudice toward and low levels of expectations from minority and low SES pupils on the part of teachers and school administrations work as "self-fulfilling prophecies."

It is not my intention here to explain all of the complex problems involved (elaborate analyses attempt at explanation; see, for example, Ogbu, 1988, 1990). I am only pointing to some aspects that have to do with misfits between traditional cultural and parental conceptions of cognitive competence and parenting and mainstream (host society, urban culture, educational institutions) conceptions. Whether we examine the situation of international migration or of ethnic minorities in the industrialized countries or of peasants and tribal people moving into urban areas or having to adjust to new economic activities or of low SES groups in a city, we find similar types of misfit.

The criteria for competence in the mainstream culture are to some extent different from those held by the minorities, immigrants, rural migrants, and lower SES people. Given the existing power differentials, it is not realistic to expect mainstream culture (schools, businesses, professions, etc.) to change much, thus readjustments on the part of the less powerful are necessary. This is not to say that nothing changes in the mainstream culture; indeed, no culture is static, and change is always with us. Furthermore, inequalities, exploitation, and so on must be corrected. And psychologists, together with other social scientists, must work for change and improvement at the macrolevel, in addition to the individual or family level. For example, a recent motto in educational intervention work is "preparing children for school *and* schools for children" (Myers, 1992).

There is an understanding here that there are many things in need of correction in the schools in both developing and industrialized countries. However, social institutional change is a slow process. Waiting for the institutions to change while doing nothing to help people (children and adults) to adjust better to institutions is unrealistic and does not prevent frustrations and failures at the individual and group level. Thus changes have to occur on both sides.

However, some aspects of the school culture are not going to change because they are functional and inherently related to other modern social institutions and the prevalent urban literate culture. School's conception of cognitive competence in terms of verbal and mathematical ability and abstract reasoning, problem solving, and so on are in line with the industrial (and industrializing) society needs to develop these cognitive skills in young people. These are the skills that effectively fit the requirements of specialized functions to be carried out in society. It is especially in these realms that any mismatch between cultural/parental conceptions of cognitive competence and school requirements need to be resolved by changes in the former.   *parents need to change*

In this context, two of the themes discussed in this chapter, learning by observation–imitation (rather than verbal reasoning) and "social definitions of intelligence," can be briefly reconsidered. Though learning through observation–imitation can be effective, the importance of other types of learning, especially through verbal reasoning, explanation, reflection, and so on need to be recognized by parents. This would bring with it other changes in orientation to the child, seen not only as a quiet observer and imitator of parental modeling but as an active participant in the learning process, who can verbalize about it. Such verbalization can involve causal relations, explanations, enquiries, and so on. Effective and extensive use of language in child socialization would be a key mediating factor here.

As for social definitions of intelligence (or cognitive competence) what appears to be called for is not a decreased emphasis on social goals in child socialization but rather an increased emphasis on cognitive goals. The mismatch between parental values and school demands, for example, seems to derive from too little parental stress on cognitive skills and too much reliance on being good (obedient, quiet) for school success. There needs to be a recognition of the importance of cognitive and language skills, as mentioned earlier. Development of social skills (if not limited only to obedience) would in fact be valuable in adapting more quickly to school, as suggested by Okagaki and Sternberg (1993). However, a recognition of the different realms of competence (social *and* cognitive), each important in its own right, would need to emerge for a better fit between the family and the school culture.

To borrow a terminology from economics and political science, what the disadvantaged groups lack is social capital (Coleman, 1990). If we understand the psychological underpinnings of the problems involved, it is possible to help ameliorate the problems even if the macrosituation does not change much. Mediating factors pointed to by models developed to describe the processes involved in disadvantage are helpful in this context. They tend to be shared to some extent in different disadvantaged situations. Some examples are a high number of risk factors (Sameroff & Fiese, 1992) and the negative impact of poverty, stress, and social disadvantage on parenting skills and parental involvement (McLoyd, 1990; Patterson & Dishion, 1988) discussed earlier. Apart from these adverse conditions, parental conceptions of competence that are at odds with mainstream ideals and the corresponding parental orientations commonly found in rural/traditional society can also act as a disadvantage, especially in periods of social change.

4 Culture and Self

In the last chapter it became clear that socialization for competence is understood differently in different cultural contexts. A social definition of intelligence prevails in contexts characterized by closely knit familial and communal bonds. Indeed, this covers most of the world outside of the individualistic "West," though showing variations in degree. Thus, for most people even cognitive competence involves social competence; and social competence certainly looms large in a general conception of socialization for adult roles in a society. At the core of social competence, in turn, is the development of the self.

This chapter examines the interface between culture and self—a nebulous topic. Being quite selective in my orientation, I deal first with how the concept of self varies with culture, reflecting it. I then discuss some psychological and anthropological approaches to the study of self and in particular the recent critical thinking in American social psychology that have brought "the self" to the foreground. These approaches, combined with the recent cultural and cross-cultural research within the individualism/collectivism paradigm, point toward a basic dimension along which there is cultural variation in self construals. This is the (inter)dependence–independence dimension, reflected in the relational–separated self. This dimension and its implications are discussed in some detail, as they constitute one of the main themes in this book.

CULTURALLY VARYING CONCEPT OF SELF

I am using "self" in this book as a construct that encapsulates the notion of the person and to some extent personality. It is a social product in the sense that it emerges out of social interaction and is socially situated at any point in time. This differentiates "self" from personality, the latter referring to rather enduring, stable characteristics, relatively unaffected by changing social situations. Self is also reflective, in the sense of the person's awareness of it as self-perception ("I," "me"), as well as interactive, including social cognition and motivation. Finally, as a social product, self is a culturally shared model of the person (Lakoff & Johnson, 1980). It is this latter characteristic of self that will be the main focus of this chapter.

The concept of self is variously understood in different cultural contexts. This is the case even though self is a basic psychological concept and is commonly assumed to have a fundamental and universal nature. By now, a vast body of research emerging from different disciplinary traditions provides definitive evidence of diversity. A well-known expression of this diversity can be found in the following oft-quoted passage from Geertz, 1975:

> The Western conception of the person as a bounded, unique, more or less integrated motivational and cognitive universe, a dynamic center of awareness, emotion, judgement, and action organized into a distinctive whole and set contrastively both against other such wholes and against a social and natural background is, however incorrigible it may seem to us, a rather peculiar idea within the context of the world's cultures. (p. 48)

In Bali, Geertz noted that individual actors were not important, but rather the roles they are assigned in society and how they enact in relation to others. Thus, "the masks they wear, the stage they occupy, the parts they play, and most important, the spectacle they mount remain and constitute not the facade but the substance of things, not least the self" (Geertz 1975, p. 50). Geertz referred to a "relational" conceptualization of self, where individuals are not known by their names (some nonsense syllable, they may, themselves, have forgotten) but in terms of whose sons they are.

Pursuing the aforementioned parallel with the social definition of intelligence, one would expect that where social definitions of intelligence prevail, some relational conceptualization of self also would be common. This is because the development of social competence, especially sensitivity to others and social responsibility, would be stressed in child training in cultural contexts where human relations are of supreme importance. I have given some examples of these in the last chapter from research in Africa (Harkness & Super, 1992; Serpell, 1977) and from Turkey (Kağıtçıbaşı, 1984, 1991b; Kağıtçıbaşı et al., 1988; Macro, 1993).

Relational conceptualizations of the self are reported from other countries as well, though probably not as striking as in the Balinese case. For example, V. G. Enriquez (1988) described the concept of *Kapwa*, the core of Filipino interpersonal behavior, as "the unity of the 'self' and 'other'" (p. 139). It embraces both the categories of "outsider" (other) and "one of us," thus it allows for the merging of the self and the other, in contrast to the common English usage pitting the two against one another. Similarly, much has been written about the Japanese "group self," originating from the early merging of the mother and the child in the *amae* relationship and continuing through life in a sense of connectedness and dependence (Caudill & Frost, 1973; DeVos, 1985; L. A. Doi, 1974; T. Doi, 1973; Yamaguchi, 1985; Lebra, 1976; Morsbach, 1980; Neki, 1976; Stevenson, Azuma, & Hakuta, 1986).

Nsamenang (1992) referred to "social selfhood" within the West African context, which starts with the naming of the infant until death in old age. "Connectedness" is also seen in the Chinese self, where the meaning of being human resides in interpersonal relationships (e.g., Bond, 1986; Hsu, 1985). More recently, Sun (1991) described "the Chinese 'two persons' matrix" in the sense that "a Chinese individual, far from being a distinct and separate *individuum*, is conceivable largely in the continuum of 'two persons'. . . . The completion of One in the matrix of the Other is also reflected in the prime symbolism of Chinese culture—the complementarity of *yin* and *yan*. . . . Confucianism is the philosophy *par excellence* of the 'Two'" (pp. 2–4; emphases in original).

Connectedness of the self is not only with others, but sometimes also with nature or the supernatural realm, as evidenced by much anthropological work, especially in preindustrial societies (sometimes preliterate; e.g., in Africa and Oceania). In these conceptualizations of the oneness of self with natural or supernatural forces, there is a continuity and extension of the self through time and space, and the individuals themselves are not necessarily in charge of their own life or actions (e.g., Heelas & Lock, 1981; Marsella et al., 1985; Nsamenang, 1992; Shweder & R. LeVine, 1984; G. R. Teasdale & J. I. Teasdale, 1992).

From a psychoanalytic perspective, Roland (1988) distinguished the "familial self" of the Japanese and the Indians, "where the experiential sense of self is a 'we-self,'" from the Western "individualized self" (p. 8). Yet, "the West" is no homogeneous, entity; for example, Gaines (1984) contrasted the Northern European (Protestant) and the Mediterranean (Latin) concepts of the person as "referential" and "indexical," respectively. The latter self is perceived "not as an abstract entity independent of the social relations and contexts . . . but as constituted or 'indexed' by the contextual features of social interaction in diverse situations" (p. 182).

Looking into history may provide further insight. In the age-old cultures of the Middle East and Anatolia, both in the Jewish and the Moslem traditions, patriarchal ideology was expressed in calling boys and men not with their own names but as sons of their fathers. The Arab words *ibn* or *bin* or the Hebrew *ben* or the Turkish *oğlu* (son of) were used with the father's name often without the person's own name (reminiscent of the Balinese practice?). Thus some historical Turkish folk poets (Köroğlu, Dadaloğlu) and famous Moslem philosophers *Ibn*

Sina (Avicenna) and *Ibn* Rushd (Averroes) are known only with their father's names. Even today the formal way a young boy is addressed at the Bar Mitzvah ceremonies in a Jewish synagogue is in terms of his name and his father's name (not with his last name).

I could go on with examples both from research and everyday experience from around the world. They all point to the pervasiveness of a relational conceptualization of self in diverse cultures. Cross-cultural studies conducted by anthropologists and psychologists provide us with many other accounts of this diversity. The main distinction drawn is between a self-contained, individuated, separated, independent self defined by clear boundaries from others and a relational, interdependent self with fluid boundaries. Furthermore, this distinction holds in both self-perception and in social perception (perception of others). A number of volumes have included this basic theme, discussed mainly from an anthropological perspective (e.g., Bond, 1986; Heelas & Locke, 1981; Ito, 1985; Marsella, DeVos, & Hsu, 1985; Marsella & White, 1984; Roland, 1988; Shweder & R. LeVine, 1984; White & Kirkpatrick, 1985). Indeed, a growing body of research and thinking on the self from different sources appears to converge on some such type of distinction.

The previous distinction may reflect more a dimension of variability than a sharp duality. At an absolute existential level every person in every society is obviously aware of being a separate entity ("body" in Chinese terms, according to Sun, 1991). In other words, some line is drawn between what intrinsically is (or belongs to) the self and what is not. However, beyond this most basic existential level, extensive variability emerges. There is variability as to *where* that line is drawn (Heelas & Lock, 1981) and as to how sharply and clearly it is drawn. American (and Western) psychology, both reflecting and reinforcing the individualistic Western cultural ethos, has drawn the line narrowly and sharply, constituting a clear boundary between self and non-self. Other cultural conceptions differ from this construal of the "self" in varying degrees. However, American psychology enjoys a dominant position and is self-contained so the knowledge it creates (based on its own empirical reality) is often assumed to be universal. Partly as a reaction to this, the tendency in cross-cultural research and writing has been to construe the cultural differences as diametrically opposed realities rather than varying in different degrees on a continuous dimension. Because much work is actually done in extremely different cultural contexts (from the West), especially by anthropologists and ethnopsychologists, sharp polarities predominate in the cross-cultural discourse on the self.

Even when this tendency is taken into account, diversity still appears to be more striking than commonality in conceptions of the self across cultures. What is interesting in this context is that psychology of the self is emerging as an area where American psychologists, especially those who are critical of the continuing mainstream conventions, make use of cross-cultural evidence (e.g., Pepitone, 1987; Sampson, 1988, 1989; M. B. Smith, 1991, 1994). The importance of cross-cultural and, in general, contextual analysis to the study of self is getting recognized. Historical inquiry is also used (e.g., Cushman, 1990; Gergen, 1991; Gergen & Davis, 1985; Sampson, 1987, 1989; Taylor, 1989). For example, Taylor (1989) showed how an "inner" segregated self is "strange and without precedent in other cultures and times" (p. 114), reminiscent of Geertz's earlier (1975) claim. However, as M. B. Smith noted, "We can pursue our questions more rigorously, with better evidence, in cross-cultural comparison than is ever possible in historical retrospect" (1991, p. 76).

TRENDS IN THE STUDY OF SELF

I want to examine briefly some trends that have brought self to the forefront of psychological inquiry. When we look at the literature, we find that two rather independent lines of thinking and research have contributed significantly to the current conceptualization of self and society relationships. One of these comprises American critical theory; the other emerges within cultural and cross-cultural psychological and anthropological thinking. The latter, in turn, covers different approaches.

Soul Searching in American Psychology

The 1970s mark the beginnings of increasing self-consciousness and soul-searching in American psychology, especially social psychology. With the rise of cognitive psychology, social psychology, despite its name, was also becoming a psychology of the cognizing individual and losing much of its social and interactionist character, stressed by its founders (such as Kurt Lewin and Muzafer Sherif). Both this trend and noncontextual, ahistorical, laboratory-based methodology of social psychology came under attack, together with a questioning of the supremacy of the individual as the unit of analysis. A recognition of the historical (contextual/ideological) nature of psychology and the dangers of excessive individualism for social well-being are important themes in this early autocriticism (Gergen, 1973; Hogan, 1975; Lasch, 1978; Rotenberg, 1977; Sampson, 1977; M. B. Smith, 1978), which extended into psychology in general.

In the 1980s and 1990s, an increasing number of critics from among American psychologists and sociologists continued questioning mainstream psychology in general and the ideology of individualism it upholds in particular. Bellah et al. (1985) wrote a seminal treatise on the current American society and its changes over time. Taking their clue from the French social philosopher Alexis de Tocqueville, who in 1930s studied American character and society, they named their work *Habits of the Heart*. It is basically a critique of individualism "that has marched inexorably through our history . . . that [ ] may be destroying those social integuments that Tocqueville saw as moderating its more destructive potentialities, that [] may be threatening the survival of freedom itself" (p. vii).

Critical thinking spread in the work of Sampson (1977, 1985, 1987, 1988, 1989), who differentiated between *self-contained* individualism (with firm boundaries of self–non-self and personal control) and *ensembled* individualism. The former is the prototype of the Western and especially American construal of the self. The latter, which he proposed as an alternative, is a definition of the self with permeable boundaries, and control located in the interpersonal *field*, and not necessarily within the person. Other critics deplore the "empty self" "because of the loss of family, community, and tradition" (Cushman, 1990); the "minimal self" (Lasch, 1984), with a psychoanalytic orientation narcissisticly turned unto itself but not able to prevent fragmentation (Lasch, 1978, Kohut, 1977, 1984); or the "saturated self" (Gergen, 1991), overwhelmed by the overload of information in the postmodern era.

M. B. Smith (1994) reviewed these critiques and talked about the vulnerability of the "inflated self" (p. 7) of which too much is expected as a source of life purpose and goals such as self-actualization, self-commitment, and so on. Given the fading of religious and moral values, the self is overburdened to replace these sources of life purpose, which M. B. Smith considered "basically unworkable as a frame for living our lives" (p. 8). This analysis is in line with those advanced by Taylor (1989) and Baumeister (1986, 1991). According to M. B. Smith (1994), the metaphors of both depletion and expansion of the self refer to the same problem. This is the problem of a self troubled with a lack of human nurturance, moral guidelines for action, and "inflated pretensions" of control and worth.

The negative social implications of this concept of self are further analyzed by critics, and psychology is blamed as a part of the problem. For example, the Wallachs (1983, 1990) deplore and make an effort to counteract psychology's sanctioning and promotion of selfishness. In his APA presidential address, Campbell had noted earlier, "Psychology and Psychiatry . . . not only describe man as selfishly motivated, but implicitly or explicitly teach that he ought to be so" (1975, p. 1104). Indeed, during the "me generation" in the United States (1970s, 1980s) many "self theories" developed, reinforcing and legitimizing the preoccupation with and exaltation of the individual self, unencumbered by any loyalties to others.

Batson (1990) noted that "each of these theories assumes motivation with an ultimate goal of maintaining or enhancing one's self image; social encounters [being] instrumental to this self-serving end" (p. 337). He also took issue with the assumed egoism of humans in psychology and endeavored to show, with a research program, the human capacity for empathy and caring. Etzioni (1993) proposed a manifesto, a new lifestyle, which he called "communitarianism," reviving communal commitments and social responsibilities without puritanism or oppression. Communitarianism has been an interdisciplinary endeavor, with philosophers (Taylor, 1989), sociologists (Etzioni, 1993), and others attempting to combine the desirable attributes of individualism and collectivism. In political theory it involves a critique of liberalism and its emphasis on individualism (Mulhall & Swift, 1992). Psychologists like M. B. Smith (1978, 1990, 1991, 1994) and Sarason (1981, 1988) devoted great effort to promoting a socially responsible psychology. A recent book by Staub and Green (1992) consists of psychologists' work contributing toward the solution of global issues. This topic is discussed further later.

Even those who consider individualism of value warn of its excesses. For example, Spence, in her APA presidential address, said that ". . . we are obligated as citizens and human beings to renew a national sense of commitment to larger causes that go beyond narrow self-interest and the search for self-satisfaction . . . I do not hesitate to hope—indeed to plead—that psychology and psychologists contribute not to the problem but to its solution" (1985, p. 1294).

It is interesting to note, however, that even the most outspoken American critics of individualism, when they propose alternatives, coin new terms that qualify individualism rather than replacing it with another construct. For example, Rotenberg (1977) proposed "reciprocal individualism" (as opposed to alienating individualism); from a feminist perspective, Lykes (1985, p. 373) talked about "a notion of the self as 'social individuality'" more characteristic of the less powerful; and Chorodow (1989), in an attempt to reconcile psychoanalysis with feminist theory, developed the concept of "relational individualism." Probably the best known and referred to among these is Sampson's (1988) "ensembled individualism." To the outsider these terms appear as a contradiction in terms because individualism connotes a particular world view (ideology), thus a term like *self* would have fitted into these formulations better than *individualism*. Indeed, the debate *is* on individualism (Sampson, 1989) and, given its importance in American culture and psychology, even its critics' alternative proposals do not seem to be able to exclude it.

The recent discussion of the self in American psychology has thus focused on individualism and its place in both society and psychology. This has also been the core of social criticism and commentary. Both the disciplinary and social criticism appear healthy for a more culturally sensitive understanding of the self and for a better recognition of the social implication of the prevalent psychological construal of the self. It is also interesting to note that the basic distinction between the related (interdependent) and the separated (independent) self finds expression both in American thinking and in cross-cultural thinking. However, these two trends of thought pursued their separate paths for some two decades without much recognition of the other. American critics continued to refer only to American research, with some occasional reference to a European, in the true spirit of "self-contained American psychology." It is encouraging, nevertheless, that there is a growing recognition of cross-cultural research to be used as evidence (Sampson, 1988; M. B. Smith, 1991).

CULTURAL APPROACHES

Much anthropological and psychological work has focused on the concept of self and its development in diverse cultural contexts. I have already touched on some relevant points, especially with regard to the context of human development, which obviously is the context of self-development. Specifically, parental conceptions of competence, involving social competence and parental goals, beliefs, and values, all have a direct impact on the development of the self. At this time I want to discuss how cultural research deals with "the self."

Anthropological Background

The anthropological antecedents of "culture and self" can be found in the "Culture and Personality" school. Culture and personality was an outgrowth of Boas' early introduction of psychological themes into anthropology, which influenced his students (such as Kroeber, M. Mead, and Benedict). Starting in the late 1920s and 1930s and spanning almost three decades, anthropologists looked into the interrelationships between culture and personality. Most of this work was designed to reveal the basic personality structure of a society, first construed as "configurational personality" (R. Benedict, 1934; M. Mead, 1928), then as "basic and modal personality" (Dubois, 1944; Kardiner & Linton, 1945), and continuing as "national character" (Gorer & Rickman, 1949; Inkeles & Levinson, 1954; Kluckhohn, 1957).

All this work was characterized by intensive and holistic study of single cultures. Starting in 1950s, a cross-cultural comparative approach was introduced into the "Culture and Personality" school by Whiting, using the Human Relations Area Files (HRAF) (Whiting & Child, 1953). The HRAF, founded by Murdock at Yale University, consisted of extensive ethnographic records on a great number of preindustrial societies that allowed for comparison.

The Culture and Personality school, which was later called Psychological Anthropology (Hsu, 1961), was informed mainly by psychoanalytic theory in psychology, which turned out to be a limitation both in terms of topics of study and methodology. For example, the heavy reliance on projective techniques was seriously criticized by Lindzey (1961), and partially as a result of this, enthusiasm faded in 1960s. Another problem involved the assumptions of stability and societal homogeneity of basic personality, ignoring individual and subgroup differences and change over time. These are unwarranted assumptions even for an isolated tribe; they are clearly wrong for contemporary complex societies (for more detailed accounts of Culture and Personality, see Berry et al., 1992; Bock, 1988).

Notwithstanding its problems, the Culture and Personality school contributed significantly to the study of self in cultural context. It introduced the notion that some personality characteristics are shared by individuals in a society because they are adaptive to living in that society. This functional approach is also used in contemporary cultural and cross-cultural thinking, and I believe provides insight into understanding the underlying reasons for cross-cultural similarities and differences.

The cross-cultural comparative work of Whiting and his coworkers, especially, has produced important empirical findings regarding the development of self and paved the way to the current ecocultural framework in cross-cultural psychology (Berry, 1976; Berry et al., 1992). Whiting and his students first started examining ethnographic data from 75 societies on five "systems of behavior": oral, anal, sexual, dependence, and aggression (J. W. Whiting & Child, 1953). The general model used involved linear causal links among ecology, maintenance systems (settlement patterns, economy, etc.), childrearing, child personality, adult personality, and projective systems (cultural beliefs, religion, art, magic, etc.). There are later revisions of the model (J. W. Whiting, 1974). However, the same unidirectional linear model remains, which does not allow for nonlinear or feedback effects.

Using this general framework, other studies looked into sex differences in child socialization (Barry, Bacon, & Child, 1957) and related child training to the economic functioning of the society (Barry, Child, & Bacon, 1959), focusing on obedience, responsibility, nurturance, achievement, and self-reliance training. Some of the findings of this research program showed that girls were socialized more for responsibility and nurturance and boys for achievement and self-reliance. Also, a general emphasis on compliance training was found in "high-food-accumulating" agricultural and animal herding societies, whereas self-reliance training was seen among the "low-food-accumulating" hunters and gatherers (Barry et al., 1957, 1959).

Though this early work was challenged by later analysis (Hendrix, 1985), socialization for compliance in sedentary, agrarian, closely knit societies appears to be a common phenomenon as evidenced in research on cognitive style (Berry, 1976, 1990; Witkin & Berry, 1975). The subsequent "Six Cultures" project (Minturn & Lambert, 1964; B. B. Whiting, 1963) also obtained similarities in childrearing among societies with subsistence agricultural life styles, following a quite different methodology (structured interviews used in different settings rather than the HRAF) . More recent work similarly noted dependency and conformity expectations from children in more traditional societies with extended or joint families characterized by closely knit bonds (Bisht & D. Sinha, 1981; Kağıtçıbaşı, 1984). These findings are akin to those about the importance given to social responsibility (and "social intelligence") in child socialization in traditional societies with closely knit familial and communal bonds, noted earlier.

Current Cross-Cultural Work

There is a general shift in current cross-cultural study of the self from subsistence (preliterate, small-scale, isolated) societies to contemporary societies (industrialized or industrializing nation states), on the one hand, and to ethnic groups within these societies, on the other. One reason for this shift is the greater involvement of psychologists, and not only of anthropologists, in cross-cultural comparative research. Second, more psychologists in non-Western countries are realizing the possibly ethnocentric orientations in Western theory and research and undertaking their own studies of psychological phenomena. Also, more and more cross-cultural research, especially studies involving many countries, are carried out in collaboration with researchers from non-Western countries. Finally, there is a greater interest in validating hypotheses among samples that can be matched in education, SES, and so on from different countries, rather than using extremely different groups in isolated subsistence societies who differ in every respect from the Western samples, thus making it difficult to reveal possible causes of any obtained differences.

Even with this shift in emphasis, however, cross-cultural variability in conceptions of the self is the rule. In particular, a "relational" conceptualization of the self is again a common finding in non-Western contexts. For example, Shweder and Bourne (1984) studied person concepts in the United States and in India. Whereas American subjects used individual ("egocentric") constructs (46% of Americans' descriptions were of this type, compared with only 20% of the Indians'), Indian subjects used more context-specific and relational ("sociocentric") person descriptions, where "units' (persons) are believed to be necessarily altered by the relations they enter into" (p. 110). This distinction reflects the Western view of the self as comprising stable and abstract traits that have generality over time and situations, as opposed to a more situational understanding of the changeable self. Thus, whereas Americans tend to use more trait descriptions ("she is friendly"), Indians contextualize ("she brings cakes to my family on festive days") (p. 119).

Relational concepts of self also figure in attributions made about others' behaviors. J. G. Miller (1984), again comparing Americans and Indians, asked her subjects to give reasons for others' deviant and prosocial behaviors. Her results showed a preponderance of dispositional (person) attributions for Americans and situational (contextual) attributions for Indians, especially marked for deviant acts (of the American subjects, 36% made dispositional, 17% situational attributions; for Indian subjects, the figures were 15% and 32%, respectively). Clearly, there is a stronger situating of the person in the interpersonal context for Indians for whom the self is affected by the situation (others' expectations, etc.). Americans, on the other hand, understand self and explain behavior in terms of context-independent, stable, enduring personality dispositions.

Relational or separated construals of the self also have implications for self-perceptions. Cousins (1989) used the Twenty Statements Test (TST) (Kuhn & McPartland, 1954; which repeatedly asks "Who am I?") with American and Japanese students. He found that the American subjects used psychological trait or attribute descriptions of themselves, whereas the Japanese subjects were more concrete (situational) and role specific. This is similar to the difference Shweder and Bourne (1984) found between Americans and Indians in describing *others*.

The reverse result was obtained, however, when a modified version of the test was applied specifying situations (in relation to others) in which to describe oneself. Because this was more "natural" for the Japanese, they could give enduring trait descriptions more easily, but the Americans felt the need to qualify their self-descriptions to make sure their self-images could be independent of the situational constraints (Cousins, 1989). Other studies using the TST also found that Americans use more trait descriptions of self than the Japanese (Bond & Cheung, 1983) and the Chinese made more references to self as a member of a group (Triandis, McCusker, & Hui, 1990).

How the self is construed also has implications for moral thinking. J. G. Miller, Bersoff, and Harwood (1990) compared Indian and American subjects' moral reasoning regarding hypothetical nonhelping situations. They found that Indians consider social responsibilities as moral issues, but Americans do not (except in cases of life-threatening emergencies and in parent–child interaction); they consider them to be matters of personal choice or decision. Thus, for the Indian "related self," the welfare of others (beneficence) is an integral aspect of moral code, invoking social responsibility. For the American "separated self," however, moral code is limited to justice and individual freedom; it does not include beneficence, as evidenced in Kohlberg's theory (1981). Indeed, beneficence can be seen to conflict with the individual freedom of choice. There are clear implications of this finding for the issue of egoism-altruism, which is salient in the recent criticism and social commentary within American psychology, as noted before.

In other areas of psychological functioning, we can find implications of the connectedness–separateness of the self. For example, with a more relational construal of the self go equality rather than equity orientations in distributive justice (Kashima, Siegel, Tanaka, & Isaka, 1988; Leung, 1987; Marin, 1985; Triandis, Leung, Villareal, & Clack, 1985); a tendency to perceive interpersonal harmony rather than competition in social episodes (Forgas & Bond, 1985); less "self-serving bias" (Kashima & Triandis, 1986); less social loafing (Gabrenya, Wang, & Latane, 1985); a more cooperative than competitive orientation (Eliram & Schwarzwald, 1987), and other tendencies in cognitive, emotional and motivational realms, as reviewed by Markus and Kitayama (1991). Most of this research has been conducted within an "individualism–collectivism" framework. However, given the nature of the behaviors studied, I believe the main determining factor in these studies is the degree of connectedness–separateness of the self.

Triandis (1989) reviewed this literature and suggested a probabilistic framework explaining when the "private," "collective," or "public" selves become more salient, over three dimensions of cultural variation (individualism–collectivism, tightness–looseness and cultural complexity). After Baumeister (1986) and Greenwald and Pratkanis (1984), Triandis defined *private self* as cognitions that involve traits or behaviors of the person ("I am introverted"); the *public self* as cognitions concerning generalized others' view of the self ("People think I am introverted"); and the *collective self* as cognitions concerning a view of the self that is found in a collective, such as the family ("My family thinks I am introverted") (Triandis, 1989, p. 507).

Most relevant for the present discussion is the prediction that the more individualistic the culture (i.e., the more self is construed as separate), the more frequent is the sampling of the private self (i.e., the private self is more salient in the person's experience); and conversely, the more collectivist the culture, the more the collective self is sampled. Societal tightness (which reflects closely knit familial-communal bonds) is also associated with the higher sampling of the collective self.[7]

It may be informative at this point to refer to individualism–collectivism briefly. This concept has stimulated much research and thinking in cross-cultural psychology within the last decade, thus extensive reviews are available (Kağıtçıbaşı, 1995; Kağıtçıbaşı & Berry, 1989; Kim, Triandis, Kağıtçıbaşı, Choi, & Yoon, 1994; Triandis, 1988, 1990, 1995). I touch on some points of relevance to the previous discussion.

From its beginnings in Tönnies' (1957) *Gesellschaft* and *Gemeinschaft*, and particularly with its inception in cross-cultural psychology with Hofstede's (1980) *Culture's consequences*, individualism–collectivism has referred to cultures. It has been considered "the single most important dimension of cultural difference in social behavior" (Triandis, 1988). Its popularity for cross-cultural psychologists derives from its use as a culture-level explanation for observed cultural differences in behavior. It can be used at the individual level of analysis as "idiocentrism–allocentrism" (respectively) (Triandis et al., 1985). However, this multilevel usage has at times caused some confusion.

Individualism–collectivism as "isms," are basically ideological concepts and have come to acquire some social-normative content, in addition to the separateness–connectedness dimension. For example, individualism is seen as akin to modernity and is associated with modern values such as sex-role equality, whereas collectivism is seen to embody traditional, conservative ideology (Kağıtçıbaşı, 1994a; K-S. Yang, 1988). Such normative attributions do not neces-

---

[7]Triandis (1989) related cultural complexity to the sampling of the "private" self, which I find problematic (see Kağıtçıbaşı, 1994a, for a discussion on this point).

sarily follow from a psychological level conceptualization of the separateness–connectedness dimension. Thus, individualism–collectivism carries much excess meaning.

Nevertheless, the important body of research conducted within the individualism–collectivism framework has provided much insight into a better understanding of the separateness–relatedness dimension of the self and self–other relations. There is much overlap in the thinking involved in the two areas. Separateness–connectedness of the self may be construed as the psychological core dimension of individualism–collectivism.

RELATIONAL SELF–SEPARATED SELF

There is a great deal of convergence in the research and theorizing reviewed in this chapter. Whether in the form of speculative theory, social commentary/criticism, anthropological in-depth culture study, or cross-cultural psychological research, spanning different academic disciplines over considerable time and space, views about the self distinguish between (degrees of) relating to and separating from others. Whether the self is well bounded and separate or whether it is expansive and its boundaries are diffuse is of crucial significance for the psychological and social functioning of the individual. Thus, the degree of relatedness–separateness of the self has emerged as a basic dimension.

I noted this dimension first at the cultural level, in terms of "culture of separateness–culture of relatedness" (Kağıtçıbaşı, 1985a), referring to general closeness–distance in human relations. Since then I have focused more on the separateness–relatedness of the self and its antecedents (indeed going back to some of my own culture contact experiences, which I related in the preface). I prefer this conceptual dimension to the more popular individualism–collectivism mainly because separateness–relatedness of the self is a basically psychological dimension, whereas individualism–collectivism is not.

The psychological domain within which I have noted in this chapter a great convergence of research and thinking on the self can be called the "psychology of relatedness" (Kağıtçıbaşı, 1994a). It has to do with general self–other relations and their integration with how the self is conceptualized. Thus, from a disciplinary point of view, this domain bridges personality and social psychology. It is also a cross-cultural psychological domain because both the self construal and also its integral interpersonal relations show cross-cultural variation, as evidenced by research. Indeed, if systematic cross-cultural variations can be established, and if they can be related to distinct antecedent conditions, we may be on our way to discovering a possibly universal dimension of human behavior.

There are clear parallels between the cultural, familial (group–interpersonal), and individual levels of analysis with regard to the psychology of relatedness. Thus the culture of separateness refers to the contexts (cultural–familial) and interpersonal relational patterns characterized by relations between separate selves, with clearly defined boundaries (making them self-contained). The culture of relatedness, on the other hand, refers to contexts and relational patterns identified by relations between connected, expanding, and therefore partially overlapping selves with diffuse boundaries. There are, furthermore, different degrees of separateness–relatedness between these two polar opposites, thus what we have here is a dimension of variation.

(Inter)Dependence–Independence

Psychology of relatedness can also be conceptualized as a dimension of (inter)dependence–independence. Indeed, in a former analysis, looking into the development of the related and the separated self, I proposed dependence–independence as a basic dimension (Kağıtçıbaşı, 1990, p. 154 ff). Quite independently, Markus and Kitayama (1991) also proposed the "independent" and the "interdependent" construal of the self to refer to the distinction I have already discussed. These are very similar concepts that have to do with basic human relations–self interface. The concepts of dependence/independence are not new; they have figured for a long time in developmental research, personality theory, and the study of childrearing and socialization. I have referred to some of the latter in this chapter (Barry et al., 1959; Berry, 1976; 1990; J. W. Whiting & Child, 1953; Witkin & Berry, 1975). However, an exclusive focus on this dimension in the study of self is rather recent.

The (inter)dependence–independence dimension can be conceptualized at different levels. At the level of the self, it is equivalent to the relatedness–separateness dimension. It can also be studied at the familial or cultural levels, similar to the culture of relatedness–culture of separateness (Kağıtçıbaşı, 1985). At this level it can be useful in understanding, for example, childrearing and socialization orientations. It is at this level, especially that of the family, that (inter)dependence–independence dimension provides the links between the background (cultural, social-structural) variables and the self. It is thus an important concept in studying the development of the self.

The (inter)dependence–independence dimension, just like the related/separated self construal, has to do with basic human merging and separation. In American psychology it finds its first expression in the "conflict theories" of personality (Angyal, 1951; Bakan, 1966, 1968; Rank, 1929, 1945), which proposed two basic and conflicting needs for merging with and separation from others. Within the psychoanalytic point of view, reinterpreted by object relations theory, it derives from the "resolution" of the individuation–separation issue (e.g., Chodorow, 1989; Mahler, 1972; Mahler, Pine, & Bergman, 1975; Panel, 1973a, 1973b). It is considered a natural early developmental process of attaining object constancy and mental representations of objects (mainly of comforting others) in their absence, thus leading to autonomy from the environment.

This view is also shared by ego psychologists (Hartman, 1939/1958), who earlier posited this process as the development of the rational, autonomous ego. From a different perspective, that of family systems theory (Guerin, 1976; Minuchin, 1974), there is an emphasis on clear boundaries separating the selves (subsystems) within the family system. Thus, both for healthy development of the self and for healthy family functioning, individuation–separation and well-defined boundaries of the self are considered crucial in much of personality theory and clinical psychology.

As I discussed earlier, some early cognitive process of differentiation must take place, because every person is aware of being a separate entity from others. However, the individuation–separation hypothesis does not deal only with this basic existential level; it goes beyond it in defining healthy and pathological human development and family functioning. It works at a psychological level throughout the life span, proscribing "symbiotic" relationships (overlapping selves) as pathological and prescribing separated selves as healthy. Other theoretical orientations in mainstream personality psychology, deriving from Freud, Erickson, and others, share similar views.

Thus, Western psychology affirms one type of self—the separated self—as *the* healthy prototype. It is the prescriptive nature of psychology that empowers it. It can be used to contribute to human well-being; but, if misguided, it can do more harm than good. This is what the critics of American psychology are complaining about: Psychology is a part of the problem, rather than the solution, of selfishness and lack of social commitment.

Autonomy, Control, Achievement

The very concept of independence and autonomy may also be affected by culture. For example, Osterweil and Nagano (1991) and Fujinaga (1991) found that Japanese mothers, like American and Israeli mothers, value independence in their children, but for the Japanese mother independence means the children are capable of interacting with other children or engaging in relationships of "mutual sympathy, trust, and consideration." Thus in a way, independence connotes interdependence in the development of the Japanese self. Befu (1986) also defined Japanese "personhood" in terms of "interpersonalism" ("definition of self in terms of the relationship one has with others," p. 22), self-discipline, and "role perfectionism." These characterizations have direct implications for the concept of control, which is parallel to autonomy and has been a topic of research and debate, especially in Japanese-American comparisons.

Specifically, Weisz, Rothbaum, and Blackburn (1984) showed that whereas in the United States "primary control" (influencing existing realities) is emphasized and valued, in Japan "secondary control" (accommodating to existing realities) assumes greater importance. This distinction is reminiscent of the earlier conceptualization of belief in internal and external control of reinforcement, respectively (Rotter, 1966). From an individualistic point of view, belief in internal control has always been considered to be better (indicative of greater autonomy). Accordingly, when the less powerful groups (women, lower SES groups, people in traditional societies, ethnic minorities) were found to have less belief in internal control (more belief in external control), they were often considered to be deficient (traditional, weak, fatalistic, etc.) (e.g., Kağıtçıbaşı, 1973). Though, depending on the situation, there could be some truth in this interpretation, the objective reality of less scope for control available for the less powerful or their possible alternative motivations were often ignored.

For example, an alternative to control may be "detachment," studied by Naidu (1983) as a form of indigenous Indian form of "voluntarily giving up control," as distinguished from "involuntary" lack of control in Western theorizing. In his criticism of mainstream psychology's "self-contained individualism" construct, Sampson (1988) was critical of the view of control as inhering in the individual and claimed that control is located in the interpersonal field in "ensembled individualism."

In the Japanese case, lack of primary control was interpreted by the American researchers as relinquishing control that may result in excessive conformity (Weisz et al., 1984). However, Azuma (1984) showed that "secondary control" involves different categories of control, and Kojima (1984) further pointed out the contextual nature of the use of control and its links with interpersonal boundaries in Japan. As Azuma (1984) noted, "In a culture like Japan, where tact concerning yielding is positively valued, highly differentiated perceptions are likely to emerge" (p. 970). In other cultures where similar values upholding interpersonal (group) harmony rather than individual autonomy prevail, similar psychological processes involving adjustments, such as yielding when needed, may also emerge as alternatives to direct control. Thus, conceptions of autonomy and control can vary across cultures that have direct implications for child socialization and the development of the self.

Whether autonomy (independence) and control are construed in a more individualistic or a more interpersonal (social) sense also has implications for the conceptualization of the achievement motive. Since the early work of McClelland, Atkinson, Clark, and Lowell (1953), achievement motivation in American psychology has been conceived in terms of individual striving, agency, and competition with others. This is congruent with an individualistic ethos but may be at odds with a culture of relatedness where interpersonal harmony and group loyalties are of prime importance. Indeed, efforts to instill higher individualistic achievement motivation in a collectivistic setting such as India were not successful (McClelland & Winter, 1969, 1971; J.B.P. Sinha, 1985). However, it is not to be assumed that achievement motives or strivings are weak or nonexistent in a cultural context of relatedness. On the contrary, some of the greatest feats of economic achievement at societal levels are currently seen in the collectivistic societies of the Pacific Rim. The industry and high achievement of Japanese and Chinese students are also well known.

Achievement motivation assumes a different meaning in a collectivistic culture; it extends beyond the self and merges with others very much parallel to the related self expanding toward others through diffuse boundaries. Thus, a "socially oriented achievement motivation" is proposed to be common in societies where interdependent human relations prevail (Agarwal & Misra, 1986; Bond, 1986; DeVos, 1968; Misra & Agarwal, 1985; K-S. Yang, 1986; Yu & K-S. Yang, 1994). When achievement is construed and measured in individualistic terms, many people in cultures of relatedness emerge as lacking it (Bradburn, 1963; Rosen, 1962). This is mainly because a different, more socially oriented achievement motivation is not tapped by measures devised to assess an individualisticly construed achievement motivation (Yu & K-S. Yang, 1994).

Thus, the achievement motive appears to be a complex construct, possibly involving different types of achievement needs, functioning singly or in combination. A socially oriented achievement motive would involve upholding group achievement, transcending the self, in such a way that achievement would not only exalt the self but also some other (social) entity encompassing the self. Note that this is not debasing the self or sacrificing self-interest for the group, but rather merging the self with the group so that achievement elevates both. For example, Phalet and Claeys (1993), in a study comparing Turkish and Belgian youth, found *combined* preferences among modern urban Turkish youth for both "loyalty" (to the family and the larger group/society) and "self-realization," contrasted with "self-realization," alone, among Belgian youth. The latter self-oriented striving is again what the critics of American psychology and society deplore, calling for "values that transcend the self" (M. B. Smith, 1994, p. 407; Spence, 1985, p. 1294).

The type of child socialization that engenders such a combination of self-and-other-oriented achievement motivation is probably itself rather complex, involving a combination of different goals. For example, Lin and Fu (1990), in a comparison of Chinese, immigrant Chinese, and Anglo-American parents, found the two Chinese groups to be higher than the Anglo group on both parental control and encouragement of independence (with an emphasis on achievement). These complex socialization orientations may be considered to be at odds with one another and to involve conflicting elements when viewed from an individualistic perspective. However, this interpretation is based on an underlying point of view pitting the individual against the group. Indeed, "loyalty to the self" and "self-realization" need not conflict with "loyalty to the group" (Kağıtçıbaşı, 1987b) in the familial–cultural context, which is conducive to the development of the relational self.

Development of the Self

How the self is construed in a cultural context has direct implications for socialization. This is because childrearing and socialization are goal directed, with the goal being culturally valued adult characteristics and optimal functioning. Several examples regarding parental values and cultural conceptions of competence were examined in the previous two chapters. Indeed, it is often possible to see the links between cultural values and even specific childrearing patterns. For example, to pursue further the American ethos of independent self, autonomy orientation in childrearing is clearly implicated. It is also widely evidenced in research, especially among the middle-class Anglo-American mainstream. For example, in parent education classes in the United States, young mothers are often taught to "let go" of their toddlers. This early separation must go against at least some (natural?) tendencies of mothers to "merge" with their young children (considered to be harmful), because they are asked to make a calculated effort to control these tendencies.

If even in an individualistic culture mothers have to consciously monitor their behavior for early independence training of their children, one can understand how strange this would be in a collectivistic culture. Yet, it is occurring because Western developmental psychology is being exported to the world as the "gospel of truth" (Dasen & Jahoda, 1986). For example, a South East Asian developmental psychology handbook (Suvannathat et al., 1985) mentions in the introduction that "many traditional beliefs and practices prevent [parents] from seeking and using the new *scientific* knowledge in child rearing. . . . The Handbook of Child Rearing may require parents to change many of their beliefs, attitudes, values, habits and behaviors . . . for example, giving the child more of the *independence* the child *needs*" (pp. 4–5; emphases mine). The issue is *what* is to change and *what* is to remain, and *how* this will be ascertained and *by whom*. I return to this important issue later.

Early caretaker–child interaction, reflecting "psychology of relatedness," can provide clues for understanding the development of the self. We do not have many systematic studies of this interaction, and much more work needs to be done across cultures to unravel the antecedents of the relational and separated selves. These behavioral antecedents mediate between the cultural (and parental) goals and conceptions of human development and the actual development of the self. A small-scale psycholinguistic study of communicative socialization processes by Choi (1992) provides some insight into these antecedents. She noted a fundamental difference in observations of Korean and Canadian middle-class mothers' interactions with their young children. The Korean mother–child interactions are found to have a "communicative pattern relationally-attuned to one another in a fused state" where the mothers freely enter the children's reality and speak for them, "merging themselves with the children." The Canadian mothers, on the other hand, are "distinguished by their effort to detach themselves from the children . . . withdrawing themselves from the children's reality, so that the children's reality can remain autonomous" (pp. 119–120).

This is reminiscent of Azuma's (1984, reported in Kornadt, 1987, p. 133) characterization of the mother–child interaction in Japan, where the mother's message to the child is "I am one with you, we can be and will be of the same mind." Choi's finding is also similar to that of Caudill and Schooler (1973). They noted that American mothers, holding culturally derived views of infants as potentially autonomous, encouraged them to express their own needs and desires. In contrast, Japanese mothers viewed their infants as "extensions of themselves" and stressed physical contact. Similarly, Coll (1990) argued that attachment and separation processes foster interpersonal dependency (rather than autonomy) if the ideal for mature relationships is relative enmeshment, "as is the case, for example, among Puerto Rican families (p. 271).

Further research along these lines is needed to reveal what types of parenting/socialization underlie the development of the self. Apparently, childrearing where the mother "merges herself with the child" paves the way for the development of a relational self, whereas childrearing that allows an "autonomous reality" to the child, mother "withdrawing" from it, engenders the development of a separated self. In cultural contexts (and social–structural–economic conditions) where closely knit familial, communal relations are important and where social responsibility training is stressed in socialization, the former type of early caretaker–child interaction may be expected to prevail.

Need for Conceptualization

The previous discussion points to some possible causal relations between cultural contexts where closely knit human bonds are important and the type of childrearing that engenders the emergence of the relational self. This is contrasted with the development of the separated self in cultural contexts characterized by individualism. Childrearing and socialization in general mediate between the cultural and social–structural–economic conditions, on the one hand, and the resultant self, on the other.

However, at times the causal links may not be apparent. This is especially the case when an individualism–collectivism perspective is used. The descriptive approaches, in particular, amount to showing that in individualistic cultures individualistic (separated) selves prevail, and in collectivistic cultures collectivistic (related) selves prevail. This type of tautological thinking does not answer the question "why?" The related question of "how" this distinction comes about is addressed by studies of childrearing, such as that of Choi (1992) on the communicative socialization processes. However, childrearing by itself does not address the question of "why?" either. A functional analysis and conceptualization is needed to understand why different sociocultural contexts have different types of childrearing.

Thus, different types of conceptualizations are possible. For example, one would show that there are different types of selves, independent–interdependent or separated–relational (varying in degrees) that differ from one another in several psychological processes, ranging from self-perceptions to emotions (e.g., Markus & Kitayama, 1991). A second type of conceptualization would throw light on the kinds of socialization engendering the different selves. A third type of conceptualization would reveal why a certain kind of socialization occurs in a particular context and when a change in this process of self-development may be expected.

Most of the current cross-cultural conceptualizations of the self do not deal with this third type of analysis. In other words, the causes or antecedents of the independent and the interdependent selves are not adequately examined. Often taxonomies in terms of individualism–collectivism are used, and the consequences or behavioral correlates of the different types of selves are examined. However, not much analysis is done on the antecedent factors underlying functional relationships and especially how changes in these occur.

Such analysis requires an examination of the functional underpinnings of the society–family–socialization interfaces. For example, there is a need to understand how family interaction patterns and socialization values are affected by the socioeconomic-cultural context and how the former, in turn, affect childrearing. Any changes in the context would have implications for changes in the chain of causal relationships. This kind of a conceptualization cannot remain only at the psychological level but has to situate the self and the family within the larger context. The family would play a key mediating role in the functional/causal relationships between the self and the society.

The next chapter presents a model of family change that aims to discover the societal and familial antecedents of the separated and relational selves. It also examines the implications of family change, through socioeconomic development, for the development of the self that can integrate both autonomy and relatedness.

5 Family and Family Change

In the introduction to this volume, I said that one of the things that I am attempting to do here is to link the self, family, and society. Up to this point I have been trying to form some links by examining human development in context and the culture–self interface. Societal conceptualizations of childhood, of competence, and of the self emerged as important, as did the corresponding parental construals of competence and of the self, mediating between societal conceptions and childrearing patterns. Though the family was often invoked in this discussion, this was not explicit. This chapter focuses on the family as the central component of the self–family–society relationship.[8] I propose a model of family and family change, through socioeconomic development, entailing a causal/functional analysis of the development of the self. This model should help throw light on some of the antecedents of the separated and the relational selves.

Though parental "ethnotheories," values, and behaviors are of great significance in understanding how societal values link with developmental outcomes, including the self, they constitute only some aspects of the family. Other aspects of the family need to be studied to complete the picture. Of particular importance is situating the family within the macrosystemic level by examining its links with social–structural–economic factors. Such an analysis, involving the family in context, should help provide some explanations for the contrasting childrearing orientations among the middle-class/urban/educated groups and the low SES/rural/marginal immigrant groups discussed earlier.

My approach to the family is multidisciplinary, and it makes use of sociologi-

---

[8]This chapter is based on "Family and Socialization in cross-cultural perspective: A model of change." In J. Berman (Ed.), *Cross-cultural perspectives: Nebraska symposium on motivation, 1989*, Vol. 37, pp. 135–200. Lincoln, NE: Nebraska University Press, 1990.

cal and demographic, in addition to psychological, concepts and evidence. This is because the family–society interface traditionally has not been studied by psychologists. Sociological perspectives are valuable in situating family processes into their socioeconomic, cultural, and historical context. Dealing with the different levels of analysis spanning individual–family–society interface is a difficult task. That is why few investigators try to link society, family, and individual systems empirically (Bronfenbrenner, 1979; Cowan, Field, Hanson, Skolnick, & Swanson, 1993, p. 479; Fişek, 1991; Grovetant, 1989; Szapocznik & Kurtines, 1993). Nevertheless, it is important to understand at least some of the relationships and possible causal links underlying the self, family, and society. Such understanding would unravel, for example, why certain socialization values and goals are seen in certain societies and not in others and how and why change comes about.

The complexity of the family as an intergenerational system moving through time has been a deterrent to its psychological analysis (McGoldrick & Carter, 1982). It has been difficult for psychologists, given their focus on the individual, to treat the family as a unit of analysis. So there is a scarcity of psychological theory on the family, except in the more applied fields of clinical psychology and family therapy. In this latter field, family systems theory (e.g., Guerin, 1976; Minuchin, 1974) has informed thinking and applications, particularly in providing a holistic approach to the family.

Given the lack of theory in academic psychology to throw light on family functioning and family change, the prototypical Western (middle-class, nuclear) family has been adopted implicitly as "the family." Therefore, the cross-cultural variations in the family, which have been studied by anthropologists and sociologists, have not been much addressed by academic psychology.

MODERNIZATION VIEWS

Family is an integral part of society and is inherently tied to its social structure, values, and norms. As these social and cultural characteristics vary through time and across societies, families vary too. Faced with family diversity, psychologists have typically either ignored it, regarding it as a topic appropriate for sociological or anthropological inquiry, or have dismissed it as transitory. The latter view adheres to the modernization theory prediction that there is a "convergence" of the diverse patterns in the world toward the Western prototypical pattern and thus whatever is different from this pattern will be modified in time to resemble it. Thus, in the absence of challenging cross-cultural theory of the family, there is an assumption of unidirectional change toward the Western model with social development, as originally proposed by the modernization theory (Dawson, 1967; Doob, 1967; Inkeles, 1969, 1977; Inkeles & D. H. Smith, 1974; Kahl, 1968). Even though modernization theory has lost its popularity in sociology, in the face of serious criticism (Bendix, 1967; Gusfield, 1967), its expectation of a unidirectional shift in the human/family characteristics toward the Western pattern is shared by many psychologists and others (Caldwell, 1977; Georgas, 1989; see Kağıtçıbaşı, 1994a, 1994c, for a further discussion of this issue). Thus, for example, developing countries are often characterized as "transitional societies," with the transition implied to be toward the Western pattern.

To reiterate the main characteristics of the "prototypical" Western family, it is a system of "independent" relationships. It is both independent of kin and forms a separate nucleated, unit and its subsystems (members) are also separated from one another with well-defined boundaries. It may be argued that not all Western families fit this pattern completely, which is certainly true. Nevertheless, this is the prototype that has been promoted, especially in psychology, reflecting the Western (particularly American) individualistic ethos (as I discussed in the previous chapter). Despite much criticism emerging from among psychologists and other social scientists, the prototype remains strong and colors much of the thinking regarding the family and family change.

The modernization view of change is tenacious. It adheres to an evolutionary model of progressive improvement, eventually to reach the fixed goal, that is, the Western prototype in the tradition of social Darwinism (Mazrui, 1968). Underlying it is the implicit assumption that whatever is different from the Western prototype is deficient and is, therefore, bound to change with development. This view has been rather influential, especially in debates regarding economic development. It is commonly assumed, for example, that collectivistic (inter)dependent orientations are not compatible with economic development (e.g., Kapp, 1963; Minturn & Hitchcock, 1966; Weber, 1958, as discussed by D. Sinha, 1988; Hoselitz, 1965). Indeed, Hofstede (1980) found a close association between individualism (at societal level) and economic affluence.

Though pervasive, this assumption is being challenged seriously today by the striking examples of economic growth in East Asia with collectivistic cultures (Japan, Korea, Taiwan, Hong Kong, Singapore, with Thailand and Malaysia following suit). The interdependent family patterns in these societies do not appear to deter development or to be "deficient" in any sense. Neither do they manifest any significant changes toward the Western individualistic–separated family patterns. Indeed, there is much evidence of continuity in human relations and family patterns (Bond, 1986; Hayashi & Suzuki, 1984; Iwawaki, 1986; Roland, 1988; D. Sinha & Kao, 1988; Sun, 1991; Suzuki, 1984; C. F. Yang, 1988). Furthermore, these family patterns are found to be conducive to economic success, as for example in Japan where they are successfully adopted into the workplace and in Chinese societies where family businesses flourish.

A second assumption underlying the modernization theory and its "conversion hypothesis" is that the Western family patterns have evolved toward nucleation and individualistic separation as a necessary outcome of industrialization. Therefore, it is claimed that industrialization will also engender the same changes in family patterns in non-Western contexts. This common assumption is also seriously challenged today by a great deal of historical evidence, which clearly documents that the nuclear family and individualism predated industrialization in Western Europe (particularly in England) by several centuries.

Historical and historical demographic records and court rolls are excellent sources for the study of the family in terms of interactions (cooperation–conflict), relations (similar surname forms), marriage patterns, residence patterns, and several family functions (Razí, 1993). This research has shown that the typical British family was nuclear rather than extended; the bond between family and land was weak; wider ties of kinship were also weak so that villagers relied on institutional support rather than on the assistance of kin; rural society was highly mobile; children often left home in their teens and spent a few years as living-in servants in other families before starting their own families; women married late and some never married (see Razí, 1993, for a review).

These are all demographic–structural characteristics associated with nuclear, separated, individualistic human and familial relational patterns. There is also evidence of secular individualism, individual control of sexuality, and of age at marriage that led to marital fertility decline starting in the 18th century. Though most marked in Britain, similar early individualistic themes predating industrialization in Western Europe and the United States are also found in historical research and travelers' records (Aries, 1980; Furstenberg, 1966; Lesthaeghe, 1980; Thorton & Fricke, 1987).

On the basis of such historical research, some historians claim that the nuclear family and individualistic patterns date all the way back to the Middle Ages (13th century) in Britain (Bennett, 1984; Britton, 1976; Hanawalt, 1986; Laslett, 1971, 1977; Macfarlane, 1978, 1986; R. M. Smith, 1979). But even those who do not trace the individualistic familial system so far back in history agree that it was prevalent by the early modern period (beginning of the 16th century) (Lesthaeghe, 1983; Lesthaeghe & Surkyn, 1988; Razí, 1993; Thadani, 1978; Thorton, 1984). Given this historical evidence, it is clear that Western individualism was not an outcome of industrialization; it predated it by centuries. Therefore, the argument by analogy that individualism will spread in the non-Western world as an inevitable outcome of industrialization does not hold.

This does not mean that the non-Western family patterns, characterized by interdependence, do not change. Change is going on in all societies at all levels of human phenomena, but it may take different forms; that is, it does not necessarily follow a single path toward the "Western model," as claimed by the convergence hypothesis. In order to ascertain what kind of change in family patterns is most likely, we must understand why and how change takes place.

CONTRASTING FAMILY MODELS

A General Model

It may be informative at this point to venture into some detailed descriptions of family patterns that may serve as prototypes in examining how families change. In doing this, I draw heavily on a model of family change I have developed (Kağıtçıbaşı, 1985b, 1990). This is a general family model that shows variations in the content of its components (family system and family structure) and of its context, constituting three different patterns.

What I propose here is a general model of family change, entailing three different models of family interaction patterns in context. This model, in its three different manifestations, is used as a heuristic device to understand the functional/causal links between society/culture, family, and the (resultant) self. It is a contextual model in situating the self within the family and the family within the cultural and socioeconomic environment. The family is treated in terms of both its social and psychological characteristics. The former is examined in terms of the family structure, and the latter in terms of the family system, including interaction and socialization. This is also a functional model as causal relations and the dynamics underlying the family interaction patterns and the socialization/development of the self are stressed.

In the general model (Fig. 1) reflected also in the following three specific models, there is a recognition of the primacy of the context in which the family is situated. The context is construed mainly in terms of the culture and the living conditions of the family and is seen as basically an influencing component. Culture is construed as mainly individualistic (culture of separateness) or as collectivist (culture of relatedness), as discussed earlier. It refers to the existing culture base underlying the socioeconomic–structural factors and the family system. Urban–rural residence, socioeconomic development levels, subsistence/affluence characteristics of the living conditions are taken up as significant indicators of context. However, they are not considered to be exhaustive.

In this contextual model there is a systemic approach to the family. The subsystems of the family are socialization values and interaction patterns in childrearing and in self–other relations. Family structure can be seen as both the context of family functioning (affecting it) and also as a part of the family system, in general. Social change and societal development impact the family with resultant changes in the family structure and the family system. Such changes may, in turn, feed back into the context, modifying some of the living conditions. This kind of a feedback loop would occur mainly through changes in family structure. Thus a dynamic interaction takes place between the context and the family system through time.

Family structure comprises the structural–demographic variables that research has established as important in affecting family functioning. These struc-

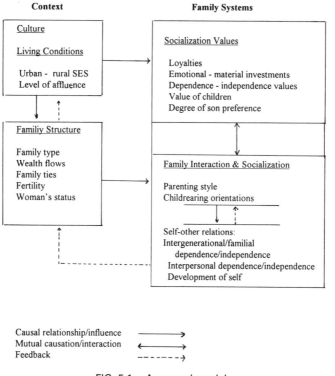

Context   **Family Systems**

FIG. 5.1.   A general model.

tural variables are also found to change systematically with socioeconomic development. For example, whether the family is extended or nuclear, with high or low fertility, and with high or low woman's intrafamily status appear to relate to socioeconomic contextual factors (living conditions).

The family system entails two interacting subsystems: socialization values and family interaction. Some of the main socialization values found to be important in research are included, again with no claim to comprehensiveness. They show variations along the independence–interdependence dimension and in terms of the emphasis put on the individual or the group and on the economic or psychological values of children for parents and the family.

Family interaction is differentiated in terms of parenting orientations and the resultant self–other relations and the development of the self. Baumrind's (1971, 1980, 1989) parenting construals are used here (as discussed earlier). The resultant familial/interpersonal independence/(inter)dependence and the relational/separated self can be considered to be the final product of the overall system.

The general model is not linear but dynamic and interactive, involving mutual causal relations and feedback loops in addition to direct causal routes. Its contents, and therefore how it works, will be more evident in its three different patterns of manifestation, which are examined next. I consider this model to be a general heuristic device that attempts to analyze family functioning in socio-cultural context as it mediates between the macrosocial–structural variables and the individual self.

The three specific family models are construed as prototypes of family systems and family functioning in different socioeconomic–cultural contexts. They are not to be seen as descriptions/characterizations of existing families, but rather as approximations toward different theoretical configurations. The three models involve different combinations of characteristics, partially overlapping, though each is discernible as different from the other two. This difference is more one of degree than of kind. They can also be seen as "human models," especially when the focus is on the type of self-development. They have to do with basic human relational patterns and their linkages to family and culture. Thus, where relevant, I refer to them as *family/human models*.

I first describe the ideal-typical family model of interdependence. Then the contrasting model of independence is examined. These two prototypes are familiar, because they figure most commonly in the literature. Some aspects of these family patterns have been discussed in the previous chapters.

The third model, emotional interdependence, is what I propose in my model of family change to be a prototype of families undergoing modification through socioeconomic change in the Majority World with cultures of relatedness. I describe this model later, after I present the two contrasting models and after a discussion of how change from the prototype of (traditional) interdependence comes about. In presenting these three different family/human models, I try to explain why they exhibit their particular characteristics. Thus, I also deal with dynamics from a contextual/functional point of view.

Model of Interdependence

An ideal-typical family/human model of interdependence (Fig. 2) is commonly found in rural/agrarian traditional societies with closely knit human/family relations, often characterized by patrilineal family structures. This is the ideal-typical culture of relatedness at both the societal and the familial levels and is a pervasive pattern in many parts of the Majority World, notwithstanding variation. I do not deal here with this variation, which may appear in family structures, kinship, and descent systems (e.g., polygamous marriages, matrilineal structures, etc).

This prototype typically entails "functionally extended family" structures (Kağıtçıbaşı, 1985a) even though most households may be nuclear. The family functions as if it were extended in carrying out such tasks as home production of goods, agricultural production or consumption, child care, and so on, jointly with kin. This is often made possible by the close proximity of immediate kin

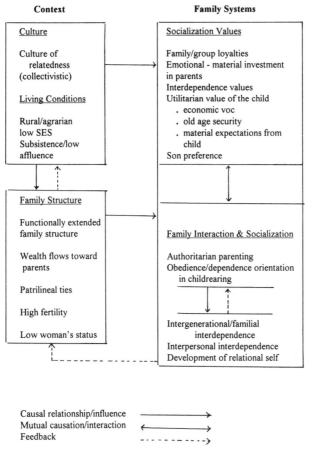

FIG. 5.2. Model of interdependence (adapted with permission from Kağıtçıbaşı, 1990).

spanning different generations. Given the low affluence levels and agricultural lifestyles, such shared work is highly adaptive for survival. Thus the family is interdependent with kin (other families).

The interdependence between generations is particularly notable, as adult offspring are the main sources of "old-age security" for the elderly, in the absence of wide-scale old-age pensions, social security systems, and so on. Thus, young adults provide financial assistance to their elderly parents; in demographic terms, "wealth flows" are toward parents, especially through patrilineage. This has direct implications for "son preference" in a patrilineal (patriarchal) context where having sons is a great asset, because these are more reliable sources of "old-age security." Such a family structure also entails high fertility, to ensure the survival of enough children and particularly sons, in the face of high infant mortality. Having sons also increases the woman's "intrafamily status," which is initially (at marriage) quite low, because she is, by definition, an outsider to the patrilineage.

This description of a prototypical family structure is a capsule summary of a complex pattern, necessarily leaving out several important aspects. Mainly, it involves characteristics that on the basis of research are theoretically important to explain family dynamics and interaction—the family system that shows predictable modifications through social change and development.

One such crucial characteristic, then, is the "old-age security value" of children for parents, which implicates *material* dependencies together with *emotional* dependencies between generations. The distinctions between material and emotional dependencies is an important one because they are differently affected by social change and development (and modifications in life styles). Although material interdependencies across generations decrease with increased affluence (urbanization, education, etc.), emotional interdependencies do not change with socioeconomic development in the Majority World with cultures of relatedness.

All of the previous points have been demonstrated in research. Of particular importance is the nine-country Value of Children (VOC) study. Some of the findings of this comparative study provide evidence.

In the VOC study utilitarian and psychological values of children (voc)[9] came to the fore. The utilitarian (economic) voc entails children's material contribution to the family both when they are young (as child work or help with household chores) as well as their old-age security value when they grow up. The psychological voc, on the other hand, is a value attributed to children by parents reflecting the joy, pride, companionship, love, and so on, derived from children. Extensive interviews were carried out in the VOC study with more than 20,000 married respondents comprising nationally representative samples in Korea, the Philippines, Singapore, Taiwan, Thailand, Turkey, Indonesia (Javanese and Sundanese), the United States, and Germany (only women in one province in Germany). Motivations for childbearing, values attributed to children, fertility preferences, and so on, were studied (Bulatao, 1979; Darroch, Meyer, & Singarimbum, 1981; Fawcett, 1983; L. W. Hoffman, 1987, 1988; Kağıtçıbaşı, 1982a, 1982b, 1982c).

A main finding of the comparative study was the greater salience of the utilitarian voc and especially of the old-age security voc in less developed countries. For example, old-age security as a reason for childbearing was considered very important among women by 93% and 98% of the two subsamples in Indonesia, by 89% in the Philippines, by 79% each in Thailand and Taiwan, and by 77% in Turkey; this sharply contrasts with only 8% each in Germany and the United States. The percentages in Korea (54%) and Singapore (51%) though still high, were significantly lower than the other non-Western countries, in accor-

---

[9]VOC (in capitals) refers to the study; voc (in small letters) refers to actual values of children (for parents).

dance with their higher levels of economic development. Other specific results and men's responses manifested similar patterns (Kağıtçıbaşı, 1982c).

Within-country variations also reflect similar patterns in terms of socio-economic development. For example, as the development level of the area of residence rose in Turkey, the salience of old-age security voc decreased (100% in the least developed areas, 73% in medium developed, 61% in more developed, and 40% in most developed large metropolitan centers). Similarly, it decreased systematically with increased women's professionalization, involving education (100% among unpaid agricultural family workers in rural areas with little or no education; 91% among small shopowners and artisans, typically traditional groups; 50% among wage earners and only 19% to 37% among white-collar workers, depending on their education levels). Again similar patterns obtain for men (Kağıtçıbaşı, 1982a).

Thus, in contexts of low affluence rural/agrarian/low SES standing with material interdependencies favoring high fertility, socialization values include a stress on the utilitarian (economic) voc, old-age security voc, and son preference. Son preference is closely associated with economic/old-age security voc because commonly, and particularly in patriarchal societies, sons are more reliable sources of economic benefits and old-age security (Caldwell, 1977; Fawcett, 1983; Kağıtçıbaşı, 1982a). Son preference is also closely associated with fertility, because high fertility assures that at least some sons survive (Darroch et al., 1981).

The economic/utilitarian voc is positively associated with fertility (child numbers) but psychological voc is not. Thus, in the Turkish VOC study, psychological voc and the number of existing children were found to be negatively associated ($r = -.26$), but economic voc and the number of children were positively associated ($r = .24$) (Kağıtçıbaşı, 1982a, p. 77). This is because the material contribution of each child (while young and as an adult) can add up to that of every other child and thus increases with child numbers, but the psychological satisfactions children provide to their parents do not add up in the same way with more children. (For example, parents can get all the love they need from one or two children without the need to have more). Thus in the Turkish VOC study, women who had two children wanted to have additional children if they stressed the economic voc but did not want more children if they stressed the psychological voc (Kağıtçıbaşı, 1982a, pp. 72–73). Similarly, in a comparative analysis of data from eight VOC countries, Bulatao (1979) found that women with five or more children and not using contraception stressed the economic voc more than women with two or fewer children using contraception, the differences being quite large (some exceeding 30 percentage points).

These findings point to the dynamics underlying high fertility. In this context socialization values also uphold family/group loyalties (rather than individual loyalties) and investment in(elderly) parents, as these values are adaptive for the livelihood of the family in a pattern of total (intergenerational) interdependence.

Accordingly, a particular type of family interaction is implicated in childrearing, entailing an obedience/dependence orientation, characterized by control, rather than autonomy. Again, such parent–child interaction and socialization are adaptive in this context for family survival through time. This is because a socialization orientation stressing family loyalties, control, and dependence/obedience of the child ensures the child's full integration in the family. When socialized this way, children grow up to be "loyal" adult offspring who uphold family needs and invest in their (elderly) parents, whereas "independent" children are more likely to look after their own individual interests. So, independence training is not adaptive in the family model of total interdependence.

Thus, in the Turkish VOC study, among characteristics most and second most desired in children, "to obey their parents" was the most prominent, chosen by 61% of men and 59% of women, contrasted by much lower importance of "to be independent and self-reliant" (chosen by 17% of men and 19% of women) (Kağıtçıbaşı, 1982a). Similarly, even more contrasting results were obtained in countries such as Indonesia, the Philippines, and Thailand. This is in line with some previous discussion (chapter 2, chapter 3), pointing to obedience and conformity orientations in childrearing in societies where these characteristics are highly valued and are adaptive (e.g., Kohn, 1969; R. A. LeVine, 1974, 1988; Serpell, 1977).

The intergenerational dependencies shift direction during the family life cycle in the model of interdependence. First, the child is dependent on the parent. This dependence is later reversed when the elderly parent becomes dependent on the grown-up offspring. The resultant familial and interpersonal relations in the family model of interdependence are characterized by interdependence along both emotional and material dimensions. The relational self, discussed in the last chapter, develops in this type of family system. Thus, the causal antecedents of socialization for a relational self are construed in this model to reside in the requirements of the family livelihood, based on intergenerational interdependence.

The socialization values and family interactions in this model further reinforce a functionally extended family structure. Thus, the general pattern is a self-perpetuating one unless the context (living conditions) changes. It is possible, of course, for the family system (socialization values and family interactions) to change in response to other influences, also, such as cultural diffusion (acculturation) or intervention. However, this contextual/functional model does not deal with such exogenous factors.

Model of Independence

I want to examine next the contrasting family/human model of independence— the ideal-typical model for the family in the Western, industrial, urban/suburban middle-class society with a culture of separateness (individualism) (Fig. 3). This

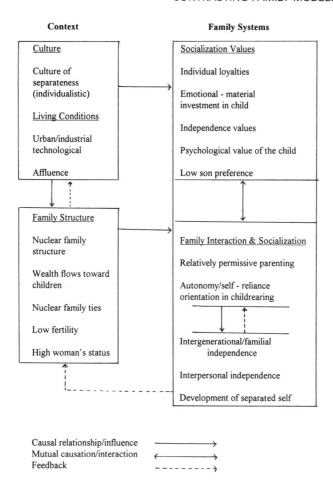

FIG. 5.3.   Model of independence (adapted with permission from Ka-ğıtçıbaşı, 1990).

model is also familiar, because it is the prototypical model of the Western individualistic nuclear family, hailed or assailed by social critics.

This is the family model of independence and separateness of both the family from other families and of its elements (members) from one another. It probably reflects more an ideal or abstraction than reality, given recent evidence regarding the existence of quite a bit of interdependence in the Western (American) family (see the section "A Different Convergence"). Nevertheless, the overall picture is obviously quite different from the model of interdependence described. Indeed, there is almost no overlap between these two prototypical models in terms of shared characteristics. The dissimilarity reflects the dissimilarity of the contexts, in terms of high levels of affluence, urban/industrial technological society in the family model of independence contrasted with low levels of affluence, rural/agricultural/preindustrial lifestyles in the model of interdependence. It also reflects the difference between the underlying cultures of separateness (individualism) and relatedness (collectivism), respectively.

The family/human model of independence is distinguished by separateness of the generations and both emotional and material investments channeled toward the child, rather than to the older generation. The unit is the individuated nucleated family. Lack of commitment to the patrilineage and affluence providing old-age security goes along with higher woman's intrafamily status, low son preference, and low fertility. In this context, especially with mass education (R. A. LeVine & White, 1986), having children entails economic costs—not assets. Accordingly, in the absence of children's economic value, their psychological value comes to the fore. Psychological voc, together with high costs of children, further implicates low fertility. This is particularly noticeable among educated professional couples for whom the "opportunity cost" of having children is considerable.

Socialization values and family interaction engender the development of the independent, separated self with clearly defined boundaries. Interactions both at the individual and the family levels are among separate, nonoverlapping entities. There is less control in childrearing; it entails a relatively permissive parenting compared with the authoritarian parenting of the model of interdependence. Autonomy orientation is stressed in accordance with the prevalent individualistic ideology. This is because independence and self-reliance are valued in a sociocultural–economic context where intergenerational material dependencies are minimal (children's loyalty to their elderly parents is not required for old-age security). This type of socialization is conducive to both intergenerational (familial) and interpersonal independence. Thus this model provides an analysis of the causal/functional antecedents of the independent separated self.

Many of the characterizations in this model, such as woman's status, permissive parenting, and independence of the family and the self, are to be understood in relative terms, especially in comparison to the family model of interdependence. They should not be taken at absolute levels and certainly they should not be considered typical of all Western middle-class families, but these characteristics are by and large reflective of the mainstream Western and particularly American middle-class family. This is in keeping with the individualistic ethos, which constitutes the cultural context for the family and the self.

Furthermore, this model does not reflect the great diversity that exists in the Western and particularly the American scene with regard to ethnic and social class variations. The same is true of the previous model of interdependence. They are provided as heuristic devices for us to understand some of the functional bases of family dynamics in varying contexts and the differences among the families. For example, there is research evidence showing quite a bit of interdependence in the American family, particularly among the working class and among women (Bronfenbrenner & Weiss, 1984; Cohler & Grunebaum, 1981; Keniston, 1985). However, there is also a commitment to independence and self-sufficiency (Bellah et al., 1985; B. Berger & P. L. Berger, 1984; Kagan, 1984), as noted in chapter 3 at times resulting in ambivalence.

WHAT KIND OF FAMILY CHANGE?

The previous section described two contrasting family models—total interdependence and independence. Given their disparate characteristics and the significant differences in their respective contexts, it is commonly assumed that there is a shift from one to the other. As discussed earlier, this is the modernization theory prediction of convergence toward the Western model. Apparently, because the family model of total interdependence is more common in rural/agrarian/low affluence contexts, and the family model of independence is more common in urban/industrial/high affluence contexts, a shift in both contexts and family patterns is assumed to take place from the former to the latter with socio-economic development.

This assumption does not take culture into account. As I have explained in some detail, both the historical and current evidence point to some continuity in cultures while social and economic structures undergo modifications. Thus, individualistic familial and human relational patterns are seen in Western Europe much before, during, and following the industrial revolution. Similarly, collectivist patterns appear to be sustained in the Pacific Rim countries alongside significant economic growth and industrialization.

The continuity of the individualistic (family) culture is substantiated by a great deal of historic-demographic research referred to earlier. The continuity of the collectivistic culture in human/familial relations is established by much current cross-cultural work, carried out especially in 1980s (again examined earlier, and in chapter 4). In referring to the Japanese, Morsbach (1980) purports that: "it is the continuity in important patterns of interpersonal relations, despite historical changes, which is so remarkable" (p. 342). And reviewing research from Mainland China, Taiwan, and Hong Kong, Kao and Hong (1988) concluded that there is a "general persistence of [the] cultural and socialization patterns, without being subject to much attenuation and erosion in spite of the impact of modern industrial life" (p. 262).

Given this continuity in basic culture, then, the question is what kind of change occurs in family patterns and why? Obviously, change is going on, and it would be rejecting reality to assert the persistence of all forms or aspects of family-human relations. As I have shown for example in discussing the Value of Children study (VOC), systematic changes are seen in values attributed to children with socioeconomic development in both international and intranational comparisons. Specifically, with socioeconomic development, the old-age security and economic/utilitarian value of children (voc) decrease. There are also parallel decrements in expectations of specific financial support from children in old age (Kağıtçıbaşı, 1982c).

At first sight, such systematic reduction in utilitarian (economic) values of children and expectations of specific help from them appears as if full nucleation and separation are occurring in the family with socioeconomic development.[10] However, a closer examination of the findings reveals that these changes are taking place only with respect to certain needs satisfied by children. Specifically, it is material dependencies that decrease with socioeconomic development, not emotional dependencies.

The VOC study findings refer mainly to material dependencies and not to emotional (psychological) dependencies. The former are reflected in economic/utilitarian values attributed to children (voc), whereas the latter are reflected in the psychological voc. The VOC study findings provide clear evidence for decreasing economic voc with socioeconomic development. This is found to be the case for different indicators of economic/utilitarian voc (children providing old-age security; specific financial support in old age; help with household chores; or material help while young) and using different indicators of socioeconomic development (Kağıtçıbaşı, 1982a, 1982c).

The fact that material dependencies decrease with socioeconomic development does not imply family nucleation–separation. Emotional (psychological) dependencies can continue even if material dependencies (on children) decrease with increased children's costs and alternative old-age security benefits. Indeed, this is evidenced by the VOC study findings, which show that in contrast to economic voc, psychological voc either does not change (Fawcett, 1983), or even increases with development (Kağıtçıbaşı, 1982a, 1982b). For example, in Turkey the salience for parents of the "companionship" value of children increases with parent education (from 33% at high school to 43% at university level) and with the development level of the area of residence (20% in the least developed areas; 26% in medium developed; 32% in more developed; and 51% in metropolitan areas).

Other research provides further evidence for decreased material (inter)dependencies without a corresponding decrease in emotional (inter)dependencies. For example, a study conducted in Turkey (Erelçin, 1988) compared the willingness of modern (young and urban) and traditional (old and rural) groups to give material and emotional resources to others. There was no difference between the two groups in willingness to give emotional resources (for example to visit a person in the hospital), but the modern group was less willing to give material resources (e.g., money). Other research examining intergenerational and kin

---

[10]This was my original interpretation of the VOC study findings (Kağıtçıbaşı, 1982a). However, later on I realized this interpretation was too simplistic and refined it by distinguishing between material and emotional interdependencies.

relations in developed/urban areas of the Majority World with cultures of relatedness shows that the close family/kin relationships continue, especially between generations. This is despite the fact that material dependencies have diminished as many urban elderly are self-supporting (through old-age pensions, etc.) and may even be financially supporting their young adult children (Olson, 1982; C. F. Yang, 1988). On the basis of his research in Turkey, Duben (1982) concluded that "the significance of kin relations seems not to be fading with increased urbanization or industrialization" (p. 94).

What are the implications of a decrease in material dependencies but not in emotional dependencies (reflected in economic voc losing importance and psychological voc gaining importance) for the family system? It would be expected that some aspects of the family system would undergo changes, whereas other aspects are sustained. Therefore, some combinations of characteristics not present in either the family model of total interdependence or the family model of independence would emerge.

Model of Emotional Interdependence

The complexities of contextual and familial changes through socioeconomic development in the Majority World with cultures of relatedness implicates a third family/human model: the model of *emotional interdependence*. This model differs, but nevertheless overlaps in some characteristics with the two prototypical models. To reiterate, the distinguishing mark of the prototype of total interdependence is familial (intergenerational) and human (individual) interdependence in both material and emotional dimensions. The prototype of independence is distinguished by independence at both familial and individual levels in both material and emotional dimensions. This model, however, manifests interdependence in the emotional realm at both family and individual levels, but it entails independence at both levels in the material realm (Fig. 4).

The model of emotional interdependence is typical in the more developed/urban areas of the Majority World with cultures of relatedness (collectivistic culture base). So what we see here is social structural and economic change (and development) alongside cultural continuity, as discussed previously. Given the continuity of the relational culture, the family in this pattern extends into other families (kin) in complex ways. However, the kind of shared activities would be different in this case than joint (agricultural) production or consumption (as seen in the case of the functionally extended family in the family model of total interdependence). These family links can occur bilaterally (with either spouse's kin), with the decreased importance of patrilineage and the correspondingly increased women's status, lower fertility, and lower son preference.

Given the sustained emotional interdependencies between generations, though not required for material survival, emotional investments of young adults go both toward their elderly parents and toward their children. Material invest-

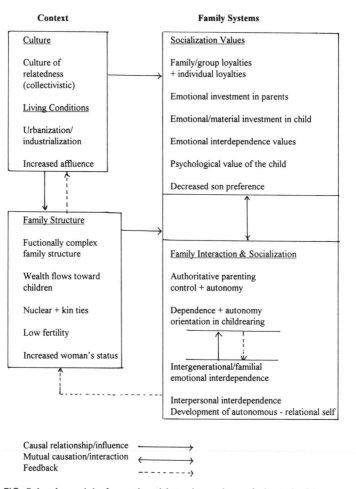

FIG. 5.4.   A model of emotional interdependence (adapted with permission from Kağıtçıbaşı, 1990).

ments (wealth flows), however, are directed mainly toward children who in this developed/urban context cost more. With the higher cost of children and their diminished economic voc, their psychological value becomes more salient. This is because economically it does not "make sense" to have children; thus the psychological satisfaction derived from children assumes greater importance as a reason for childbearing.

Socialization values continue to emphasize family/group loyalties, given the sustained emotional interdependencies. However, individual loyalties are emerging as well. This is especially important in implicating modifications in family interaction patterns, that is, childrearing entailing autonomy. Alongside parental control and dependency orientations in socialization, reflecting the continued importance of closely knit family/human bonds, there is room in this family system for individual loyalties and autonomy as well. This is because with decreased material dependencies, complete dependency of the child (and subsequent total loyalty of the grown-up offspring) is no longer required for old-age security of the parent and thus for family well-being.

Thus, this model reveals the causal antecedents of the development of the autonomous–related self through societal/familial change. This type of self integrates both autonomy and relatedness within itself. The two basic human needs for agency and communion (Bakan, 1966, 1968) appear to find expression in the self engendered by the model of emotional interdependence.

The individual interests (of the growing child) can be accommodated in this model alongside group (family) interests. The autonomy of the growing child is no longer seen as a threat to family livelihood. Comparisons of childrearing values in different SES groups provide some evidence. For example, Imamoğlu (1987) found urban upper SES mothers in Turkey to value independence and self-reliance, whereas most middle and lower SES mothers emphasize obedience and loyalty to parents. Similarly, whereas upper SES parents do not want their children to feel much gratitude toward them, lower SES parents do. In terms of the old-age security and economic voc, "it is highly functional that children feel a high degree of gratitude toward their parents to keep up the family bond" (p. 143).

The modifications in values and orientations in the family/human model of emotional interdependence do not mean that group (family) interests are unimportant or secondary at best, as in the family pattern of independence. A *combination*, or *coexistence*, of individual and group (family) loyalties is the case here (Kağıtçıbaşı, 1987b). Accordingly, the familial/interpersonal relations continue to be interdependent ones, though in the emotional realm only, and the resultant self is again the "relational self," though also entailing autonomy—"the autonomous–related self." For example, Imamoğlu (1987) found that all parents, even upper SES ones who do not want their children to be grateful to them, want them to be more loving and close. Parents also desire that children become more respectful as they grow older, pointing to the continuing emotional interdependence and relatedness.

The childrearing orientations and socialization values entailed in this family model may at first sight appear as conflicting, even mutually exclusive. However, such an interpretation would probably reflect a Western individualistic world view pitting the individual against the group. Indeed, there is nothing illogical about the coexistence of interdependence and independence orientations, and quite a bit of research and thinking provides evidence for such coexistence. Nevertheless, conflicting tendencies can cause problems of adjustment. To some extent, this is probably inherent to a conflict (or dialectical model), given the existence of conflicting human needs. However, this conflict can also be the source of dynamic change and growth, rather than static equilibrium. In this process of change, conflicting tendencies, confronting one another, would lead to new solutions (syntheses) reflecting new adjustments to changing environmental demands.

It is also possible to construe these combinations of contrasting tendencies in another way. This could be in terms of considering a single dimension of parenting, for example, with the opposite poles of control and autonomy.[11] In this case, the authoritative parenting in the model of emotional interdependence would fall within an average midpoint on that dimension, which could be called "medium level of control." Similarly, a single childrearing dimension with the opposite poles of dependence and autonomy orientations in the model of emotional interdependence would again fall within an average midpoint on this dimension. It could be called medium level of dependence orientation in childrearing.

This type of conceptualization might be easier to operationalize, for example, by constructing a single scale. This would also allow for comparisons with the other models in terms of degrees of control in parenting or degrees of dependence–autonomy orientation in childrearing. Researchers can approach the issue in this way, and I see no problem with alternative ways of conceptualizing and operationalizing the components of the model.

Indeed, as mentioned earlier, the coexistence of opposite trends may be seen as conflicting and unstable, especially for Westerners with an intellectual heritage of Cartesian dualism. Sinha and Tripathi (1994) noted that "use of dichotomies is a heuristic device popular in the West" (p. 123). With such an orientation it may be difficult to construe the coexistence or combination of apparently contrasting behavioral categories or individual characteristics. It may be easier to conceptualize them as polar opposites of a single dimension.

I, nevertheless, prefer to spell out both the contrasting tendencies in the model. I want to stress their coexistence in the same person or family, though one or the other orientation may take over at different times and regarding different issues (over time and behavior episodes, the net result may indeed be one of average standing on a single dimension of variation). Second, I want to be able to show how a model of family change comes about and for this, the introduction of autonomy or individual loyalties, for example, into the family model of emotional interdependence alongside continuing dependence and (family) group loyalties is of crucial importance. Finally, to integrate some of the combinations such as family/group loyalties and individual loyalties into a single dimension is unwarranted. Construing individual and family/group loyalties as opposite poles of a single dimension assumes they are mutually exclusive. This is not evidenced in research (see Kağıtçıbaşı, 1987b).

---

[11]This was suggested by Ype Poortinga (personal communication).

Support for the Model
of Emotional Interdependence

Quite a bit of research and theory provides support for the coexistence of some apparently contrasting orientations. Before turning to this evidence, I would first like to point to the parallels between this pattern of family/human relations and the conflict theories of personality, as espoused by Rank (1929, 1945), Angyal (1951), and Bakan (1966, 1968). These theories posit two basic and conflicting human needs for independence from others and for interdependence with others, variously called "autonomy," "agency" or "separation–individualization," versus "surrender," "communion," "union," "fusion," or "dependency," respectively. A dialectic synthesis of these merging and separating tendencies is considered to engender a healthy personality, whereas too much stress put on one of these needs, at the cost of the other, is seen as a problem. However, Angyal and especially Bakan (1966, 1968) stressed particularly the dangers of denying only one of these needs—communion, possibly in reaction to dominant American individualism.

Other theoretical views carry similar themes: for example, Deutsch's (1962) promotive interdependence (cooperation) versus contrient interdependence (competition); Benedict's (1970) high or low synergy societies; and expressiveness versus instrumentality in gender theories (Chodorow, 1974, 1978; Gilligan, 1982). The previous chapter mentioned several critical views of the individualistic stance of American psychology. Each proposes a formulation combining the two basic needs for dependence and independence, reminiscent of the model of emotional interdependence: for example, "ensembled individualism" (Sampson, 1988), "reciprocal individualism" (Rotenberg, 1977), "social individuality" (Lykes, 1985), and "relational individualism" (Chodorow, 1989). A recent analysis, utilizing an evolutionary perspective (Guisinger & Blatt, 1994), proposes two basic developmental lines through natural selection: "interpersonal relatedness" along with "self-definition," which interact in a dialectical fashion. This is very much in line with the thesis proposed here.

In each one of these views a "relational" conceptualization of the self is proposed, similar to the resultant "relational self" in the family model of emotional interdependence. Furthermore, in both these formations and also in the model of emotional interdependence, autonomy is attributed to the relational self. The relational self also figures importantly in postmodern discourse (N. Young, 1992), which sees the reconstruction of the self "through compassionate, abiding and deeply rooted relationships with others" (p. 144). Excesses of individualism (and independence from others) are deplored by these critics as well as by others within American psychology and social science to whom I have already referred (Batson, 1990; Baumeister, 1986, 1991; Bellah et al., 1985; Campbell, 1975; Cushman, 1990; Etzioni, 1993; Hogan, 1975; Lasch, 1978, 1984; Sampson, 1985, 1987, 1988, 1989; M. B. Smith, 1994; Taylor, 1989; M. A. Wallach & L. Wallach, 1983, 1990).

In contrast, in cultures of relatedness, particularly among the more traditional groups where the family model of (total) interdependence prevails, the opposite holds. For example, in Turkey, critics and educationists deplore the excess of connectedness (collectivism) and call for more emphasis on individual autonomy (e.g., Eksi, 1982; Gectan, 1973). Indeed, it appears that individualistic societies have typically stressed the need for independence often at the cost of the need for interdependence, and the reverse has been true for collectivistic societies. The family model of emotional interdependence is distinguished from the other two models (total interdependence and independence) in recognizing and satisfying both of these basic human needs.

The distinguishing characteristic of the family model of emotional interdependence in better recognizing and fulfilling the two basic human needs may be considered a reason in itself for shifts toward this model. Because this model of family and human relations allows for the expression and fulfillment of both basic human needs, it may be more optimal than the other two models for human development.

This type of a shift toward the model of emotional interdependence is evident in the developed/urban contexts of the Majority World (e.g., Duben, 1982; Erelçin, 1988; Fawcett, 1983; Imamoğlu, 1987; Kağıtçıbaşı, 1982a, 1982c; Olson, 1982; K-S. Yang, 1988). Other research also points to such shifts or coexistence of (inter)dependence–independence orientations. For example, as discussed earlier, the concept of a socially (rather than an individually) oriented achievement motivation emerged from research conducted in different countries, showing a drive to exalty both the self and the group (social entity transcending and encompassing the self) (Agarwal & Misra, 1986; Bond, 1986; Misra & Agarwal, 1985; Phalet & Claeys, 1993; J.B.P. Sinha, 1993; K-S. Yang, 1986; Yu & K-S. Yang, 1994). This would entail a "relational" self in an emotionally interdependent relationship with others, striving to uphold both the self and the other. D. Sinha and Tripathi (1994) proposed "the coexistence of opposites" regarding individualistic and collectivistic orientations, quite similar to independence–(inter)dependence. A study from Japan points to the combined importance of individualism and group goals (D. W. Shwalb, B. J. Shwalb, & Murata, 1991) among adolescents. It also provides some insight into the temporal emergence of these orientations, specifically, social preoccupation emerging in childhood and individualism emerging in early adolescence.

The coexistence of dependence and autonomy (independence) in the model of emotional interdependence is also reflected in some childrearing research. Apparently, contrasting childrearing orientations, as proposed in the model, are found together. For example, Lin and Fu (1990) in a comparison of Chinese, immigrant Chinese, and Anglo-American parents showed that the two Chinese groups were higher on both parental control and encouragement of independence than the Anglo group. Authoritative parenting (Baumrind, 1971, 1980, 1989), which combines order-setting control and autonomy (together with love), also entails some of these apparently conflicting orientations. Baumrind noted that "authoritative parents represent a balance between agency and communion, as does the competent child type" (1989, p. 370).

Other research has also found authoritative parenting to be more conducive than authoritarian and permissive parenting to both cognitive development and academic success and also to psychosocial competence (Dornbusch et al., 1987; Lamborn et al., 1991; Lau & Cheung, 1987; Lau et al., 1990; Steinberg et al., 1989). This type of parenting is proposed to replace authoritarian (restrictive, obedience-oriented parenting) in the family pattern of emotional interdependence. As discussed earlier, with decreased material dependencies in this model, complete obedience (and loyalty) of the child is no longer needed for family survival, and there is room for autonomy in childrearing. However, at the same time, there is still firm control (rather than permissive childrearing as in the family model of independence) because full independence–separation is not the goal in the context of continuing emotional dependencies.

In an entirely different area of research and application—in family psychology and clinical practice in the United States—similar formulations combine independence and interdependence. For example, Vannoy (1991) found that stable marriages are more likely to be achieved only by those individuals who develop capacities for both autonomy and intimacy, and Selman (1989) focused on fostering intimacy and autonomy in psychotherapy with children. Similarly, F. L. Hoffmann (1989) called for conceptions of adolescent development that simultaneously pose goals of relatedness and interdependence with autonomy and self-reliance. From a gender-role perspective, Barciauskas and Hull (1989) called for a new integration of individualism and relatedness, of independence and interdependence, both in the home and at the workplace. And Fu, Hinkle, and Hanna (1986) considered dependency a valued trait in adulthood, as it helps maintain close family ties. Going a step further, Silverman and Weinberger (1985) showed that the gratification of symbiotic needs (of dependency) in psychotherapy can enhance adjustment.

Thus emerging from a different (applied) academic tradition, the previous views are similar to the criticisms of mainstream American psychology reviewed in the last chapter. They decry an excessive preoccupation with the self and call for greater social concern and interdependence, as for example in Sampson's (1988) "ensembled individualism" or in Etzioni's (1993) "communitarianism."

A DIFFERENT CONVERGENCE?

All this research and thinking follow parallel though nonintersecting paths, both in American psychology and social science, and in cross-cultural psychology. In the cross-cultural scene, the research points to continuities in human/familial relational patterns despite socioeconomic changes. These changes tend to decrease material interdependencies, which are no longer necessary with changing lifestyles (especially with urbanization). However, they do not affect emotional interdependencies, because these latter continue being adaptive and functional psychosocial mechanisms in the context of economic-industrial growth. The shift in family/human patterns, therefore, is toward emotional interdependence (entailing the autonomous-related self). In the American scene, there is a recognition of the desirability of the emotional interdependence model and a search for it, in reaction to the dominant independence model. The common underlying assumption here is that the family model of independence is prevalent in the Western (American) society and is legitimized and reinforced by psychology.

It is indeed the case that the independence model is advocated by most Western psychologists, which has a lot to do with the pervasive individualistic ideology in the West and particularly in the United States. Nevertheless, whether it is really prevalent has been questioned. As I have mentioned earlier, the family model of independence may reflect more the "ideal" (or ideology) than the reality.

Bellah et al. (1985, p. 144), in their observation of the American family, noted an ambivalence between professed ideology and actual behavior. While individualism, self-sufficiency, and independence are highly valued (B. Berger & P. L. Berger, 1984), there appears to be much interdependence between generations and kin in many American families (e.g., Bronfenbrenner & Weiss, 1983; Cohler & Grunebaum, 1981; Fu et al., 1986; Mogey, 1991), so much so that Keniston (1985) talked about "the myth of family independence." Cohler and Geyer (1982) reviewed a great deal of evidence pointing to mutual support between generations, among relatives or nonkin (e.g., neighbors) functioning as kin in providing economic help, health care, child care, and moral support. This is especially strong among women, who are socialized more than men into interdependence and relatedness in Western society (Chodorow, 1978) and have greater responsibility for homemaking, and among the low income families who lack alternative sources of support. Family support and three generational "extended" families (especially of women) are particularly notable among lower income Blacks in the United States (Slaughter, 1988; Washington, 1988).

Nevertheless, given the cultural ideal of independence and self-sufficiency, interdependence tends to be psychologically problematic. Being dependent on someone can lead to feelings of inadequacy, loss of self-esteem, resentment, and so on. The ambivalence involved has been found to cause even family pathology (Boszormenyi-Nagy & Spark, 1973) and discomfort for each generation (Cohler & Geyer, 1982). This is indeed different from the situation that is common in the culture of relatedness, especially in the family model of total interdependence. There, intergenerational interdependence is not only required for family survival (material dependencies), but is also a requisite of family honor.

Thus, in the Value of Children study (Hoffman, 1987; Kağıtçıbaşı, 1982a, 1982b) a common response of the traditional rural Turkish respondents to questions asking if they expected their children to take care of them in old age was, "Of course, if my son is worthy of his family name, he would take care of us." There was no sentiment of ambivalence or resentment; on the contrary, they were offended that we would even question the loyalty of their children. The same questions in the United States and Germany annoyed parents, and a common response was, "I don't want anything from my children; if they can take care of themselves, I'll be glad." Thus, in the culture of separateness, dependence on anyone, particularly on one's children, may be seen as a sign of weakness or failure, even if it may be a reality of life among some groups.

I have reviewed research from several societies with cultures of relatedness undergoing economic development, which provides evidence for a shift toward the model of emotional interdependence. This is often manifested in terms of coexistence of seemingly opposing characteristics of human and familial relations and in the continuation of the relational self, which also entails autonomy. Thus, in the model of emotional interdependencies, combinations of control and autonomy orientations are posited in childrearing. Again, this is what is found in research conducted in the United States to be characteristic of authoritative parenting. Similarly, the human/family interdependencies are reported in American research, and the relational self is called for by the American critics of American psychology.

What does all this mean? With economic development there is a shift in the Majority World from a family model of total interdependence to a model of emotional interdependence. Is there also a shift in the postindustrial society from a family model of independence to one of emotional interdependence? As the model of emotional interdependence reflects a dialectic synthesis of the two basic human needs for merging and separation (relatedness and autonomy), such a shift may indeed be the case. Thus a new type of global convergence may be emerging, characterized by a shift toward the model of emotional interdependence from the model of interdependence in the Majority World together with a shift in the Minority World, also, from the model of independence to the model of emotional interdependence, rather than the other way around. The latter shift is quite possible, though counterintuitive.

Some evidence in fact supports this view. Shifts from the family model of independence to even more individualistic nonfamily living arrangements may also result in a swing back into more interdependent patterns approaching the model of emotional interdependence. For example, Saal (1987) described such alternative housing and living arrangements as "additional group house," "chosen neighborhood relations," and "boarding community," and Jansen (1987) reported the "explosion" of communal living since the early 1980s, both in the Netherlands. These arrangements appear to reflect a need to recreate the community. L. H. Ekstrand and G. Ekstrand (1987) found that Swedish parents stress the value of group relations more than Indian parents (because the former miss them more). In Israel, Weil (1987) showed how proximal households function as alternatives to joint families among the "Bene Israel," who migrated to Israel from India.

Studies of postmodern values in the posttechnological society (Inglehart, 1991; N. Young, 1992) find the increasing importance of human relational values, rather than individualistic competitive values. Apparently, particularly in Europe, the austere Protestant work ethic of the modern era is giving way to some "softer" postmodern values. Greater concern with the environment, decreasing importance of work and fewer working hours, more leisure, and in general "a search for community" are some of the defining characteristics of this era in the Western *post*technological society. If we consider the specific elements of the two models, that of independence and of emotional interdependence, the latter appears to better fit the characteristics of the postmodern era.

I must admit that this prediction of a shift from the model of independence to one of emotional interdependence in the Western world is tentative given the still-pervasive individualistic ethos in the Western world. Nevertheless, the signs of change are telling, indeed. In any case, whether or not there is a shift from independence to emotional interdependence, there is no question that some synthesis similar to that found in the model of emotional interdependence is currently being seriously searched for in the Majority World. C. F. Yang (1988) defined it as "something creative that takes in the new element of individualism while keeping the old family tradition intact" (p. 117).

Such a synthesis of autonomy and interdependence (of agency and merging) have been recognized by others (Holzman, Diaz-Guerrero, & Swartz, 1975; Lenero-Otero, 1977; S. R. Sinha, 1985; Werner, 1979; K-S. Yang, 1986). At times it has been considered utopic. For example, Westen (1985), in his scholarly social-historical treatise on self and society, traced societal developments through four main phases: primary communitarian collectivism of primitive society; secondary communitarian collectivism (similar to Durkheim's mechanical solidarity seen in peasant societies with classical historic religions); individuated collectivism (similar to Durkheim's organic solidarity; characterized by self-interest and modernity); and synthetic collectivism in which both collectivity and the individual, both sociality and self-interest, and both self-interest and group feeling are legitimate (pp. 280–281). The last phase is seen by Westen as a logical possibility, though probably more a utopia than a reality. I believe recent research and thinking show that such a synthesis may indeed be a reality. It is what the human/family model of emotional interdependence involves.

A caveat is needed here. The model of family change proposed in this chapter is based on a functional analysis and refers to what is to be expected on the basis of ongoing socioeconomic changes, as evidenced in research. It is possible, however, that other factors not dealt with in the model can interfere with this "natural" process. One such factor could be the resistance of culture to change or "cultural lag."

It is possible, for example, in the urban developed contexts in the Majority World with collectivistic cultures that authoritarian, obedience-oriented child-rearing persists even though not required for family livelihood, because socio-economic changes have decreased material dependencies on the offspring. In this context, the obedience-oriented childrearing would not be functional for the family or adaptive for the growing person whose future lifestyle will require autonomy and individual decision making. This is an example of a mismatch between the requirements of (new) lifestyles and (traditional) childrearing.

Another factor that can counter the "natural" process of change, based on functional dynamics, could be "cultural diffusion." Global media are dominated by Western, mainly American, establishments, which project a particular world view. Diffusion of the Western model may be so pervasive as to promote the emergence of the human/family model of independence, even though it is not necessitated by or even functional for the lifestyles in most specific contexts in the world.

The model of family change I have proposed here cannot deal with such exogenous influences, but it is important to keep in mind that they may play a role. Nevertheless, the functional relations underlying the internal dynamics of the self–family–society interface appear strong enough to cause the proposed changes in most cases. The supporting evidence further confirms them.

II INDUCED CHANGE: EARLY ENRICHMENT

6 Induced Change: The Role of Psychology

Part I dealt with the linkages between the self, family, and society focusing mainly on human development within cultural context. The discussions have been mainly theoretical though I often looked into the implications of the academic and theoretical viewpoints for applications and policies. This chapter elaborates on this point further and serves as a link between the first and the second parts of the book. In Part II, the linkages between theory and application come to the fore, but the emphasis is on applications. This chapter examines in particular the role of psychology vis-à-vis applications/interventions/policies designed to improve human well-being in the world. This discussion leads to the examination of intervention studies in the next chapter.

PSYCHOLOGY AND DEVELOPMENT

For most psychologists development means child development or human development through the life span, at most. In either case, the unit of analysis is the individual, though there is a growing recognition of the context of development. These issues have been examined in some detail in the previous chapters. Here I want to focus on a different conceptualization of development in current usage by social scientists, planners, and policymakers in the world. This is the construal of human development at the societal level.

For some time, development, in this sense, was equated with economic growth and operationalized in terms of purely economic indicators, such as the per capita GNP. Today there is a questioning of economic growth as the main indicator of societal development and a growing recognition of the dynamic link between human development and societal development. For example, the World Bank is focusing more and more on the role of education in improving efficiency and motivation of the labor force and on the well-being of women for child care and lower fertility. This long overdue recognition that social development cannot be subsumed under economic development has paved the way for a new concept of *Human Development* (at macrolevel) to emerge from the United Nations Development Program (UNDP).

Since 1990, UNDP has been publishing *The Human Development Report* on an annual basis to present the global situation and to rank the countries by selected human development indicators. The following indicators are used for this purpose: life expectancy at birth, access to health services, access to safe water, access to sanitation, daily calorie supply (% of requirements), adult literacy, combined primary and secondary school enrollment rates, daily newspaper circulation, televisions, GNP per capita and real GNP per capita. The Human Development Index (HDI), which is used as the overall indicator, can further be adjusted for gender disparity. For example, Japan ranks first in HDI among 160 countries in the 1993 *Human Development Report*, but Sweden ranks first on the gender-sensitive HDI, with Japan ranking 17th.

Is this all beyond the scope of psychology? At first glance it appears so. However, a closer scrutiny of some of the indicators involved and their wide-ranging implications discloses the relevance of psychology, alongside the other social science disciplines, to the issues under question. This is as it should be, because the focus is on human development, even if macro (aggregate) criteria are being used in its conceptualization and operationalization. Yet, psychologists themselves appear to have hardly recognized the relevance of their discipline for global human development.

There are a number of reasons for this situation. These are reviewed here briefly as they relate to some of the issues in the global applications of psychology to be discussed in this chapter:

The definition of psychology as a pure science and the condescending attitude toward applied research have caused a "distancing" from real problems. This has also led to the perceived and at times real conflict between scientific rigor and social relevance. The original adoption by psychology of the physical science model, aspiring to discover universal laws of behavior, has meant the abstraction of behavior from its total environment and its reproduction in pure form in the laboratory. Though this scientific orientation has served psychology well for decades, particularly in certain areas of specialization, it has at the same time entailed a neglect of the existing diversity in the world and the "real-life problems" not easily amenable to the scrutiny of the experimental laboratory.

These basic characteristics of psychology as it developed first in Europe and then moved to North America and flourished there, were soon after transferred ready-made to the rest of the world. They were accepted by the

Western-trained psychologists in the Majority World with acquiescence and without questioning. Though there are significant exceptions today emerging in the Majority World, the overall picture remains more or less the same.

The traditionally applied area within psychology—clinical psychology—has not been relevant for development efforts, given its individual focus and exclusive involvement with psychopathology.

Psychology has remained rather "estranged" from the important societal issues in the Majority World because it is an imported discipline. As such, it has typically adopted Western psychology's theories and problems, being content in "transferring" rather than "producing," knowledge. Often the transferred knowledge has been of limited use, being the product of another cultural milieu.

Majority World psychologists, trained in the West,continue to work on similar issues when they return to their countries. This is because of their Western socialization into the field and because Western psychological circles remain their main reference groups and American journals are their main publication targets.

Even when dealing with issues of social importance, psychologists, given their basically individual level of analysis, tend to locate the "problem" in the individual and do not deal adequately with contextual factors. For example, Nunes (1993) complained about school psychologists' explanation of school failure in Brazil in terms of lower capacity of the working-class children (who score lower on adapted intelligence tests), ignoring the social context in which they grow up and the misfit between the home and the school cultures. Such a tendency toward "blaming the victim" does not help to change the unfavorable environmental conditions either at home or at school.

Indeed, the individualistic stance of Western psychology can be used (or misused) to justify existing social inequalities by "blaming the victim," or in terms of the "just world hypothesis," which claims that people get what they deserve. This is a problem related to seeing individuals as solely responsible for what happens to them and can be relevant for a wide range of explanations spanning from psychological health/pathology to attributions of economic success/failure (Leahy, 1990). This view presupposes initial (equal) opportunity and choice; where this assumption does not hold, it is not warranted.

Given the previous characteristics of psychological research, psychologists have typically shied away from confronting problems of development, such as population, education, health, migration, and so on. The large-scale proportion of such problems, not amenable to individual level of analysis, has been a deterrent for psychologists. Yet, these are all human problems with distinct cognitive, motivational, behavioral aspects in fact requiring psychological inquiry to be better understood.

Finally, the lack of involvement of psychologists with large-scale human problems also derives from an unawareness of the relevance of their knowledge for such problems, on the one hand, and a hesitation to act on the basis of insufficient knowledge, on the other. Yet, psychology *is* relevant to human problems, and there is indeed accumulated psychological knowledge, even if insufficient in some respects, which can be used to solve them.

These interrelated factors all play a role in the low levels of involvement of psychologists in development efforts in the Majority World. This situation has meant that psychologists have not in fact contributed what they could and should to the solution of important human development problems. Correspondingly, it has also had some significant implications for psychology as a discipline. Because societal development is often the first item on the agenda in developing countries, scientific disciplines that are seen to contribute to societal development have a high status and enjoy priority in allocation of resources for research, recruitment in large-scale projects, and so on. J.B.P. Sinha (1993) noted that "psychology has yet to develop as a policy science. . . . It has neither a macro database, nor a national perspective, nor a planning model to claim any attention" (p. 146). It lags behind because it is deemed irrelevant to societal development issues.

Just as serious are some of the implications of psychology's noninvolvement for social policies drawn in the Majority World. In effect, it means that social policies are not informed by psychological knowledge and expertise. There is commonly a lack of scientific expertise in Majority World government agencies and ministries (Wagner, 1986). If the existing expertise in a few universities is not tapped either (because it is not considered relevant), poorly formulated policies emerge, entailing great waste of economic and human resources. There are many examples of such poor policy making in population, health, and education areas in the Majority World. I deal with some of these areas and discuss how psychological participation can improve policy programming.

The result of all this is often social development that tends to lag behind economic development (Moghaddam, 1990). One factor is the relatively low contribution of human sciences, especially of psychology, to social development efforts, compared with the great contribution of physical sciences and engineering to economic and technological development. Psychology has tended to be "modulative" (in reacting to societal change) rather than "generative" (in instigating societal change) (Moghaddam, 1990; UNESCO, 1982); this timidity has been costly. To remedy the situation, it is incumbent on the psychologists in the Majority World to take the initiative without waiting to be asked, to make their knowledge available, and to partake in policy-relevant projects.

Theory and Application

The previous discussion is not just a call to Majority World psychologists to get involved in applied research. There is actually a call for a problem-oriented, non-theory-driven approach for developing countries (Connolly, 1985; Moghaddam

& Taylor, 1986). But this is a patronizing stance, reflecting the conventional habit of looking "West" for theory and "East" for data (Kağıtçıbaşı, 1994b). More importantly, theoretical work is crucial in informing policy-relevant research. There is much wisdom in K. Lewin's (1951) words: "There is nothing as practical as a good theory" (p. 169). As mentioned in the introduction, applied work not informed by theory has the risk of turning into blind empiricism that cannot be afforded, especially not in the Majority World.

To be of value, the theory should be culturally valid. This is an issue of crucial significance, given the fact that most psychology in the Majority World is imported. Formulating a theory with cultural validity requires production of knowledge. Both cross-cultural theory testing and indigenous theory construction would contribute to this process. Indeed, this is well recognized by a number of socially concerned psychologists from developing countries in a call for a more integrative approach involving endogenous psychological knowledge and culture-sensitive theory development (e.g., Kağıtçıbaşı, 1994b; Nsamenang, 1992, 1993; D. Sinha, 1983, 1989; D. Sinha & Kao, 1988; 1993; J.B.P. Sinha, 1993; Wang, 1993). The concept of *endogenous development* proposed by UNESCO (Huynh, 1979) is now receiving wide acceptance. It centers on human beings and takes into consideration the characteristics and inherent strengths of the societies involved.

However, when theories or models are used implicitly in development plans, they tend to be those transferred from the West. Thus in development "recipes," there are often tacit assumptions about the underlying human factors—a human model for development. This, in turn, is often based on the Western experience and is informed by Western psychology. Though the model is assumed to hold universally, it may in fact be quite at odds with the local reality. An example of such a misfit is the failure of attempts at promoting economic growth through an individualistic competitive achievement motivation model in collectivistic cultures such as India (J.B.P. Sinha, 1985) where "social achievement motivation" is pervasive (Agarwal & Misra, 1986; Misra & Agarwal, 1985). A different human model combining achievement with extension is needed. The need for extension refers to relating to others, thus when combined with the need for achievement, the need for social achievement emerges, "which is shown to facilitate collective efforts for development (J.B.P. Sinha, 1993, p. 145).

This example fits in with the family/human models discussed in the previous chapter. Specifically, an individualistic achievement motivation model is in line with the family/human model of independence, whereas social achievement motivation fits in better with a model of emotional interdependence. Given the unidirectional change expectations (toward the Western model) of the tenacious modernization theory, most tacit assumptions about human factors in development models subscribe to the family/human model of independence. Yet, as I have shown, the main shift in the world with socioeconomic development is not toward the model of independence but toward the model of emotional interdependence. What is needed is culturally valid theory to be developed and used in development models rather than tacit assumptions, based on imported knowledge.

Up to this point, I have been discussing the problems of lack of involvement of psychologists in development efforts and the need for the integration of culturally valid theory into applied work in the Majority World. But there is a related issue, not as readily apparent, that nevertheless has something to do with the modulative rather than the generative stance of psychology noted by Moghaddam (1990). This is the role definition of the psychologist-scientist as the "student" of human behavior trying to understand and explain phenomena, with the ultimate ambition of predicting them, which is to be contrasted with another possible role definition that would also entail being an "agent of change." Obviously, this is again the distinction between "pure" and "applied" research orientations. However, it is also worthy of discussion in its own right, for it becomes relevant in the types of interpretations made of any research results and has to do with values, standard setting, and relativism.

Again, remember that this chapter focuses on the situation in the Majority World in particular. Similar complaints may also be made about the rather inactive role of Western psychology in social policy making and societal issues, combined by an overactive emphasis on the individual. It should be noted, however, that there are some psychologists who are keenly aware of social issues and who have been involved in pioneering service-oriented research in such areas as public health, family planning, education, rehabilitation in war and conflict, and so on. For example, recently *The American Psychologist* (February 1994) contained reviews and evaluations of psychological contributions to early educational intervention in the United States. Still, the numbers are limited, especially in the Majority World where such involvement is most needed.

VALUES, STANDARDS, AND RELATIVISM

This discussion begins with examples of two contrasting approaches. Nutrition researchers who study the nutritional status of children in a village in a developing country may encounter malnutrition. They would note the situation, establish the severity of the problem, analyze the type of nutrition deficiency, and so on. Together with such analysis, they would most probably recommend that some measures be taken to ameliorate the malnutrition, such as the provision of nutritional supplementation, and so on. The level of malnutrition is established using growth monitoring techniques based on age-specific norms, though there may be problems in devising norms appropriate for the specific population in question. The nutritionists pass a judgment based on a standard, even if approximate, and often try to induce change to correct an unhealthy state. They do not construe this situation in relativistic terms, for example, viewing the children's malnutrition in comparison to their possible normal status in some other sphere of development, such as finger dexterity in pottery making.

An example of actual research with such an approach, where an *involved* orientation of the researchers is seen, is the large-scale nutrition research carried out by Kotchabhakdi and others (Kotchabhakdi, Winichagoon, Smitasiri, Dhanamitta, & Valya-Sevi, 1987) in a number of villages in northern Thailand. The presence of wide-scale malnutrition was established in this study. In addition to providing nutritional supplementation to children, the researchers also undertook to sensitize mothers to the importance of early psychosocial stimulation and more effective feeding techniques to decrease malnutrition.

The other example is one related in chapter 3 and reflects the contrasting approach of the cultural psychologist/anthropologist who studies child development. Specifically, Harkness and Super (1992) noted the inability of children in Kokwet (Kenya) to retell to an adult a story or to do other simple cognitive tasks. This low level of performance is viewed with a relativistic stance, however, as compared to their developed skills in child-care or household chores. Explanations of this situation are made (rightly) in terms of parental ethnotheories and their expression in the organization of daily life settings and customs of childrearing, and no action is taken to induce any change to "correct" the low level of performance in cognitive tasks.

Yet another example of an uninvolved approach is the study of childhood in a weavers' community in India by Anandalaksmy and Bajaj (1981) (also presented in chapter 3). The authors noted the restrictive and cognitively unstimulating environment of the female child, who is deprived of schooling. However, no action is taken to induce change.[12]

The contrasts between the two approaches are obvious. In the first case, a judgment is made about normal (acceptable) and subnormal (unacceptable) growth on the basis of a standard, and change is induced to bridge the gap. This is not done in the second approach. From where does this difference emerge? Are the issues involved so different in kind that a comparison is nonsensical? It is unlikely. Some of the points discussed in this chapter are relevant here, especially the role of the psychologist (and also of the anthropologist) as distant scientist who observes (understands, explains) phenomena but does not instigate change.

Apart from this definition, however, there is the additional factor that to instigate change, one needs a standard with which to compare the case under study, much like the nutritionist's standard of normal growth, based on growth norms. Are psychologists (or anthropologists) able or willing to develop such standards? This is a basic issue I have touched on in this book in different contexts, especially with regard to relativism-universalism in the study of social-

---

[12]It should be noted, however, that later on Anandalaksmy (1994) has actually gotten involved in an action research to improve the situation of the girl child in the family.

ization for competence (chapter 3), and in the cultural versus cross-cultural approaches in the introduction.

It also became clear in chapter 3 that there is a general unwillingness to pass judgments or to use standards on the part of psychologists and especially of anthropologists engaged in the study of human development in cultural context. A number of factors appear to play a role here. One is a fear of being ethnocentric (or Euro-American-centric). Because most of the child development researchers doing cross-cultural/cultural psychology/anthropology are in fact Euro-Americans, this is understandable (the smaller number of non-Western researchers are also so imbued with the Western psychological/anthropological outlooks that they are mostly not very different).

This is actually a respectable sensitivity, especially in view of the remnants of the colonial past and the social evolutionary views of the "primitives" as "childlike," "prelogical," and "less developed," in general. Thus, passing judgments about the (inferior) capacities of non-Western preindustrial groups on the basis of their poor performance on Western tests (or even on any tasks which are not culturally meaningful to them) is not warranted. It is reminiscent of a biased colonial outlook that cross-cultural and cultural researches would rightly want to avoid. However, is the only alternative to this unacceptable position a rampant relativism where anything is as good as anything else?

As discussed in chapter 3, this appears to be the view of some cultural psychologists and cognitive anthropologists. It is particularly strong in hermeneutic anthropology and in postmodernism, in general, which are so committed to subjectivity and therefore relativism that even the existence of any "facts" or "knowledge" is denied (Kvale, 1992). Gellner (1992) criticized postmodernism seriously as an "ephemeral cultural fashion . . . of interest [only] as a living and contemporary specimen of relativism which as such is of some importance and will remain with us for a long time" (p. 24). Relativism is of course not confined to postmodernism. It is quite noticeable in the "specific learning model" (LCHC, 1983) and "everyday cognition" tradition informed by Vygotskian sociohistorical school of thought. In this approach all learning is "goal-directed action," which is functional for adapting to the context and for practical problem solving required by the particular context in which it takes place. Thus, a great deal of everyday learning "through guided participation" within the child's "zone of proximal development" is studied in context, and the context-specific requirements on the development of specific cognitive skills are emphasized (see chapter 3).

This body of research has provided us with rich description and insight into the functional nature of cognition. However, if this view of context-specific learning is seen to define all learning (Shweder, 1990), then we are left with no shared attributes, no common standards, and no possibility of comparison—total relativism.

Schooling and Religious Education
as a Case in Point

School is considered by some cross-cultural researchers as just another context for learning and not superior to any other specific learning (Greenfield & Lave, 1982, p. 185). It is this relativistic approach that does not see any problem with a child who cannot perform simple cognitive tasks but, for example, is skilled in carrying out household chores or, in the case of girls, capable of developing skills for household chores and filling spools for weaving but stays illiterate. It is interesting to note that this type of a relativistic interpretation (nonjudgment) tends to be made for children (or adults) in preindustrial, less developed contexts, but not for those in industrial environments. For the latter, comparative standards are used, involving cognitive skills and school performance, and arrears in these are not interpreted in relative terms, compared with their skills in noncognitive, nonschoollike tasks.

It could be claimed that this is as it should be, because noncognitive tasks are more adaptive and valued in preindustrial traditional settings whereas schoollike tasks are more adaptive for living in urban industrial society. Though this may be true, it is also the crux of the matter. Indeed, by *not* using comparative standards and *not* passing judgments (making value judgments) about the state of the children in the preindustrial traditional society, ironically, a value judgment *is* being made by default. Expressed rather bluntly, this value judgment states that in the industrial society with mass schooling, (universal) cognitive standards of achievement apply, but in preindustrial societies they do not. What we have here is relativism leading to double standards.

There are a number of problems here. A basic one is social change. As mentioned earlier, preindustrial, even preliterate societies, like all societies, undergo change. Change often involves opening up traditional economies to cash economies, greater integration with national (and international) markets, rural to urban migration, introduction of public schools,and so on. Many of the traditional skills lose their adaptive values in the process of change. Relativistic values stressing the importance of these traditional skills presume static societies, which do not exist, especially today, given the tremendous ongoing socioeconomic structural changes and globalization. Furthermore, emphasizing these skills alone would help perpetuate the status quo.

This can be a dilemma, especially in contexts where people want to change their lifestyles (e.g., rural peasants aspiring to migrate to cities). In such situations researchers should be careful about their conclusions and interpretations. It can be just as patronizing and intrusive to claim that the traditional ways are valuable and should not change (when people would like to change them) as it is to insist that people change when they do not want to change. This type of a dilemma can be resolved if the researcher does not make interpretations of the situation on purely theoretical (academic) grounds but tries to find out people's genuine preferences. Collaboration with local researchers and experts in equal-status partnership (D. Sinha, 1983) would be a great asset in this endeavor.

A related dilemma has to do with the hesitation to impose middle-class values on non-middle-class populations. It is interesting to note here that the so-called middle-class values or behaviors are those that research shows to be beneficial for children's development in general (S. A. Miller, 1988, p. 271) and for their cognitive competence and school performance in particular. I have reviewed a great deal of research showing this in chapters 2 and 3, especially in dealing with the concept of disadvantage. The question to be asked is why such positive parental values and behavior should be in the monopoly of the middle classes? If they are beneficial for children, then it is desirable to promote them in all parents as much as possible. *Not* to do this is again to affirm the existing inequalities, which work against the children of the marginalized groups. It is important to make sure that tolerance of diversity and relativism do not impede efforts to improve the environments of socioeconomically disadvantaged children.

Related to this is the commonly observed misfit between indigenous skills and the requirements of formal schooling. An example is the traditionally valued social skills of quiet obedience, and so forth, which do not guarantee and may even detract from school success. The same is true for the contrasting case of cognitive skills, such as preliteracy skills, including verbal reasoning and vocabulary, which are conducive to school performance but are not typically valued or stressed in traditional childrearing. For example, research in Nigeria points to the mismatch between the concrete language and classification skills at home and the abstract and representational language and classification skills required in school (Haglund, 1982). Other similar cases were discussed in chapters 2 and 3.

It does not help to claim that school learning is just another specific learning, not superior to any other. First of all, school learning is more conducive to generalization and transfer to new learning situations (LCHC, 1983; Scribner & Cole, 1981; Segall et al., 1990), though some higher level everyday cognitive skills are also transferable (T. N. Carraher et al., 1988; Nunes et al., 1993). And just as important, schooling (school attainment and performance) is often more instrumental than traditional skills for advancement in changing societies. Ironically, then, whereas cultural psychologists and anthropologists shun using Western-type (school-related) standards in their research with traditional peoples, in those same societies, those standards are often used as yardsticks for advancement in social status, economic well-being, and so on.

The point I am trying to make here is that research may be conducted for academic purposes only. However, because it is conducted in the real world, it cannot stay at a distance from social values and policies. Indeed, social science cannot be "value-free." As Bellah et al. (1985) rightly noted, "To attempt to study the possibilities and limitations of society with utter neutrality, as though it existed in another planet, is to push the ethos of narrowly professional social science to the breaking point" (p. 302). Absolute neutrality is not possible anyway, for even when the researchers do not intervene or prescribe change, they are in fact taking a stand with political implications. As in the earlier example, stressing the importance of traditional ways may have the effect of perpetuating the status quo and not change, which is a value-laden view and even a political stand.

It might be argued that social science research does not really have the power I am ascribing to it. Such power may not be readily observable, but it is there, at least potentially. In fact, given the high prestige of science, any conclusions or interpretations made by a researcher carry quite a bit of weight, especially when published and available through the mass media. They are certainly liable to use by politicians and policymakers to legitimize their positions. Thus, social science research carries social responsibility, whether or not it chooses it.

Actually, a socially responsible role is also demanded of social science. This is certainly the case in the Majority World where effective development models, including human models, are being searched for, and human potential development is high on national agendas. Most cross-cultural research in child development, for example, has been knowledge driven (Masters, 1984), mainly with the goal of testing "universal" theories of child development or developing new theories. Though highly beneficial for academic advancement (in the West), this substantial amount of research has contributed little to the well-being of children or to societal development in the Majority World (Dasen, 1988b; Kağıtçıbaşı, 1994b; Wagner, 1986).

There is some resentment in the Majority World of research conducted by foreigners (especially anthropologists), which only gathers information and thus benefits from the local resources but gives back nothing in return. What is searched for are insights into how improvement in human conditions and human potential can be achieved. This is because societal (national) development is the most important goal in these societies, and human resources are often their most important resources for development. Yet, this is what many cultural psychologists and anthropologists are *not* equipped or willing to provide, given their relativistic views avoiding judgments based on (comparative) standards and their role definitions as uninvolved scientists.

Societal aspirations need to be taken seriously. Universal literacy and schooling are pervasive aspirations in the Majority World. The World Conference on "Education for All" met in Jomtien (Thailand) in 1990. A second meeting was held in New Delhi in 1993, focusing on "quality education for all" (1990 was declared the International Literacy Year). In early 1994, "The Education for All Summit" witnessed the governments of some of the most populous nations of the world (China, India, Indonesia, Bangladesh, Pakistan, Brazil, Mexico, and Egypt) commit themselves to provide schooling to all their children. All this is in response to gross inequalities in educational opportunities and provisions in the world that are too painfully recognized in many parts of the Majority World. For example, whereas in North America school enrollment at all levels reaches 91.8%, it is only 41.9% in Sub-Saharan Africa (with tertiary enrollment 70.4% in the former and a mere 2.1% in the latter) (UNESCO, 1991, p. 94).

Education is also a basic human right. Article 26 of the Universal Declaration of Human Rights states: "Everyone has the right to education. Education shall be free, at least in the elementary and fundamental stages. Elementary education shall be compulsory." Accordingly, all efforts to expand literacy and schooling must be supported and governments should be urged to invest more in education to increase significantly educational opportunity for over 150 million children, more than two thirds of them girls, who at present have no access to basic education (Bennett, 1993, p. 12). Apart from the vast proportions of the problem, there are other reasons for concern. For example, the 1980s witnessed declining investments in health and education with economic difficulties in the world, especially in Africa and Latin America, which prompted some to call it "a lost decade for development" (Jolly, 1988). In this context, the negative effects, of the International Monetary Fund and World Bank policies of structural adjustment and privatization of education should also be mentioned. Finally, most foreign aid of the affluent industrial societies is not to education; only Sweden allocates more than 5% of its aid to education.

Together with the urgency and the serious nature of educational issues in the world go controversies and political debates on education. For example, governments may invest inadequate resources to formal education, which is a long-term investment, allocating resources instead to other areas with faster returns. Thus, they may fail to meet their commitments and be eager to relegate the responsibility to nonformal communal organizations, religious groups, and so on. Every effort should be made by psychologists, among others, to force governments to face their responsibilities. Or genuine efforts by governments to make education available to all may be frustrated or counteracted by conservative or reactionary forces who oppose modernization and especially the education of girls (women).

An example of the latter is the rising political power of religious fundamentalism in the world, especially in Moslem societies (Gellner, 1992). Wagner (1983) noted that today "Koranic schooling [is] in more direct competition with the modern secular school systems of many Moslem societies" (p. 80). Indeed, there are efforts to *replace* regular schooling by Koranic schooling, often financed internationally by theocratic governments such as those in Iran, Libya, and Saudi Arabia with the intention of undermining secularism in Moslem societies. Such reactionary movements are impediments to societal development, as for example measured by the human development indicators of the United Nations Development Program (UNDP). It is also to be noted that wide-scale religious education is being advocated only in Moslem societies in the world, which appears to point to some political issues involved.

Many governments and particularly the educated sectors in Moslem societies are struggling hard and against great odds to overcome the rise of fundamentalism. Much is at stake, with fundamentalist terror also emerging in the picture. Yet, research by Western cross-cultural psychologists and anthropologists can come up with statements supporting and legitimizing Koranic schooling (Santerre, 1973; Wagner, 1983, 1988).

At the preschool level or as supplementary education (not replacing formal schooling), Koranic schooling can contribute to literacy in Arab countries (Wagner, 1988). However, it cannot serve this function in other Moslem societies with other languages. Even in the case of Arabic-speaking countries, however, the goal should be "education for all" in modern public schools. In fact, some of the highest proportions of illiteracy are found in Arab countries (49%), which are close to those of the much poorer countries in Southern Asia (54%) and Sub-Saharan Africa (53%) (Verhoeven, Rood, & Laan, 1991), especially among women.

Actually, any positive effects of Koranic schooling (at the preschool level) obtained in research were very limited and specific: only on a serial memory task using digits. Even this specific effect diminished "when Koranic names were used instead of digits or when these items were used incrementally rather than in longer randomized spans" (Wagner & Spratt, 1987, p. 1217). Among adults, Koranic schooling did not improve overall memory but only specific incremental recall (Scribner & Cole, 1981). In Moslem societies with languages other than Arabic, it is doubtful that it would even have this specific effect because it amounts to memorizing text in an incomprehensible language. In contrast, pervasive and consistent positive effects of formal schooling are found on diverse cognitive and memory tasks (LCHC, 1983; Oloko, 1994; Scribner & Cole, 1981; Segall et al., 1990; Serpell, 1993).

Given the flimsy evidence of any positive cognitive effects, it appears unwarranted to draw conclusions about traditional education as "appropriate education," which has a definite contribution to make "given the needs of Third-World countries" (Wagner, 1988). Again, we are faced with relativistic double standards. Religious education has declined in the world, especially in the industrialized West, and no one is proposing a return to it; but it is seen as "appropriate" for the Third World (Moslem societies). Religious education cannot serve the functions of public schooling in promoting societal development, therefore it should not be considered as an alternative, but only as a supplementary form of education to universal schooling.

I have discussed education in some detail within the Majority World perspective both because it is very important and also because it presents a particularly striking example of the political implications of research. Schools are possibly the most important institutions for societal development, despite their weaknesses. They do not just provide cognitive skills or specific learning. For example, there is much evidence indicating that formal education, especially of girls, has far-reaching long-term effects, such as later age at marriage, lower fertility, lower infant mortality, and better nutrition/health of future children (Caldwell, 1979, 1980; Cochrane & Mehra, 1983; R. A LeVine, 1983), in addition to the obvious benefits such as better literacy skills, higher levels of employment, and so on. Furthermore, these long-term benefits obtain with only primary school education, even with a few years of formal schooling, particularly in the least developed countries (Cochrane & Mehra, 1983). Min (1994) reviewed a great deal of research pointing to the empowering effects of public schooling for girls/women.

Thus, belittling interpretations, such as school learning not being superior to any other kind of everyday specific learning, are not helpful to global efforts to provide "education for all." On the contrary, psychologists can contribute to efforts to expand schooling by also disseminating scientific evidence regarding the enhancement of human performance through schooling, as well as through everyday learning outside the school. Similarly, religious education does not just impart specific memory skills. It inculcates a religious world view that is often antithetical to a scientific world view. This is particularly the case in Islamic education, because Islam encompasses not only "the faith" but also "the law," which regulates everyday life (including gender roles, economy, government, etc.). In countries such as Turkey, Egypt, and Tunisia, which have opted for secularism, religious education tends to promote reactionary conservatism. In an early research with adolescents in Turkey (Kağıtçıbaşı, 1973) I found "religiosity" to be associated with authoritarianism and belief in external control of reinforcement and to correlate negatively with optimism and achievement motivation.

Given the serious issues involved, it is incumbent on cross-cultural researchers to be aware of the politics of education in the world and the far-reaching implications of their own work.

As mentioned earlier, schooling has its problems as well, and has been criticized for them. Indeed, in most of the Majority World public schools are inadequate (Myers, 1992; Serpell, 1993). The inequality of access to schools; the poor quality of instruction, often involving rote learning and recitations; lack of educational materials; at times the irrelevance of the curriculum to local/national realities; and overcrowded classrooms are among the many problems in the Majority World. This calls for greater efforts to invest in schools to work toward improving them.

However, these problems reflect the existing societal problems rather than cause them, as is sometimes assumed. For example, it is not schooling that causes rural to urban migration but basic social–structural and economic changes—such as the mechanization of agriculture replacing human labor, too high a population pressure on cultivable land, and so on—which push people out of rural areas in search of urban jobs. Again, it is not schooling that creates unemployment, but mainly economic and population problems in a society. However, schooling may be inadequate in solving issues; for example, unemployment calls for more investment and better planning to upgrade schools and to enable them to train youth in line with the employment requirements in the society.

Schooling is found to induce individualistic orientations, which in collectivistic societies can result in the weakening of interdependent family ties (Greenfield & Cocking, 1994; Oloko, 1994; Serpell, 1993). However, this may not be inevitable, for interdependence values can be integrated into school learning, as for example generally seen in East Asian cultures (Greenfield, 1994) or in the Pueblo Indian classrooms (Suina & Smolkin, 1994).

Schooling promises to be a powerful instigator of societal development when it is rendered socially relevant and culturally appropriate (e.g., getting rid of colonial components where applicable). I would further propose not to use the term *Western schooling* in most Majority World societies where national educational policies and plans have been established and are in application for some time. What used to be Western (or the property of the Western world) is now globally shared education. It is an inherent part of "endogenous development" (Huynh, 1979; Tripathi, 1988) that can encompass *both* the culturally relevant *and* the globally shared knowledge.

WILL PSYCHOLOGY HELP?

Up to now I have been discussing issues involved in linking theory and application, with a special focus on the role of the cross-cultural researcher. I have also stressed the problems of values and politics inherent in research informing policy and social action. There is, of course, no guarantee that research findings will be used to promote human well-being. Because science is public, it can be used or misused and there is probably not much that the scientist can do about it.

Social scientists or psychologists who are involved in cultural/cross-cultural research have the additional problem of evaluating and interpreting research findings within the cultural and political context of the society or societies in which they work. A call for an "involved" stance is not a sanction for foreign visitors to intervene whenever they find something disturbing. A good way of preventing misunderstanding is to work in partnership in team research with local researchers (D. Sinha, 1983). Indeed, as noted by Greenfield (1994, p. 23), "an insider's perspective [may be] essential to the valid description of socialization and development." This is not to say that an insider's view is perfect; it has its own weaknesses. Nevertheless, it can serve as a corrective to the outsider's possible ethnocentrism. It promises to be valuable in policy-relevant research and interventions.

A second way of avoiding imposing one's own views on the situation is involving "subjects" of the research as participants in evaluation/interpretation, as well as asking their opinions and aspirations regarding the issues relevant to the research in question. These approaches are particularly helpful in tackling some difficult decisions in applied research. For example, in intervention or applied research designed to provide some solutions to human problems, decisions about change are involved. Difficult questions, such as " what is to change, what is to remain, how is this to be ascertained, and by whom?", can be better handled by using the informed opinions and insights of the insiders.

Caution is called for in intervention research. We should be able to differentiate between what constitutes good social science involvement in social policy and what constitutes psychological imperialism and unwelcome paternalism. This is not always easy to do, and some of the procedures recommended earlier may help by bringing in the insider's perspective.

"Endogenous development" does not mean perpetuation or strengthening of traditional ways. Indeed, this type of an indigenization may carry the danger of turning into a revivalistic movement (Dalal, 1990, p. 116), as in the case of religious fundamentalism. Though, on the one hand, endogenous development involves aligning development with societal values, on the other hand, it also entails development of effective systems that can cope with global changes. Both "openness" and "embeddedness" are thus required for social change to qualify as "development" (Tripathi, 1988).

Examples of such development are reflected in "integrative syntheses," some of which I have been discussing. They are the nurturant-task leadership (J.B.P. Sinha, 1980); social achievement motivation (Agarwal & Misra, 1986; Misra & Agarwal, 1985; Phalet & Claeys, 1993; Yu & K-S. Yang, 1994); the family/human model of emotional interdependence, also entailing autonomy and interdependence (chapter 5); and emphasis on language-cognitive development alongside "social intelligence" in childrearing (chapter 3).

These issues are relevant, for example, in intervention research designed to improve the early environment and to promote optimal human development. Chapter 3 examined "disadvantage," and chapter 2 discussed some models relating human development to context. A main point made was that because (adverse) socioeconomic conditions at the macrolevel affect the growing child through the mediation of parental behavior (and the family), psychological intervention is possible. Such interventions at the family level, extending into other ingroups and the community, are even more likely to be effective in collectivistic cultures than individual level interventions (D. Sinha & Kao, 1988, p. 25).

School Readiness and Early Development

A serious human development problem many countries in the Majority World face is school failure and school dropout. It leads to high rates of repetition of first year classes and low retention rates to the end year of the basic educational cycle (UNICEF, 1991; UNESCO, 1991; e.g., Bangladesh retains only 20%; Bennett, 1993, p. 12). Especially in the context of underdevelopment, where universal schooling is not yet achieved, this problem entails great economic and human costs. Thus, the World Bank (1988, p. 50) reported that the cost of each completer of primary school in Sub-Saharan Africa is on the average 50% higher due to repetition and dropout; in some countries in the region it is much higher.

Obviously, many factors are involved—low quality schools with overcrowded classrooms, uneven distribution of schools necessitating long commuting distances for some children, and so on. Among the factors involved also are inadequate school preparation (of the child) and inadequate family support (of the child's "student role" and school performance). I discussed this issue in chapters 2 and 3. Here I want to examine how psychological research can address the issue, together with other issues of human development. As Myers (1992) noted, "improving the readiness of children for school can improve the quality and efficiency of school systems . . . [for] children are probably the most important 'input' into schooling as well as its most important 'output'" (p. 221).

Inadequate preparation for school can be seen as a developmental problem based on the assumption of some standard of adequacy that can be established and measured. "Readiness for school" is currently defined in terms of the child's activity level (health and nutritional status, affecting both school attendance and concentration in class); social competence and psychological preparedness (affecting adaptation to and coping with school requirements); and cognitive abilities, including preliterary and prenumeracy skills. Readiness is also reflected in the positive outlooks and expectations of the family as well as their support (Myers, 1992, p. 216). Though different terms may be used for some of the previous concepts, and/or some slightly different or more refined categories may be utilized, these concepts constitute a characterization of the child's school preparedness.

Within developmental psychology and psychometrics there is much accumulated knowledge regarding both the conceptualization and the assessment of the aforementioned aspects of human development. Much research has informed us about language/communication; problem solving, concept formation, and other cognitive processes; social competence/maturity; emotional development; life skills development; and so on in the years preceding school entry. Altogether these contribute to "school readiness." However, all this knowledge and expertise is yet to be used optimally in intervention work in different sociocultural contexts. Culturally sensitive and appropriate measures of age-specific development in different spheres needs to be developed in order to ascertain any retarded development, which needs to be acted on to promote school readiness. These measures would need to be based on culturally valid conceptualizations of human development, which, in turn, would be informed by both international research in the field and also research within each sociocultural context.

The current dependence on Western conceptualizations and especially on Western measures is an impediment for advancement in this area. Related to this is the problem of the lack of measures that do not require much time and expertise for their application to large numbers of children. Given the scale of the problem in many developing countries, large numbers of children are involved. Screening and detection instruments are often needed to pick out children at risk of debilitated or delayed development in order to attend to their needs. Individual intelligence tests or other assessment techniques, which are costly in terms of time and professional expertise for their application, are not suitable for such use. This is the type of assessment in which psychologists have been traditionally involved. Therefore, a different kind of approach is called for to address the needs arising in real-life situations.

For example, a 1985 UNICEF workshop in Brazil concluded that "a simple instrument to measure children's psychosocial development needs to be perfected and applied in the different countries of the region. Current methods are considered, by and large, to be inadequate" (Consultative Group, 1986, p. 2).

It is unlikely that any such single instrument can be developed. Nevertheless, the statement is instructive in reflecting the needs felt by field workers. Psychological expertise, especially in psychometrics and cross-cultural developmental psychology, can contribute a great deal to efforts to devise reliable and culturally sensitive assessment instruments—for example, to ascertain school readiness. This is a new challenge for psychologists that has to be met (Landers & Kağıtçıbaşı, 1990).

It is typically the health professionals, mainly nutritionists and pediatricians, who have been involved in large-scale assessment of children for screening and detection purposes. There is a growing need to devise psychological developmental assessment techniques to parallel the existing measures of physical growth. Similarly, there is a need to establish culturally valid norms of psychosocial development to parallel (physical) growth norms. Such norms are crucial for monitoring child development (very much like growth monitoring) and for ascertaining developmental delays.

So far psychologists have not had a significant presence in large-scale health projects and have not made a "niche" for themselves in multidisciplinary efforts for promoting health and education in the world (for a rare exception, see Dasen, Berry, & Sartorious, 1988). Nevertheless, significant attempts have been made in research (e.g., in Latin America, India, and Turkey) to establish culturally valid age-specific developmental norms (Kaur & Saraswathi, 1992; Landers, 1992; Landers & Kağıtçıbaşı, 1990; Myers, 1992; Pandey, 1988; Savasir et al., 1992).

In some large-scale projects involving several developing countries, establishment of psychosocial indicators of development is pursued within health or mental health contexts where mainly health professionals are involved. One of these is the World Health Organization project for the development and use of psychosocial indicators, started in 1983 and carried out in Argentina, China, India, Pakistan, Senegal, and Thailand. By 1990, more than 31,000 children had been measured for both growth and psychosocial development (World Health Organization, 1986, 1990). This large-scale undertaking has involved test development, reliability checks, tester training, repeated administration and refinement, including the integration of culture-specific items, and so on. It promises to be a major international effort toward cross-cultural conceptualization and assessment of early (age 0–6) human development. However, the academic psychological community is hardly involved, even hardly aware of what is going on.

In addition to indicators of psychological development, environmental indicators are also greatly needed. These entail the assessment of the physical environment, environmental stimulation, caretaker attitudes and behavior, child–caretaker interaction, and so on. A most important component of intervention work involves parent education and community programs designed to act on the environment to make it more conducive to healthy human development. Thus, environmental indicators are crucial to ascertain high-risk environments for interventions to be effective. General indicators such as socioeconomic status are not adequate; more refined indicators are needed because there is much variation, for example, in parental behaviors within the same socioeconomic context.

Psychological expertise is also called for in the establishment of environmental indicators. The very concept of environmental risk is in need of better conceptualization and operationalization. This is a challenging task in cross-cultural context. Culture-specific measures need to be developed, but it may be possible to establish some basic categories in areas like caretaker interaction styles, expectations, beliefs; cognitively stimulating environment, verbal stimulation; physical characteristics of the environment; autonomy and affection in childrearing; and so forth. Environmental indicators are also being integrated into some large-scale health projects, again mainly by health professionals (DeSilva, Nikapota, & Vidyasagara, 1988; Nikapota, 1990; Sockalingam, Zeitlin, & Satato, 1990; World Health Organization, 1986, 1990).

An adequate conceptualization of human development has to be complex, integrating both physical growth-maturation and also total psychological development (including socioemotional, language, cognitive development) within context and through time, starting from the very beginning. With the serious problems of infant mortality in the Majority World, for some decades a heavy emphasis was put on nutrition and health needs of children, concentrating on early ages (0–3). With recent shifts from medical to social science models of health (Mosley & Chen, 1984), there has been a greater recognition of the social-behavioral aspects of health and well-being. Thus, the World Health Organization constitution defines health broadly as "a state of complete physical, mental and social well-being, and not merely the absence of disease or informity." The broader conceptualization of health is both in terms of the synergistic relationship among nutrition, health, and psychosocial development (Myers, 1992), and also in terms of the contextual-interactional aspects of human development. Thus, psychological development and the importance of the mediating factors in the environment are now recognized as important. Research conducted in different parts of the world has contributed to this long overdue recognition.

The interactive relationship among nutrition, health, and psychosocial development and the direct impact of environmental factors are relevant from the very beginning and affect children's school readiness. For example, research shows that malnourishment breeds malnourishment, unless counteracted by caretaker sensitivity and behavior. Because sick and malnourished children are less active and demanding, they end up getting less food; active, healthy babies demand and therefore get more food. The immediate environment is a part of this synergism because reluctant babies can be fed more if, for example, mothers stimulate them during breastfeeding; whereas a less stimulating environment is less conducive to nutrition-health and psychosocial development from early on (Brazelton, 1982; Myers, 1992).

A study conducted in a Mexican village found that the mothers of malnourished children had less exposure to the radio, provided lower quality of home stimulation, and were less responsive to their children than the mothers of normal children (Carvioto, 1981). A child stimulation project by the Ford Foundation in Central Java (reported by Landers & Kağıtçıbaşı, 1990) found that the quality of maternal–child interaction (mothers' level of understanding of and responding to their children's developmental needs) was related to positive growth and development outcomes (better nourishment, higher physical and cognitive development of children), in spite of distressful environments. Finally, a large-scale nutrition intervention project in Thailand provided mothers in villages also with awareness of the importance of early stimulation and interaction with infants, with beneficial results for nutrition, health, and development (Kotchabhakdi et al., 1987).

The concept of "positive deviance"[13] has been proposed by Zeitlin, Ghassemi, and Mansour (1990) to refer to children who survive and even thrive in adverse environments. Reviewing 16 studies, they concluded that positive caretaker–child interaction "enhances the child's tendency to exercise its developing organ systems and hence to utilize nutrients for growth and development" (p. 33). Psychological stress has adverse effects on the use of nutrients while psychological well-being stimulates the growth-promoting hormones. "Psychosocial factors, such as the affect between mother and child, are associated with adequate growth and development" (p. 34). This is important evidence for the synergy between nutrition, health, and psychosocial factors and for the role of the mediating environmental (caretaker–child interaction) variables in counteracting negative macrolevel influences such as poverty.

The synergistic relationship between nutrition, health, and psychosocial development is also noted in research conducted with school or preschool-age children with direct relevance for school readiness or school performance (Moock & Leslie, 1986; Pollitt, Gorman, Engle, Martorell & Rivera, 1993;

---

[13]"Positive deviance" is a more specific construal of the concept of resilience within the context of nutrition.

Pollitt & Metallinos-Katsaras, 1990; Seshadri & Gopaldas, 1989). All these studies point to the need to assume a wholistic as well as an interactional–contextual approach to human development in both conceptualization and operationalization. Such an approach promises to provide both a better understanding of the factors involved and more effective interventions to promote healthy human development, also involving better school readiness.

NATURE–NURTURE UNDERPINNINGS

Underlying the discussions in this chapter is the basic principle of malleability of human nature by environmental influences. This is assumed in any applied research. From a contextual-interactional perspective, and in line with the evidence I have reviewed, the familial factors (e.g., caretaker–child interaction) that mediate between the macrolevel social structural factors and the individual child appear to be the best targets for psychological interventions.

This view does not imply a rampant environmentalism, rejecting constitutional influences (including genetic factors). Recent conceptualizations of the effects of environment and genetics to psychological outcome stress "the multiple contributions of organismic and environmental variables to the processes that result in particular behaviors and particular developmental outcomes" (Horowitz, 1993, p. 350), and "non-additive synergistic effects in genetic-environment interaction" (Bronfenbrenner & Ceci, 1993, p. 314). Wachs (1993) called for "multideterminant research" to develop a better understanding of the covariance and interaction among the genetic, biomedical, nutritional, environmental, and individual determinants. The long-standing debate on nature versus nurture is a misnomer. As Anastasi (1958) urged more than 25 years ago, instead of seeking to establish how much of the variance (in outcome variables) is attributable to heredity and how much to environment, the question "how?" should be addressed. Indeed, neither genetic nor environmental determinism is correct because their influences are intermingled (Gottlieb, 1991; Oyama, 1985).

The recent advances in behavior genetics and a general shift toward organismic explanations in psychology, however, have tended to undermine the role of the environment, with far-reaching implications for social and political agendas. Specifically, if environment is inconsequential, then interventions are not needed or even justifiable. It is a short step from this to asserting that intergroup differences, say in intelligence, cannot be helped, because they reflect the natural unfolding of the different genetic pools—thus it is a "just world," with those having lower genetic potentials doing less well. Even though responsible behavior geneticists are careful to note the limitations of the claims that can be made from data regarding genetic control of behavior (Plomin, 1989), easily popularized statements can be misused, with significant potential harm to the marginal groups in society. Though the current debate is mainly occurring in American psychology (Plomin & McLearn, 1993), it also has global implications.

There is a recent assertion that environment has an influence on developmental variability only at the extremes (Scarr, 1992). In "normal families," therefore, environment is considered to be unimportant. A real problem here is the determination of what is "normal" and what is "extreme." Scarr defined normal "families in the mainstream of Western European and North American societies" (p. 10). Obviously, the Majority World remains outside and yet this is proposed as a "developmental theory for the 1990s." A further claim of the theory is that individuals choose their environments, and therefore it is their genetic endowment that creates the environments they constitute for themselves. This is a "genotype-environment" theory. Though in a footnote Scarr admitted the theory is based on the assumption that people have varied environments from which to choose their experiences, she did not seem to think it detracts from the external validity of the theory that a great many people in the world are not in a position to choose much at all.

The previous view reflects the individualistic stance of American psychology, which explains outcomes in terms of individual characteristics (even innate ones) and holds the individual responsible for them. This type of outlook assumes equal opportunity (and the existence of choice). When we consider the varied environments children are born into—some with great opportunities and choices, others with very meager ones—the limitations of the theory become apparent.

Actually, as Wachs (1993) noted, there is much evidence that even in normal, nonextreme families, specific environmental factors relate to specific aspects of development, as shown for example by Bornstein and Tamis-Le Monda (1990), A. Gottfried and A. Gottfried (1984), and Wachs (1987). A great deal of the evidence presented in chapters 2 and 3 is also relevant here. All this research shows that when specific mediating variables in the environment are adequately conceptualized and operationalized, they are found to relate to developmental outcomes.[14] One of the problems of genetic deterministic explanations is a rather global treatment of the environment, with inadequate assessment. Better and more standardized measurement of specific environmental components is therefore badly needed and promises to throw light on some of the "masked" influences (Horowitz, 1993). This needs to be done cross-culturally.

The fact of the matter is that a great number of children in the world grow up in environments that do not promote their potentials; that is why environmental intervention is important. Bronfenbrenner and Ceci (1993) put it succinctly, "Humans have genetic potentials . . . that are appreciably greater than those that are presently realized, and [ ] progress toward such realization can be achieved through the provision of environments in which proximal processes can be enhanced, but which are always within the limits of human genetic potential"

---

[14]Wachs (1993) also provided other criticisms of Scarr's (1992) theory, claiming that it is incorrect in a number of areas.

(p. 315). Not much can be done about unfavorable genetic influences, however, adverse environmental influences can be ameliorated to a considerable extent. So a positive and constructive role psychology can play is to show how this can be done effectively. This is how psychology can help promote better human functioning and human well-being—"human development" in the world.

7 Early Childhood Care and Education (ECCE): An Overview

The previous chapter examined the role of psychology in inducing change and linked theory and application in a number of different areas. Issues of applied research came to the fore. In this chapter I want to narrow down the focus and to take up a particular area of research and application in which I have conducted an intervention project with my colleagues over the last 10 years. This is the area of early intervention or enrichment to promote better child development and competence. This chapter aims to provide the background theory and research as well as the state of the art in the field for the intervention research to be presented in the next chapter.

Early childhood care and education (ECCE) is the term adopted internationally (Van Oudenhoven, 1989) to describe education-related services to the young child. ECCE is assuming increasingly greater importance as a field integrating theory, application, and program development. First in the United States and growing in numbers and expanding to other countries, a great deal of research has been conducted in this field. This chapter provides an overview of some of the main research issues and a brief review of the state of the art in ECCE as a general background for our intervention project.

The large body of literature on intervention projects and ECCE programs has been reviewed in some detail, covering work in the United States (Meisels & Shonhoff, 1990) and in the Majority World (Myers, 1992). Earlier partial reviews are also available (King & Myers, 1983; M. Woodhead, 1985, 1988; Zigler & Berman, 1983; Zigler & Weiss, 1985). I do not attempt a systematic or comprehensive review here but rather focus on some of the main historical developments and the basic issues involved.

STATE OF THE ART IN ECCE RESEARCH

Most of the reviews and evaluations of early intervention work have been conducted in the United States. This does not mean that the most comprehensive ECCE programs exist in the United States. For example, there is a higher coverage in "pre-primary education" in Europe (including the former Soviet Union) than in the United States (67.8% and 62.7%, respectively, in 1988, UNESCO, 1991, p. 93). These formal figures are probably underestimations, because how much of nonformal care is included is not clear. A recent comparative study of ECCE in 11 countries (Belgium, China, Finland, Germany, Hong Kong, Nigeria, Portugal, Spain, Thailand, and the United States) shows that in many countries nonformal care has greater coverage than center-based care. Thus, for example, whereas 4-year-old children spend an average of 6 hours a day in formal care (preschool or day-care center) in Belgium, and 4.6 hours in Spain, this type of care constitutes only 2 hours a day in Finland, 2.1 hours in Germany, and 1.8 hours in the United States. In turn, the highest hours of daily parental care are seen in Germany (12.5 hours) and the United States (12.3 hours) (Olmsted & Weikart, 1994).

These figures reflect provisions of formal care, together with parental preferences (and the two may also be related). For example, in Hong Kong where there is universal provision of half-day preschool for 4-year-olds, daily parental care comes down to 8.4 hours. In many European countries there is universal, or close to universal, formal (center-based) ECCE provision, particularly in France (écoles maternelles), Sweden, and some Eastern European countries (Kamerman, 1991; Kamerman & Kahn, 1989; Olmsted & Weikart, 1989). However, systematic evaluation of and research on these programs are not easily available. This may be because in these countries preschool education is considered as an inherent part of normal (public) education, and citizens feel little need to test its effectiveness. Nevertheless, there are some recent studies from Europe looking into long-term effects of early day care (Andersson, 1992) and early enrichment programs for ethnic minorities (Eldering & Leseman, 1993). Compared with the almost universal provision of center-based ECCE in Europe for 3- to 5-year-old children, there is greater diversity in the services for the 0- to 3-year-olds. Family day-care homes and increasingly care in the home through parental leaves are widespread for this younger age group (Himes, Landers, & Leslie, 1992; Kamerman, 1991).

ECCE in the Majority World lags behind. The UNESCO (1991) figure for developing countries in general is 20.3% in 1988, less than one third of the figure for the developed countries (65.3%). This average figure is not very meaningful because of great internal variation. In Latin America and the Caribbean the figure reaches a high of 38%, followed by developing countries in Eastern Asia and Oceania at 31.2%. It is down to 14.9% in Arab countries, 9.6 % in Southern Asia, and a mere 5.1% in Sub-Saharan Africa (UNESCO, 1991, p. 93). Again these statistics do not cover informal care. Still, the very low coverage of ECCE, particularly in Africa and Asia, is notable, and should be taken seriously in view of the importance of early stimulation for school readiness.

With the impetus provided by the International Year of the Child in 1979, great strides have been made in many developing countries, doubling and tripling available ECCE services (for example in Brazil and Thailand), increasing even five- or sixfold in some (Burkina Faso, Oman, and the Dominican Republic) (Myers, 1992, p. 24). However, because in many countries the baselines were very small, the present coverage is still grossly inadequate. Given this situation and the limited available funds, alternative nonformal ECCE programs (non-center-based services and innovative community-based programs often involving caretakers) are being tried out in many countries in the world. In this context the American programs and their evaluations again serve as a model.

The American Experience

The roots of the ECCE programs in the United States are to be found in the War on Poverty initiative of the Johnson era. It aspired to open up opportunities for poor families (especially poor black families) and to enable them and their children to benefit from these enhanced opportunities. Head Start, sponsored by the Office of Economic Opportunity, synthesized several aspects of this massive endeavor, including preschool education, meals, service brokerage for families, and parent participation (but not parent education). Detailed accounts of Head Start are available both in the several extensive reports and evaluations coming out of the program and in other writings (Halpern, 1990; McKey, Condelli, Ganson, Barrett, McConkey & Plantz, 1985; M. Woodhead, 1988; Zigler & Berman, 1983; Zigler & Weiss, 1985).

An early evaluation of Head Start, the Westinghouse Report (Cicirelli, Evans, & Schiller, 1969) prematurely concluded that Head Start had failed; this was followed by a review by Bronfenbrenner (1974) also expressing disappointment. These early reviews focused mainly on the problem of the dissipation of immediate gains in IQ scores over time. A subsequent report prepared for the World Bank (Smilansky, 1979) was so critical of early enrichment programs, based on the initial evaluations, that it resulted in a policy decision by the World Bank not to allocate funds to early intervention. This is an example of the heavy social responsibility carried by the social scientist. The main problem with the report was that it referred mainly to the first wave of rather negative evaluations, based on the work of the 1960s. It did not use the later information providing evidence for positive long-term effects. Nevertheless, it had a significant effect directing the World Bank away from ECCE.[15]

The unfavorable early evaluations of Head Start and other ECCE programs in

---

[15]The situation has recently changed, and the World Bank is now actively involved in ECCE (see M. E. Young, 1993); it has taken a long time to reverse its policy.

the United states had a number of conceptual and methodological problems. Among these were the vague criteria of success; exclusive dependence on IQ measures; thus a unidimensional conceptualization of child development in terms of cognitive competence (narrowly defined in psychometric terms); abstraction of the child from the environment and focusing only on individual child outcomes; and the short time span used for evaluation. I deal with these issues later on. Underlying these problems was an unrealistic and unnecessary goal attributed to Head Start—raising IQs. This was greatly reinforced by the popular media as well (Woodhead, 1988). IQ as a "magic" yet concrete target was singled out and held on to, at the exclusion of other beneficial outcomes.

Later evaluations brought forth a different and more positive picture. Over 1,600 documents on Head Start formed the basis for the Head Start Synthesis Project, which utilized a metanalysis on 250 research reports. Effects from 72 studies showed evidence of gains in cognitive competence, school readiness, and school achievement that were sustained for 2 years after attending Head Start. There is also evidence of positive effects on children's socioemotional development and health status (McKey et al., 1985). However, IQ and achievement differences (from the control groups) tended to dissipate over time.

The great diversity of Head Start programs and the methodological flaws of some of the studies involved—notably, noncomparability of groups (Woodhead, 1988)—detract somewhat from the overall value of the metanalysis. Nevertheless, the trends all point to positive effects, especially notable in large-scale studies. For example, a study with thousands of sixth through eighth graders who had attended Head Start in Philadelphia found that they had better school adjustment than peers without such experience (Copple, Cline, & A. Smith, 1987). Another study of three Head Start cohorts, totaling over 1,900 children, at the end of high school found the oldest cohort to perform better academically than a control group (Hebbeler, 1985).

Carefully planned early enrichment projects utilizing experimental designs produce scientific evidence of sustained effects. Such studies predated Head Start, paving the way for it, and they have continued. Some involved massive and costly intervention, often starting out in infancy. Some examples include the Early Training Project (Gray, Ramey, & Klaus, 1982; Klaus & Gray, 1968), the Milwaukee study (Garber & Heber, 1983), the Abecedarian Project (Ramey & Campbell, 1991; Ramey, Yeates, & Short, 1984; Wassik, Ramey, Bryant, & Sparling, 1990), Ypsilanti Perry Preschool Project (Berrueta-Clement, Schweinhart, Barnett, Epstein, & Weikart, 1984; Schweinhart, Barnes, Weikert, Barnett, & Epstein, 1994; Schweinhart & Weikart, 1980), and the Mother–Child Home Program (Levenstein, O'Hara, & Madden, 1983).

The longitudinal results of these studies show better school performance and social adjustment for the experimental group of children compared with control groups (including lower rates of grade retention and referral to special classes; higher rates of high school completion and employment; and lower incidence of crime and teenage pregnancy). There are also indications of motivational gains and psychological well-being (higher achievement motivation; higher occupational aspirations and expectations; and more positive self-concept). These are reflected in parental outlooks, which also show higher aspirations and expectations for their children, as well as indicating more satisfaction with their children's school progress, even when grade retention and referrals to special classes are controlled. These results come from some single study evaluations, especially of the Ypsilanti Perry Preschool Project (Berrueta-Clement et al., 1984; Schweinhart et al., 1994; Schweinhart & Weikart, 1980). They also derive from pooled findings, in the form of metanalyses conducted by the Consortium for Longitudinal Studies, (Lazar, Darlington, Murray, & Snipper, 1982; Royce et al., 1983). Bronfenbrenner (1979) also conceded that his earlier conclusion, that there were no lasting intervention effects, had been premature (p. 169).

The explanations proposed for the positive long-term effects have focused on interactions between immediate cognitive gains from enrichment programs and environmental factors such as teachers' and parents' expectations and school requirements (Lazar et al., 1982; Woodhead, 1985). Specifically, it appears that children who go through preschool enrichment programs gain immediate cognitive skills as well as other skills such as attentiveness to teachers, ability to follow instructions, task perseverance and sustained focused attention, and the ability to work in groups and relate well to others. All these school-relevant skills help them adjust to the demands of classroom procedures and the public school system better than children from similar socially disadvantaged backgrounds. These positive attitudes and behaviors are in turn perceived by the teachers and further reinforced, producing feelings of competence and higher aspirations for success in children, as well as higher expectations on the part of teachers and parents, thus triggering a virtuous circle leading to sustained satisfactory school performance. Although these effects do not involve raising children's IQs, they are at least as important in terms of long-term real-life consequences.

Majority World Experience

As I have indicated before, ECCE lags behind in the Majority World, with great diversity in the provision of services. Nevertheless, the recent increases are notable and the sheer numbers of children in programs are impressive. Thus, several million children are served in Brazil, Indonesia, and India. China provides preschool services to 16.3 million children (a number larger than many European countries' total populations, but nevertheless constituting a relatively low percentage coverage) (Myers, 1992).

There is great variety in programs. Some involve integrated health, nutrition, and early education services, as for example in the massive Integrated Child Development Service (ICDS) in India, which covered some 3 million children in 1985 (UNICEF/India, 1988). This number has grown tremendously in recent years; in 1989 it was estimated that ICDS reached 11.6 million 0- to 6-year-old children (reported in Myers, 1992, p. 103). Others are smaller range experimental programs; some entail mainly nursery school activities; many include home and community involvement. The quality of care and early education provided varies greatly.

Myers (1992) provided a comprehensive review of the different programs in the Majority World. I point to some examples of ECCE programs and relate recent developments. An important trend is toward coordinating different approaches and diverse orientations underlying services for young children, women, and families. An example of this is the Thai Nutrition Project (Kotchabhakdi et al., 1987), which was discussed briefly in the last chapter. In this large-scale project by the Ministry of Health in Thailand, a community-based primary health care program was integrated with growth monitoring, supplementary food program and nutrition education, and a psychosocial education program (sensitizing mothers to the early development of sensation-perception in the infant, the value of early stimulation and the importance of mother–child interaction). Other integrative attempts have searched to meet the intersecting needs of (working) women and children (Engle, 1986; Evans & Myers, 1985).

In general, early childhood programs have been conceptualized in formal preschool terms, following the traditional Western experience. However, preschools tend to be expensive because they entail building/grounds maintenance, expensive materials, and professional salaries. Consequently, in less developed countries they are limited in number and those that do exist cater to the children of the urban middle-class families who can afford them. Thus there is much need for innovative and cost-effective approaches in ECCE in the Majority World to reach large numbers of poor children who need these services the most. This need has been recognized and alternative ECCE models are being tested, sometimes in large-scale service programs.

Myers (1992) differentiated five different approaches and program options: center-based programs; parent support/education; community development; strengthening institutions; and creating awareness and demand for ECCE. Following this grouping, I present a short summary of the different types of ECCE programs that are found and are being promoted in the Majority World.

Center-based programs provide services to children within an institutional context and constitute the traditional model of ECCE. They vary greatly, however, in terms of their degree of formality, ranging from formal preschools to nonformal home day care, where a caretaker (child minder) cares for a number of children, including her own.[16] Preschools focus on education, whereas home care is oriented toward custodial care. Between these two extremes are different types of centers. Some are designed to support children's health and nutrition

---

[16]This type of care is considered "center-based" because a woman takes care of other people's children in her home and gets paid for this service. Her home functions as a center.

needs and others try to integrate early education and school preparation with food supplementation and health care. Some centers function at the workplace, mainly to support working mothers, and some are "mobile creches," serving the children of seasonal workers who move from one site to another (such as construction workers).

Moving beyond centers, parent/caretaker support and education is an important approach to ECCE. Here the target is the caretaker and the goal is to support that person in order to promote better child development. A holistic contextual orientation underlies this approach. Educating/supporting caretakers can be done through home visits, adult education in groups, through the mass media, or through child-to-child programs. The last alternative is a typically non-Western model where older children are trained/supported to care for younger children and prepare them for school.

Another approach to the provision of ECCE services is to integrate them into community development programs. Community development programs aim to strengthen the material conditions of a community and its capacity for self-help. So, they build up resources and build on existing resources, and the whole community, together with the children, benefit. But there is the danger that early child development may be treated simply as a residual in a larger program and will not be attended to adequately.

Strengthening institutions and creating awareness and demand for ECCE in populations are other complementary approaches. In general, they have to do, on one hand, with integrating (psychosocial) child development into the formal training of medical professionals, nutritionists, and others whose work is relevant to children. On the other hand, improving child-care provisions by building up educational materials (which need not be expensive) (Swaminathan, 1986) and better care/training skills among caretakers all promote good ECCE services. Finally, creating a higher level of awareness of the importance and requirements of ECCE among parents and in the general public is of crucial significance.

A general issue in evaluating early intervention programs is whether they work in the Third World conditions and whether the "Western experience" can be generalized to non-Western contexts (Woodhead, 1985). Indeed, given the great contextual differences, this type of generalization is problematic. However, there is a growing body of evaluation research emerging from the Majority World that needs attention.

Myers (1992) reviewed the evidence regarding the effects of early educational interventions in developing countries on progress and performance in school. Six of the 13 studies examined showed a difference in school promotion rates, being dramatic in some cases. For example, in Brazil, repetition of the first grade was only 9% for children who had had a nutrition and education intervention, compared with 33% for a control group. Another study from Brazil showed a high first-grade repetition rate of 36% for children with a kindergarten experience but a much higher rate (66%) for those without such experience. Studies from Colombia showed higher gains from intervention among the most impoverished groups of children, where 60% of the program children reached fourth grade, compared with only 30% of the comparison group. Similarly, in India and Argentina, the most impoverished groups benefited the most. In Argentina, 36% of poor rural children repeated first grade if they had a preschool experience, compared with 77% of those without such experience. Finally in 6 of the 10 studies where information was available on academic performance, children who had had early educational intervention performed better than comparison groups.

These results from the Majority World show that early interventions can improve children's school performance. Though long-term effects are not available, the shorter term results are encouraging. They are particularly notable for the most disadvantaged children, and they appear to be materializing despite unfavorable conditions in primary schools. Multifaceted programs integrating nutritional-health aspects together with early education are found to have a greater impact, particularly in most impoverished areas. These findings have clear policy implications for promoting human development in the Majority World.

The Situation in Turkey

I would like to review briefly the state of the art in ECCE in Turkey, as a background to the Turkish Early Enrichment Project presented in the next chapter.

In Turkey a standardized widespread system of preschool education does not exist. Only about 7% of Turkish preschool-age children attend a formal preschool institution. The shortage is even more critical for children from deprived socioeconomic backgrounds because most of the preschool facilities available (nursery school, day-care centers, nursery classes, child clubs) are privately owned and charge tuition. National resources have been allocated to the primary school system in order to raise literacy levels, leaving government sponsored preschool services at a rudimentary level. Turkey has been undergoing rapid social change involving massive migration from rural to urban areas. The number of women, including mothers of young children, employed in nonagricultural jobs outside the home has increased rapidly. This has created the demand for institutionalized preschool care and a consequent increase in the number of child-care centers.

In 1978–1980 the Turkish Preschool Project was undertaken (Kağıtçıbaşı, 1981) in cooperation with the Turkish Ministry of Education to study the state of the early childhood development and education in Turkey; to develop alternative working models for preschool services; and to prepare materials for use in preschools, teacher training, and parent education. The materials included sourcebooks for use by teachers and parents, such as *Child Development, Yearly Program in the Preschool, Preschool Activities, Cognitive Activities, Your Child and You* (all in Turkish). These books, published by the Turkish Ministry of Education, have provided valuable source material for preschool and parents, but they have not reached a very large-scale audience. The project also provided the ministry with detailed recommendations and proposals regarding the promotion of preschool services and their synchronization with primary school education and teacher training. Though this project failed to mobilize the government to increase its ECCE coverage substantially, it paved the way for our subsequent longitudinal study—The Turkish Early Enrichment Project—and to policy-relevant outcomes emerging from this latter work.

Looking further into the state of the art in ECCE in Turkey, a number of points are to be noted. The ECCE provisions for the children of the working classes mainly provide custodial care, in contrast to the educational preschools catering to the middle classes. The former are often creches at the workplace to provide working women (mostly factory workers) with child care during work hours.

The ECCE provisions in Turkey are much too limited considering the country's level of development. In this respect social development lags far behind economic development and the coverage of ECCE is as low as in the Sub-Saharan African countries with much lower levels of economic development. This has to do with conservative values about the family, still low levels of urban women's employment and a general lack of public opinion with regard to the importance of the early stimulation/learning/school readiness for later school performance. It may be said that psychologists, child development specialists, and educators have not yet succeeded in sensitizing the public to the needs of the growing child, especially of the one growing up in adverse conditions.

More recently, there have been attempts by women's groups to advocate greater public provision of ECCE. Universities (especially education, psychology, and child development departments and in particular our Early Enrichment Project) and nongovernmental organizations have also played a role in creating favorable public opinion and urging government to increase ECCE coverage. At least partially in response to the recent demands and as an outgrowth of a decade of work in needs assessment, materials development, and public opinion formation, a General Directorate of Preschool Education was established in 1992 within the Ministry of Education. This is a promising policy change in a state that hitherto had invested exclusively in primary schooling and above, considering early education to be a family responsibility.

Nevertheless, this development alone cannot solve the problem. First of all, public funds are too limited to reach even the low levels of target coverage (indicated as 14% in the sixth 5-year plan, 1993). Second, not all public ECCE provisions are under the Ministry of Education. Day-care centers are under the General Directorate of Social Services and Child Protection within a separate Ministry of State. There are also other public ECCE provisions connected with other ministries such as the Ministry of Health. There is a great need for better coordination within the public sector both to increase ECCE provisions and to improve them.

There is a recent development in alternative ECCE services in Turkey. This is significant, because it represents a shift away from the traditional center-based preschool model, which is costly and limited in coverage. It entails home- and community-based nonformal enrichment through mother–child training. It is an outgrowth of our Early Enrichment Project.

ISSUES IN ECCE RESEARCH

The previous overview of ECCE research both in the United States and in the Majority World shows that the main debate has revolved around the question of whether preschool intervention works. This is a problem of evaluation and entails several conceptual and methodological points. I mentioned these briefly in discussing the problems with early evaluations of Head Start. I want to elaborate on them in this section to put the issues into perspective.

One such problem is the unidimensional conceptualization of development solely in cognitive terms. The easy availability of intelligence tests and other cognitive measures, and their wider acceptance in comparison with the less well-established measures of personality and social development, have contributed to the disproportionate emphasis on cognitive development.

Apart from the methodological weakness of single criterion measures, and their vulnerability to statistical artifacts such as ceiling effects and regression toward the mean in repeated testing, a unidimensional conceptualization is theoretically too simplistic. Cognitive development is but one aspect of total human development. There is an inherent interdependence among the different aspects of this development. Thus a "whole child" approach (Zigler & Berman, 1983) is called for. Focusing attention exclusively on IQ gains diverts attention from other possible developmental benefits of preschool intervention programs. An impoverished environment that is not conducive to the full development of the child's cognitive potential is also detrimental to his socioemotional development. For example, a child's lack of self-confidence may underlie a low level of motivation to excel in intellectual tasks, which may in turn result in low IQ scores and poor school achievement. This low self-confidence is itself a reflection of how "significant others" in the environment view the child.

The dissipation of IQ gains after the completion of enrichment programs may, ironically, be due to the exclusive concern of these programs with IQ gains. The cognitive development spurred by the "directive cognitive approach" is often not supported by the induction of corresponding growth of the child's self-confidence, initiative, motivation, and autonomy, so that the cognitive gains cannot be self-sustained after the completion of the program. It is therefore necessary to support the child's *overall* development. If the child's immediate social environment, which could provide the child with continued support, is not fostered by the intervention, cognitive gains are likely to be short-lived.

This points to a related problem of conceptualization, namely, the problem caused by focusing on the child out of context. There is much evidence showing that support of the child's immediate social environment is of great importance (e.g., Bronfenbrenner, 1979; Halpern, 1990; Seitz & Provence, 1990; Weiss & Jacobs, 1988; Zigler & Berman, 1983; Zigler & Weiss, 1985). Specifically, helping the mother build self-esteem and competence so that she can engage in cognitively oriented, affectively based communication with her child can help to support the sustained cognitive development of the child. Thus, both the mother (caretaker) and the child benefit from the intervention.

Particularly in sociocultural contexts where close-knit family, kinship, and community ties exist, as in most parts of the Majority World, it would make sense for an enrichment program to build on these ties as support mechanisms. Such an approach would be more likely to succeed than an individualistic orientation that treats the child separately from the environment and ignores the existing family and community ties. A holistic contextual approach, which includes support of the child's immediate environment, provides other advantages as well. For example, it avoids the creation of two different and possibly incompatible environments—the preschool and the home/community—for the child. Another advantage is the possibility of generalization of gains from enrichment efforts to other individuals in the family, particularly siblings, and possibly other relatives, neighbors, and other members of the community.

Despite these advantages of contextual models of early intervention, there is a continuing debate about the relative effectiveness of child-focused versus caregiver-focused approaches. This is because child-focused approaches also have some advantages, such as direct impact on the child, which can include the enhancement of the child's autonomy and reflectiveness, as seen in the high quality Perry Preschool Program (Schweinhart & Weikert, 1980). In Sweden, where child care is of high quality, it is found that the earlier a child enters day care (within the first year of life), the more beneficial the long-term benefits (at 8 and/or 13 years of age) (Andersson, 1992). Thus, quality in care in child-focused center-based approaches appears to be of key importance. Finally, a problem with a home-based approach has been noted in that parents may not be competent teachers (Eldering & Vedder, 1993), decreasing the impact of parent-focused interventions.

Seitz and Provence (1990) noted that without longitudinal research it is difficult to resolve this debate. They concluded, nevertheless, that on the basis of the existing limited evidence, at least for poverty populations, caregiver-focused approaches are more effective, because by changing the family environment, they can bring about a broader range of beneficial outcomes for children. A recent review of community-based early intervention (Halpern, 1990) concurs in pointing to the value of more holistic/contextual approaches and provides evidence of success in recent programs where specific outcome domains are stressed.

Actually, even so-called child-focused approaches inevitably involve parents, at least to the extent of informing them and getting their endorsement. In many cases, parent involvement is of a much higher level. For example, the 11 studies that were combined and reported as the Consortium for Longitudinal Studies were child-focused programs (Lazar et al., 1982). However, more than half entailed home visits to involve parents, and the rest got parents involved and informed in other ways. Noting this situation, Seitz and Provence (1990) stated that it is not practical to ask whether child-focused or caregiver-focused programs are more effective but to look into how the needs of both parents and children can be best met.

A third problem of evaluation in intervention research is timing. As human development is a continuous process, we are faced with the question of deciding when to assess an effect. Typically, immediate effects of an intervention program are measured, yet this approach leaves questions of sustainability unanswered. This is especially problematic given the fact that immediate gains in IQ scores tend to dissipate over time. Ideally, long-term effects in different spheres of development should be assessed. This is seen in few studies. When such evidence is available, it can provide a better understanding of whether lasting effects obtain and how (e.g., through motivational and better adjustment mechanisms). Thus, with early enrichment, the child's positive orientation to school, initial good performance (cognitive skills), and parents' high aspirations may combine to initiate a positive cycle of development (Berrueta-Clement et al., 1984; Lazar et al., 1982; Schweinhart et al., 1994; Schweinhart & Weikert, 1980; Woodhead, 1985).

Assessing long-term effects can also reveal "sleeper effects," or effects consolidated over time, which may not be apparent at program completion. For example, a particularly intensive caregiver-focused program, the Yale Child Welfare Program, obtained stronger long-term than short-term effects (Provence & Naylor, 1983; Seitz & Provence, 1990; Seitz, Rosenbaum, & Apfel, 1985).

Another problem related to some of the points already discussed is the definition of the outcome variable (dependent variable) in intervention research. As indicated before, this is commonly construed in terms of the child's cognitive development, most narrowly operationalized in terms of IQ. Somewhat broader conceptualizations may entail other indicators of cognitive capacity, such as Piaget tasks. Expanding further, school-related performance (school success and attainment) is included in the dependent variable. Assessment of noncognitive psychological development as outcome variable is quite rare, though it is gaining importance especially in longer term evaluations. An example is the longitudinal results of the Perry Preschool Program providing evidence for better social adjustment of the experimental group compared with the control group over time (Berrueta-Clement et al., 1984).

Even with such expansion, however, it is clear that the dependent variable is commonly construed in terms of the child alone. This is despite the fact that increasingly interventions are being directed to the family and parents (caretakers) as well as the children. As noted earlier, in many cases parents are involved in one form or another, and they are influenced by the intervention. However, such impact is often not construed as an outcome variable and is not assessed. This is a conceptual and methodological weakness, particularly in home- and community-based programs (Bronfenbrenner, 1979; Zigler & Weiss, 1985).

For example, a positive outcome of Head Start is on families and the employment of parents. Each year thousands of low-income parents obtain jobs through Head Start and over 35% of the staff are parents of Head Start children or graduates (Collins, 1990). Head Start programs are also found to enhance communities' capacities to meet local needs (McKey et al., 1985). Thus, both a "whole child" approach and a more contextual approach, entailing different types of dependent variables, are needed. They would throw light on the dynamics of change produced in different spheres and levels of outcome variables.

Another issue in intervention research has to do with program implementation. Often conclusions are drawn regarding the effectiveness of a type of intervention (e.g., child-focused vs. caregiver-focused) on the basis of the results obtained from a program. But the impact of the program may have more to do with the quality of implementation than with the approach used. The intensity of the intervention, the level of training and supervision of the field workers (paraprofessionals), the availability of good materials, the rapport between the targets (families, caregivers) and the implementers of intervention, the participation level of the caregivers (including their attrition rates), and so on, are all important in affecting the outcome.

At times the same program content together with the same approach, used in two different programs, may bring forth different outcomes, mainly due to variations in implementation. For example, the Home Instruction Program for Preschool Youngsters (HIPPY) (Lombard, 1981) achieved good results in Israel and in Turkey (as a part of our Early Enrichment Project; presented in the next chapter). However, its effects in a program in the Netherlands with Turkish, Moroccan, Surinamese, and Dutch groups were negligible (Eldering & Vedder, 1993). Among the reasons for such different outcomes were implementation problems in the Netherlands (such as high attrition rates, language problems in program application, etc.) Even though it is recognized that quality of implementation is as important as the curriculum of intervention per se (Zigler & Weiss, 1985), it tends to be overlooked in drawing conclusions about programs.

On the basis of this discussion, it may be concluded that there is no one best early enrichment approach, but different approaches have their relative strengths. The characteristics of the situation, the description of the problem at hand, and the goals set for intervention all need to be taken into consideration. Better conceptualization of child development as a multifaceted process is of crucial importance, as well as a contextual construal of this development.

A final issue in intervention research is cost-effectiveness and, related to this, the potential for expansion of a program. The (long-term) goal of intervention research and in general of ECCE programs is to reach the families and children who are in greatest need of such services and who can benefit most from them. Thus, large numbers are potentially involved and the cost-effectiveness of the program assumes great importance. For example, in his highly critical report on preschool interventions, Smilansky (1979) recognized that some good programs could produce longer term results, but he dismissed them as too costly.

Calculations of cost-effectiveness of intervention programs are not common. A notable exception is the Perry Preschool Project. As part of the follow-up evaluation when program children reached age 19, a cost–benefit study was carried out (Barnett, 1985). Benefits were construed in terms of cost savings and increased economic productivity (earnings) over the life time. Cost savings included child-care savings, reduced school costs due to less remedial education, savings in welfare expenditures, and savings due to reduction in crime and delinquency. Increased earnings were both actual earnings of program children between the ages of 16 to 19 and also projected earnings after age 19.

The overall benefit-to-cost ratio was found to be very high (7 to 1), indicating a very high payoff from the program. This is despite the very high actual cost of this intensive, high quality program. The main point here is that much more important than the absolute cost of a program is its cost-effectiveness or its benefit-to-cost ratio. An expensive program is a good investment if it produces highly beneficial outcomes, whereas an inexpensive program may be a poor investment (and more "costly") if it produces no effect.

Nevertheless, absolute costs cannot be ignored, either, especially in the Majority World where resources are very limited. It is also to be noted that, given the very different conditions, cost-effectiveness findings, such as those of the Perry Preschool Project, are not generalizable from developed to developing countries. Nevertheless, similar types of cost–benefit analyses can be done in different contexts, taking into account the specific characteristics of the context. Thus, Myers (1992) provided some examples of cost calculations from India, Peru, and Chile, and a cost–benefit analysis from Brazil.

In general, nonformal home-community-based programs, employing paraprofessionals (as well as volunteers, parents, etc.) tend to be less costly than formal, center-based preschool programs employing professionals. This is despite the fact that the former usually involve a broader provision of services, including nutrition, health, and education, whereas the latter focus mainly on education. Because the formal preschool model is traditionally associated with early enrichment, many governments in developing countries have typically considered early education a luxury. This view does not hold up any longer, given the recent evidence all over the world on less expensive but effective alternatives to the formal traditional preschool.

Programs with multiple outcomes (promoting cognitive and personality-social development of children, as well as their physical growth, better school adjustment and performance, better social-economic competence later on, etc.) and with multiple beneficiaries (children, their parents, siblings, whole families, communities) appear to be good investments. Particularly in the Majority World, such multipurpose approaches to early intervention and ECCE have great potential to contribute to "human development," defined in societal terms. The next chapter presents the Turkish Early Enrichment Project as a example of a multipurpose intervention study.

8 The Turkish Early Enrichment Project

The previous chapter presented an overview of early childhood care and education (ECCE), where psychology can contribute to applications designed to promote human development. This chapter presents the Turkish Early Enrichment Project as a case in point. This project also serves as a case study of intervention and as an "involved" orientation with a central place in this book. The theoretical perspectives set out in part I serve as the theoretical underpinnings of the intervention presented here.

The Turkish Early Enrichment Project[17] is in the tradition of the ECCE studies and spans a period of 10 years (1982–1992). The original study was a 4-year intervention project, utilizing a field experiment. The follow-up study was carried out 6 years after the end of the original study (7 years after the intervention). My colleagues Bekman, Sunar and I conducted both studies (Bekman, 1990, 1993; Kağıtçıbaşı, 1991b, 1994b; Kağıtçıbaşı et al., 1988). This chapter presents both the original study and the follow-up.

[17]Funded by the International Development Research Centre (IDRC) of Canada. Project Director: Çiğdem Kağıtçıbaşı. Research Associates: Diane Sunar and Sevda Bekman. See Kağıtçıbaşı, Ç., Sunar, D. and Bekman, S. (1988). *Comprehensive preschool education project: Final report*, Manuscript Report 209e, IDRC, P. O. Box 8500, Ottawa, Canada KIG 3H9.

The follow-up study was funded by the MEAwards Program of the Population Council (Grant No. MEA 272). It was conducted by the same research team.

Throughout the different phases of the project the personal support of Sheldon Shaeffer, Anne Bernard (IDRC), and Frederic Shorter (Population Council) are greatly appreciated.

THE ORIGINAL STUDY

The original study was a 4-year longitudinal project involving early childhood enrichment and mother training in the low income areas of Istanbul. The effects of both center-based and home-based enrichment were studied, separately and in combination. The center-based child care was not introduced by the project, rather existing day care centers were selected in terms of their basic orientations (custodial or educational day care). Groups of children in each type of center and a third group of children in home care were studied. Because children were not randomly assigned to these three contexts, this aspect of the study involves a quasi-experimental, rather than an experimental design. In each of these groups 3- and 5-year-old children were included.

The intervention introduced by the project was mother training for a randomly selected number of the mothers of each group in the second and third years of the project. The research design used, therefore, was of three (context: custodial, educational, home care) by two (age: 3 or 5) by two (mother training or no mother training) factorial design (Table 1). In the first year of the project, base-lines were established through assessments of children, mothers, mother–child interaction, and demographic/socioeconomic variables. In the second and third years, the project intervention was applied, and in the fourth year reassessments were carried out.

The sampling was done in terms of the districts of Istanbul, where factories employing large numbers of women ran day-care centers for their young children. There were five such low income areas mostly on the periphery of the city. Initially, 3- and 5-year-old children were selected randomly in the day-care centers and, in some where the numbers were small, all the 3- and 5-year-olds were included in the project. Their mothers constituted the mother sample. Families of the home-reared children, most of whose mothers did not work outside the home, were neighbors of the families where the mothers worked at

TABLE 8.1
Design of the Original (four-year Study

Number of Subjects in Each Group

	Educational Day Care		Custodial Day Care		Home Care		Total
Age of child	3	5	3	5	3	5	
Mother training	11	16	23	17	16	7	90
No mother training	18	19	30	35	34	29	165
Total	29	35	53	52	50	36	255

the factories. The mean age for mothers (in the first year) was 29 (32.8 for fathers). The mean years of school attendance for mothers was 5.36 (5.81 for fathers). All the families had low income and similar living conditions with mostly squatter housing.

The majority of the population in these five regions are blue-collar workers or are involved in cottage industry or marginal economy. The sample of parents consisted mainly of former villagers who had moved into the city. Only 27.4% of the mothers and 26% of the fathers were born in the city. Nevertheless, most of the sample had been living in the city for a substantial period, having migrated in their teens. Previous research in Turkey has shown that where individuals live and where their family originates (large city, small town, or village) is an important factor in the degree of their modernization (Kağıtçıbaşı, 1982a, 1982b). The sample can thus be characterized as "semi-urban." The majority (two thirds) of the sample of mothers were unskilled or semi-skilled factory workers; one third were nonworking women (some of whom were involved in home production or cottage industry).

Procedure and Measures

The study was originally planned with a sample of 280 mothers and children (each). By the end of the fourth year, the number dropped to 255 with about 10% attrition; most of the attrition took place during the first year of the intervention.

Mother training constituted the project intervention. After the establishment of the baselines through assessments in the first year, a randomly selected portion of the mothers of children in educational, custodial, and home care were provided with mother training in the second and third years of the project. They constituted the "experimental group" in the project design. Those mothers not selected for mother training (and their children) constituted the "control group." This was the main independent variable, the other being preschool context (custodial, educational, home care).

It is to be noted that all the mothers in the project had similar socioeconomic and demographic characteristics (including low levels of education, income, mostly rural origin, rather young age, etc.), and because they were randomly assigned to the experimental and the control groups in the second year, they were well matched.

In the fourth (and last) year of the original study, reassessments were carried out to establish both pre–post and experimental (mother trained)–control (nontrained) group differences. Most of the first-year assessments were repeated, except for those that became inappropriate for use with the now older children (7 and 9 years old). Additionally, a few other measurements were carried out, including extensive school-related assessments.

In line with our "whole-child" and contextual orientation, a great number and variety of assessments were carried out to obtain detailed and comprehensive information on the children, mothers, and families. Another reason for using a variety of assessments was not to depend on any single measure and the value of getting confirmatory information from multiple measurements. Thus, various assessment techniques were used, including testing of children, observation of children's behavior and of mother–child interaction, and extensive interviews with mothers.

Assessments of the children and their families were conducted in four main areas: cognitive development, socioemotional development, family context, and day-care context. Cognitive measures included: IQ scores (mainly with a Turkish adaptation of the Stanford–Binet Intelligence Test); Piaget tasks of classification and seriation (also multiple classification in the fourth year); complexity of behavior (assessed through time-sampled observations at the day-care centers in the first year); cognitive style and analytical thinking (the "analytical triad," consisting of "Block Design" from the Wechsler Preschool and Primary Scale of Intelligence, WPPSI; "Object Assembly" and "Picture Arrangement" from the Wechsler Intelligence Scale for Children–Revised, WISC–R; as well as the Children's Embedded Figures Test, CEFT; academic achievement (standardized tests of achievement in mathematics and Turkish and a general ability test in the fourth year); and school grades: One year of primary school grades for the younger group (original 3-year-olds) and 3 years of grades for the older group (5-year-olds) were available in the fourth year of the study.

Measures of socioemotional development included autonomy/dependence (assessed through time-sampled observations at the day-care centers and through mothers' reports); aggression (again through observations and interviews with mothers); level of social participation (observation and mother interviews using a subscale on aggression from R. Rohner's, 1980, Parental Acceptance–Rejection instrument, PARI); indicators of emotional problems (Goodenough Draw-a-Person test with the Koppitz, 1968, scoring system); and self-concept/self-esteem (some items from Rohner's, 1980, PARI asked in mother interviews).

Measures of family variables included background demographic and socioeconomic information; home environment (an "environmental stimulation index," including father's and mother's education, mother's language skills, frequency of reading/telling stories to child, number of toys present, and whether there are any books in the home); information about the mother, including her childrearing attitudes and behaviors, lifestyle, self-concept, satisfaction with her life/environment, (assessed through the interviews), and teaching style (measured by the Hess and Shipman, 1965, Toy and Block Sorting Task observations). In the fourth year, mothers' intrafamily status was also assessed in terms of decision making, role sharing, and communication between the spouses.

Measures of day-care and teacher variables included ratings of the day-care centers in terms of their main orientations—providing preschool education or only custodial care. The ratings were based on direct observation of centers and teachers and on interviews with directors.

Every effort was made to ensure reliability of the measures and to make them acceptable to the mothers and the children. Much time was spent in developing "rapport" for testing and interviewing and in rendering these "normal" activities. As much as possible, nondemanding observation situations were created, for example, with the Hess and Shipman Toy and Block Sorting Task. In general, there was a good level of acceptance of these assessments on the part of the subjects, and no significant problems were encountered.

The reader may find an inconsistency between a main theme in this book: the importance of cultural context and culture-sensitive orientations in research and the use of mainly Western measures in this research. Three explanations are in order here. First of all, as has been stressed repeatedly, common standards of cognitive development need to be used for school preparation. However, they have to be made ecologically valid (Bronfenbrenner, 1979), which we tried hard to achieve. Thus, there is an attempt here to integrate universal standards with cultural appropriateness. Second, for some of the variables, we decided to use already existing measures (with established reliability and validity), if we judged them to be appropriate for use with our subjects, rather than make up new ones from scratch. For each such measure, however, we conducted further reliability tests in a pilot study. Third, particularly for the noncognitive variables, such as family variables, parental orientations, and so on, we developed our own measures. This is because the cultural context was of more direct relevance here.

Assessment of the socioemotional development of children proved to be difficult. For example, a self-concept index (Larsen & Leigh, 1977) that looked promising had to be dropped because it did not work. Mothers' perception of the child (expressed in the interview) was found to be more reliable.

Mother Training

The project intervention comprised "mother training" given to a randomly selected group of mothers for 2 years (30 weeks each year). Mother training was composed of two programs: the Cognitive Training Program and the Mother Enrichment Program.

The Cognitive Training Program.   To foster the cognitive development of children, the Home Instruction Program for Preschool Youngsters (HIPPY) was used. This program was originally developed by the Research Institute for Innovation in Education at the Hebrew University of Jerusalem (Lombard, 1981). We translated and adopted it for use in Turkey. HIPPY focuses on three main areas of cognitive development (language, sensory and perceptual discrimination skills, and problem solving) for 4- to 5-year-old children. It can be considered a school preparation program, including preliteracy and prenumeracy skills.

The materials were supplied to the mothers on a weekly basis, one week at home and one week in a group setting. Explanations and role playing were used to teach the mother how to use the materials with her child. The mothers then worked with their own children on a daily basis (15 to 20 minutes a day) to complete the week's task, including in total 60 weekly work forms (of 25 to 30 pages each) and 18 storybooks. Mainly paraprofessionals worked in the program, trained and supervised by the research team. Two levels of paraprofessionals were employed. "Group Leaders," who were also the "local coordinators" (one for each of the five areas), were rather well educated (at least high school education) and were specially trained and supervised by the research team. "Mothers' Aides" were community workers not different from the mothers in education and SES status, who were selected to provide the program to the mothers at home and also to help them in the group setting. They were trained and closely supervised by the group leaders on a weekly basis. Mothers' aides first applied the program to their own children before teaching it to the mothers at home.

The Mother Enrichment Program.   At the biweekly group meetings, guided group discussions were conducted, in addition to work on the Cognitive Training Program. Group discussions were designed to sensitize mothers to the needs of the growing child and to develop effective communication skills of the mothers to promote better verbal interaction with the child. The goal was to enhance the child's overall development, but supporting the mother was also important. The group leaders led the group discussions, and the mothers were active participants; they asked questions, expressed opinions, and shared ideas and experiences. Frequently, following group discussions, group decisions were taken regarding some course of action to be taken in the homes. In the following meeting, the results of the decision would be discussed, reassessed, and possibly a new decision would be made.

Thus, techniques of group dynamics (in the Lewinian tradition) were utilized to enable the mothers to provide their children with greater support for healthy development. In the first year, the emphasis of the group discussions was on children's health, nutrition, and creative play activities. In the second year, the stress was on discipline and mother–child interaction and communication. Also, expressing and "listening to" feelings while interacting both with the child and with others were emphasized. Throughout the program, the mothers were encouraged to develop a positive self-concept and to attend to their own needs. Specifically, health and family planning needs were addressed.

Empowerment of the mothers in coping with problems and attending to their children's as well as their own needs was the goal. A special effort was made to render the program culturally sensitive. For example, the close-knit family ties and the relatedness values were reinforced, but a new element, "autonomy," was also introduced in childrearing. The fact that the program was original, rather than imported from abroad, was an asset in rendering it culturally sensitive. In the group, usually 1 hour was spent on HIPPY, and 1 to 1½ hours was spent on the Mother Enrichment Program. All mothers were expected to attend the group meetings; this was emphasized from the start, and therefore absenteeism was quite low.

Throughout the 2 years of the mother training program there was close supervision of the group and home activities to ensure adequate implementation of the program. In addition to the project team, students also participated in group observations. Every effort was made to ensure regular monitoring, supervision, and good record keeping of the progress of the program.

FOURTH-YEAR RESULTS

As mentioned earlier, extensive assessments were used in the Turkish Early Enrichment Project, in line with our "whole-child" and contextual orientations. Accordingly, a multitude of results were obtained. They are summarized here in terms of both child outcomes (cognitive and socioemotional) and mother outcomes. The findings pertaining to the project intervention (mother training) are stressed, though the effects of context (educational, custodial, home care) are also briefly summarized. All the results reported refer to statistically significant findings, unless otherwise specified. Most outcomes are reported in text, with a minimum of tables, which are included only if helpful in summarizing findings.

Cognitive Development (Child Outcomes)

On the Stanford–Binet Intelligence Test in the fourth year a significant difference was obtained between the children whose mothers underwent training and the control group of children whose mothers did not have training in the second and third years of the project (see Table 2).

This is notable, given the fact that no direct child-centered approach was used in the project, but mothers trained their own children. Especially for the children at home, mother training made a substantial difference (Table 2). The effect was less for children in educational day care, because they received cognitive training in day care (possibly showing a ceiling effect). This is in line with other research, mentioned in the last chapter (Myers, 1992), showing greater effects of enrichment programs on the more deprived children.

The analytical triad results are parallel to IQ scores. The educational preschool children whose mothers were trained had the highest scores, and significant effects were found for both mother training and context (educational/custodial day care or home care) (Table 2). Similar positive effects of both mother training and context are found on the Block Design and the CEFT tests. Finally, the children of the trained mothers performed better than the control group on Piagetian classification tasks ($\chi^2 = 7.54$, $p = .02$). These differences on cognitive performance show that the experimental group of children not

TABLE 8.2
Fourth-Year Comparative Standing of Children on Various Cognitive Measures by Context
and Mother Training

Measure		Educational	Custodial	Home-Cared	Total	
I. Q.	Mother trained	94.19 $n = 27$ 89	90.80 $n = 41$ 82.72	92.89 $n = 22$ 86.12	91.21	$F = 18.36$
	Not trained	$n = 34$	$n = 60$	$n = 60$	85.43	$p = .0001$
	Total	91.30	86.00	87.66		df 1,244
		$F = 3.55$	$p = .03$	df 2.244		
Analytical triad	Mother trained	14.85	11.76	8.35	11.82	$F = 7.81$
	Not trained	11.63	9.84	8.09	9.58	$p = .0006$
	Total	13.03	10.60	8.16		df 1,245
		$F = 16.09$	$p = .0001$	df 2,245		
Block design	Mother trained	16.06	15.22	13.54	14.86	$F = 16.68$
	Not trained	14.39	13.57	10.45	12.63	$p = .0001$
	Total	15.14	14.32	11.16		df 1,246
		$F = 22.97$	$p = .0001$	df 2,254		
CEFT	Mother trained	8.41	5.98	7.22	7.22	
	Not trained	7.37	5.40	6.66	6.32	
	Total	7.82	5.63	6.84		
		$F = 5.68$	$p = .004$	df 2,254		

trained directly by the project team but by their mothers benefited from this approach.

In the fourth year, further assessments were undertaken with special age-graded specific achievement tests in general ability, mathematics, and Turkish. School performance was also assessed through first grade for the younger group and through third grade for the older group. On all the achievement tests the children whose mothers had been trained performed better than the control group. In particular, the younger children who were in the first grade during the posttesting in the fourth year of the project surpassed others in mathematics ($F = 10.59$, $df = 1, 91$, $p = .002$); and the mother-trained group surpassed the control group on the general ability test ($F = 3.9$, $df = 1, 212$, $p = .05$).

The positive effects of mother training began to appear in the children's school grades even after only 1 year of training, with higher grades achieved by this group in all subjects though not reaching significance levels. After the second year of mother training, the effects increased overall, and significantly better grades were achieved in Turkish and nearly significant in social studies ($F = 11.19$, $df = 1$, 80, $p = .001$; and $F = 3.29$, $df = 1$, 79, $p = .074$, respectively). Furthermore, even 1 year after the end of mother training the positive effects on children's school achievement continued to increase, with the mother-trained group having a higher academic average ($F = 4.5$, $df = 1$, 80, $p = .037$) involving better grades in all subjects. Their deportment/ adjustment grades were also better ($F = 4.22$, $df = 1$, 79, $p = .043$), pointing to better school adjustment.

As for preschool context, again the superiority of the educational day care over the others (custodial and home care) is seen. Children from educational day care outperformed the others on the achievement tests, as well as in school achievement and school deportment/adjustment grades (Kağıtçıbaşı et al., 1988).

Overall, the results pertaining to cognitive development and school-related achievement show the positive effects of mother training and educational day care. The children trained by their mothers surpassed the control group on all measures of cognitive development and school-related achievement, significantly so on most. Similarly, educational day-care context was found to be superior to custodial and home care on almost all of the cognitive measures. Children from the educational day-care setting whose mothers were trained consistently performed the best on virtually every measure. However, an interaction effect was not found. This shows that the effects of mother training and educational day care were additive and/or that there may have been a "ceiling" effect for the educational day-care children, given their initially higher level of cognitive performance.

Socioemotional Development (Child Outcomes)

The socioemotional developmental outcomes are not as notable as the aforementioned cognitive outcomes. Perhaps the measures of socioemotional development are not as highly developed, valid, and reliable as measures of cognitive development. The differences between the mother-trained and control groups of children on socioemotional measures are all in the expected direction, showing some benefit from the mother training program. However, they barely reach significance. The effects of child-care context are less clear-cut, though children cared for at home were found to be more dependent than children in day care ($F = 4.29$, $df = 2$, 196, $p = .015$) and to exhibit more emotional problems ($F = 4.82$, $df = 2$, 198, $p = .01$).

On the R. Rohner (1980) subscale of aggression, used in mother interviews, the mother-trained group of children were rated as less aggressive than the control group ($t = 2.59$, $p = .01$). Similarly, on the R. Rohner (1980) subscale of autonomy/dependence, the mother-trained group of children was rated as less dependent, though the difference did not reach significance ($t = 1.75$, $p = .08$). On the Rohner subscale of self-concept, the mother-trained group was rated as having somewhat higher self-concept than the control group, approaching significance ($F = 3.19$, $df = 1$, 191, $p = .07$). Finally, on a measure of school adjustment, the mother-trained group received slightly higher scores ($F = 3.06$, $p = .087$).

Mother's Orientation to the Child

A number of items in the structured interviews with mothers had to do with mother's orientation to the child, both attitudinally and behaviorally. Fourth-year results showed a number of important differences in these orientations between the trained and nontrained mothers.

The trained mothers were more attentive to the child (34.7% vs. 18.6% of the control group showing "frequent" or "very frequent" attention to the child at other than meal times). They also reported more interaction while at home with the child (26.6% vs. 9.6% of the control), whereas 57.1% of the nontrained mothers (compared with 38.9% of the trained mothers) reported that the child played alone ($\chi^2 = 14.6$, $df = 4$, $p = .005$).

The trained mothers reported reading or telling stories to the child more than the nontrained mothers (87.7% vs. 62.6%; $\chi^2 = 40.8$, $df = 3$, $p = .0001$). They also helped the child with homework more ($t = 3.54$, $p = .001$), and cognitive activities figured more prominently in what they taught to their children compared with the nontrained mothers (32.2% vs. 25.6%), even though there was no difference between the two groups in teaching practical skills to their children.

Attitudes toward and expectations of the child also differed between the trained and control group of mothers. Trained mothers had higher expectations for their children, especially regarding success in school ($F = 2.84$, $p = .09$), years of schooling aspired for ($t = 2.03$, $p = .04$), and realistically expected of children ($t = 2.11$, $p = .04$) compared with the control group. Similarly, expectations of things the children should be able to do on their own without asking for help differed between the two groups ($\chi^2 = 14.85$, $df = 5$, $p = .01$), with school success being the most frequent response for the trained mothers (48.8% vs. 18.6% for the control group). Clearly, such high expectations have something to do with the higher school-related achievement of the experimental group of children discussed before.

In systematic observations of mother–child interaction on structured problem solving (Hess and Shipman task), conducted by raters blind to the study hypotheses, trained mothers were found to have more positive and supportive interaction styles, involving encouragement, praise, positive feedback, reasoning, and cognitive/rational appeals in teaching the task to their children, compared with nontrained mothers ($t = 1.67$, $p = .09$). Trained mothers also had more positive current general evaluations of their children compared to the past (2–3 years earlier) than the nontrained mothers ($t = 2.16$, $p = .03$).

Finally, mothers exposed to the enrichment program were found to verbalize (communicate verbally) with their children more than nontrained mothers. This was apparent in both expressing satisfaction (73.5% vs. 58.1%, $\chi^2 = 6.01$, $df = 1$, $p = .02$) and dissatisfaction with the child (especially the latter, 40.7% vs. 21.9%, $\chi^2 = 9.79$, $df = 1$, $p = .002$), compared with greater use of physical punishment among the nontrained mothers (36.8% vs. 17.6% among the trained mothers; $\chi^2 = 10.11$, $df = 1$, $p = .002$). Also, more of the trained (61%) than nontrained mothers (39%) took into consideration the children's intentions in responding to their behavior, and they used "induction" (reasoning and making the child understand the consequences of her behavior) in child discipline more than the nontrained mothers (26.4 and 16.1%, respectively; $\chi^2 = 3.77$, $df = 1$, $p = .05$).

These differences between the experimental (trained) and control (nontrained) mothers emerging from the mother interviews appear to be indicative of different orientations to parenting in the two groups. In view of theory and research in developmental psychology, some of which has been discussed already, the kind of parenting demonstrated by the experimental group can be characterized to promote the child's development and school performance (involving less physical punishment and more reasoning/ verbalization with the child; being more responsive to the child; supportive interaction with the child with reasoning, praise, and encouragement; high expectations from the child; reading or telling stories to the child; helping the child with homework; being more pleased with the child, etc.). It is quite similar to what Goodnow (1988) called "parental modernity" (see chapter 2). It is to be noted that both self-report results and those based on observations of mothers' behaviors (interaction with child) on structured tasks point in the same direction, providing confirming evidence for the positive effects of training on parenting.

Apart from experimental-control group comparisons, before–after comparisons also provide insights. The first-year baselines showed strong relational needs of the mothers together with much value put on social–harmonious–compliant child orientations. For example, when asked about children's behavior that pleased them, "being good to mother" was mentioned most frequently. Together with showing affection, being obedient and getting along well with others, relational behavior comprised almost 80% of desired behavior in children. In contrast, "autonomy" was among child behaviors that annoyed mothers; it accounted for more than half the unacceptable behaviors (seen as self-assertion and disobedience). Complaint about dependence (of the child on the mother) was strikingly low (1.2%). In describing a "good child," mothers stressed being polite (37%) and obedient (35%) more than any other characteristic; being autonomous and self-sufficient were again negligible (3.6%).

In the fourth year it was found that trained mothers valued autonomous behavior in their children more than the control group ($F = 12.5, p = .02$). Additionally, in responding to an open-ended question about which child behaviors mothers find pleasing, more than twice as many trained mothers as nontrained mothers mentioned autonomous child behavior as pleasing them (21% vs. 9.7%; $\chi^2 = 6.04, df = 1, p = .01$). It is to be noted that even within the trained group the percentage spontaneously mentioning autonomous behavior as pleasing is quite low. However, compared with the first-year baselines, there is a noticeable change. The great majority of mothers in both groups continued stressing affectionate and relational behavior in children as pleasing and otherwise demonstrated close-knit ties as reflected in their behaviors and values. Thus, some of the trained mothers appeared to acquire a new positive orientation toward the child's autonomy while remaining as close to their children as the nontrained mothers.

These before–after comparisons provide some clues to possible changes among the trained mothers that may be seen as indicative of integration or synthesis of some new values stressing autonomy with continuing relatedness values. It is in line with the family/human model of emotional interdependence proposed in chapter 5. This finding shows that such a synthesis of autonomy and relatedness orientations (of individualism and collectivism) is possible, and, furthermore, that it can be brought about through an intervention program.

Direct Effects on the Mother

The mother training program was also found to have direct effects on the mother even though this was not the professed goal of the program. In the fourth year, the trained mothers enjoyed a higher intrafamily status vis-à-vis their husbands, compared with the control group. This was seen in their greater participation in family decision making, as well as in more role sharing and communication with their husbands (Kağıtçıbaşı et al., 1988). I had developed an index of intrafamily women's status in earlier research, comprising (shared) decision making, role sharing, and communication with the spouse (Kağıtçıbaşı, 1982a, 1982b, 1986). Compared with the national averages I obtained earlier, the trained mothers in this project fared quite well on this index, as well as in comparison to the control group. It should be noted that high intrafamily status of the woman does not mean a status higher than that of the man, but rather an egalitarian relationship between the two. A high score on this index shows shared decision making between the spouses (rather than exclusive husband decision making), communication, and role sharing between them (rather than man's and woman's roles being clearly different, with separate activities and functions).

The trained women also expressed greater satisfaction with their current life situation, compared with 3 years earlier ($t = 1.98$, $p = .05$), and they had more positive expectations for the future ($t = 2.61$, $p = .01$), both in comparison to the control group. As a reason for the more favorable evaluation of their present condition, compared with 3 years earlier, the trained mothers said they were now "better educated" and better able to cope with problems as a result of the "mother enrichment" program.

DISCUSSION AND RATIONALE FOR FOLLOW-UP

The fourth-year results of the Turkish Early Enrichment Project provide evidence of beneficial effects of both mother training and educational day care on children's overall development. All the findings are in the expected direction and in none of the measures used did the non-mother-trained (control) group of children do better than the experimental group, nor did the children in custodial and home-care outperform educational day-care children. The gains in school performance from mother training started to be seen within the first year of the intervention and continued to increase even a year after the completion of the program.

As discussed in the previous chapter, a common problem in intervention research is the dissipation of immediate gains over time (especially in IQ scores) from a directive approach. The Turkish Early Enrichment Project attempted to meet the challenge of long-term sustainment.

As argued earlier, among the factors underlying the dissipation of gains is the double approach of focusing on cognitive development alone and focusing on the individual child alone, more typical in center-based programs. Because cognitive gains are not supported by other gains in the "overall development" of the child and the child's environment does not provide continued support, the positive effects of the program may not be sustained over time. With a whole-child and especially a contextual–interactional approach, we tried to overcome these weaknesses.

We reasoned that the changes brought about in mother's orientation to the child and parenting behavior would constitute important environmental changes for the child. Furthermore, to the extent that these changes persist over time, they would continue to support the changes brought about in the child. Thus, the gains from the program would be self-sustaining. This reasoning is based on the assumption that mother training does not only affect the child but also the mother. The findings related to mothers' orientations toward their children as well as direct effects on mothers provide evidence for changes in mothers.

Indeed, the Turkish Early Enrichment Project can be characterized to have a multipurpose approach aiming to support both the mother and the child. Particularly, the mother enrichment program was an empowerment program that apparently enabled mothers to develop better communication skills (with their children and others, especially their husbands), to express their own needs, and to understand others' needs better. The mother enrichment component best reflects the contextual–interactional orientation of the project. The cognitively oriented program (HIPPY) appeared to further enhance mothers' sense of efficacy by providing them with the role of their children's teachers. The cognitive activities (such as reading books to their children, following instructions, etc.) actually improved many mothers' rather poor literacy skills as well. Thus mothers benefited from the program as much as the children.

Mother–child interaction constitutes a most important core element of the Turkish Early Enrichment Project. Another core element was the use of group discussion as the main instrument of mother training, especially of the mother enrichment program component. Group dynamics greatly facilitated learning and attitude-behavior change sustained over time. Group discussion is examined as a promising technique to bring about innovative change in analyzing the policy implications of the project in the next chapter.

To reiterate the main findings of the study, the project intervention (mother training) had a positive impact on both mothers and children. Educational preschool was also found to be beneficial for children. The effects of mother training, in particular, were expected to be self-sustaining through time because they would entail a continuing supportive interaction with the immediate social environment. A "virtuous cycle" may underlie such sustained positive development, as indicated earlier.

There was every indication from the fourth year assessments (posttesting) of the Turkish Early Enrichment Project that such a positive cycle had started when the children began primary school. Children whose mothers had been trained and those who had been in educational day care adjusted to school better, liked school, had higher scores on achievement tests, and had higher school achievement. In addition, the trained (experimental) mothers' expressed greater satisfaction with their children, higher expectations of their children's school success, and both higher aspirations and expectations for more years of schooling.

In addition to the aforementioned school-related behaviors and orientations, the trained mothers' interaction styles with and general orientation to their children were also found to be conducive to overall success and well-being of the child (particularly valuing autonomy in the child, being more attentive to and interacting with the child, helping with the child's homework, more verbalization and reasoning with the child, and more reading/telling stories to the child).

The fact that the mother-trained children's school performance continued improving even 1 year after the end of mother training provides evidence of self-perpetuating positive change. However, even though this finding and the others presented are encouraging, the real test of sustained impact requires a longer term follow-up study.

A follow-up study was planned to establish if there were long-range effects. It was envisaged as a test of the comparative durability of the effects of the educational preschool (center-based, child-focused enrichment) and the mother training (home-based, caretaker-focused) intervention. Our expectation was that the effects of mother training would hold up better than those of educational day care. This expectation derived from our contextual orientation, as has been discussed. It was based on the assumption that the changes in the mothers would be sustained over time, which the follow-up study undertook to test.

One reason for this assumption was that the mother training program was a community-based intervention capitalizing on women's networks in group discussion sessions. These networks would be expected to continue after the completion of the program and to provide support to the women. Another reason for expecting sustained effects was the functional (adaptive) nature of the changes in women and in their interactive styles with their children and spouses. Because the mother training program provided the mothers with better interpersonal skills, these newly acquired skills should be inherently reinforcing in solving problems effectively and might therefore be expected to "stamp in" and be self-sustaining. For example, in the fourth year, the trained mothers reported that when they learned to express their own feelings instead of blaming the other person or when they learned behavior modification techniques to change some undesirable behavior of their children (instead of resorting to physical punishment), they were more effective, more in control of the situation, and less frustrated.

THE FOLLOW-UP STUDY

The follow-up study was initiated 6 years after the completion of the original study (7 years after the end of the project intervention—mother training). The aim was to assess the overall condition of the children (experimental and con-

TABLE 8.3
Design of the Follow-Up Study

	Number of Subjects in Each Group			
	Educational Day Care	Custodial Day Care	Home Care	Total
Mother training	24	37	22	83
No mother training	31	50	53	134
Total	55	87	75	217

trol), who were now adolescents, and of their mothers and families, and to relate these findings to the original intervention.

The design of the follow-up study was essentially the same as that of the original study (see Tables 1 and 3) except that the age category was dropped. It is a 3 × 2 factorial design with three categories of early context (educational day care, custodial day care, and home care) and two categories of mother training (training or no training).

A major task was tracing the original families, which is difficult after so many years, especially for these low income groups who move about with job changes, unemployment, and so on. Out of the original 255 families we were able to reach 225 (with a very low attrition rate of 10%), with 217 agreeing to participate in the follow-up study (Table 3). At the time of the interviews, 108 of the young adolescents were about 13, and 109 were about 15 years old; there were 117 boys and 100 girls. Of these, 161 were still in school and 56 had dropped out. Compulsory education was 5 years when these children were in fifth grade (now being increased to 8 years).

Extensive individual interviews were carried out in the follow-up study with the adolescents, with their mothers, and with their fathers. The adolescent interviews covered topics such as attitudes toward school/education, relations with parents (current and retrospective), expectations for education and occupation, self-concept, and social adjustment. The mother interviews included questions on the child's educational orientation and social adjustment, childrearing, family relations, mother's educational and occupational aspirations for her child, mother's self-concept, and role sharing/communication/decision making vis-à-vis the spouse (intrafamily woman's status). The fathers were given a shorter version of the mother interview.

The adolescents were also administered individually the vocabulary subtest of the WISC–R, which was standardized for Turkish subjects (Savaşir & Sahin, 1988),[18] and the Embedded Figures Test (EFT), also standardized for Turkish subjects (Okman, 1982). Their full school records were obtained.

---

[18]We decided against an academic achievement test or an individual intelligence test, given the dependence of such measures on schooling. Because compulsory education was only 5 years in Turkey, a good number of the adolescents (36% of the total sample) were out of school, some for a number of years. This would have been a confounding factor. Also previous research (Berrueta-Clement et al., 1984; Schweinhart & Weikart, 1980) showed that the IQ differences between trained and nontrained groups did not persist after the sixth grade. A vocabulary measure was therefore chosen. Vocabulary is also subject to the same problem of being affected by schooling, but less so at this age (13–15) in an urban center where adolescents are constantly exposed to the radio, television, magazines, and so on. Also research on human abilities in this part of the world (reviewed by Kağıtçıbaşı & Savasir, 1988) has pointed to the greater disadvantage of lower SES subjects on performance tests in general and the higher variance explained by the verbal factor of the WISC–R, as evidenced by research from Greece, Israel, and Turkey. Finally, the Turkish standardization of WISC–R has been done with urban low SES norms, which fits with our sample. It is also reported (Savasir & Sahin, 1988, and personal communication) that the vocabulary subtest, which has been

THE FOLLOW-UP RESULTS

Extensive results were obtained in the follow-up study. They are presented in different categories. Each includes both the findings relating to mother training and also to preschool context (educational/custodial day care and home care).[19] Interview items were rated on a 1 to 5 scale, unless otherwise noted.

Cognitive Development and School Performance

In a context where compulsory schooling is only 5 years, as was the case for these children, probably the most important indicator of a positive orientation to education in low income areas is "being in school" (school attainment). This is because given the economic pressures, especially the children who do not do well in school and those who are not highly motivated, get out at about age 11, after completing the compulsory primary school. On this crucial indicator of educational attainment, a significant difference was obtained between the children whose mothers had been trained in the original study and those whose mothers had not been trained, with 86% of the former and 67% of the latter still in school ($\chi^2 = 9.57$, $p = .002$).

This is a finding, which in itself, as an objective outcome measure, speaks for the policy implication of our contextual model of early enrichment (mother training). No significant difference was found in school attainment among the children who had educational, custodial, or home care.

Primary school academic performance is the second objective academic indicator on which significant differences were obtained between the experimental (mother-trained) and control groups. Based on report card grades over 5 years of primary school, the mother-trained children surpassed the control group on Turkish, mathematics, and overall academic average (Table 4).[20] This finding also provides clear evidence for the value of the intervention model utilized. It shows that the gains obtained from the intervention were not short lived. Five years of better school performance must have contributed to the higher level of school attainment of the experimental group. It signifies a better school experience in the beginning, which paves the way for higher educational achievement and more years of schooling.

---

devised on the basis of Turkish word counts and extensive research, had high validity, reliability, and discriminating power.

[19]Probability values (p) are given on a one-tailed test of significance, because we had clear theoretically based expectations regarding the direction of the differences between the experimental (mother trained) and the control groups (nontrained), favoring the former.

[20]It is to be noted that children attended many different primary schools in different areas. Their teachers were not informed about the project intervention; they did not know about the children's previous day-care (custodial/educational/home) contexts either.

TABLE 8.4
Adolescent's Academic Performance

Primary School GPAs	Trained N = 83		Not Trained N = 134			
	Mean	SD	Mean	SD	t	p
Turkish	8.85	1.36	8.18	1.41	3.08	.001
Mathematics	8.15	1.75	7.32	1.75	3.01	.001
Overall academic	8.56	1.45	7.89	1.53	2.82	.002

The difference between the academic performances of the two groups is not significant after primary school. This is probably due to the self-selection factor in the control group, where the less successful students tend to drop out after primary school, and the better ones continue in school.

The preschool context does not relate to grades either. However, the custodial care group had significantly greater number of retentions in grade (failed 1 or more years of school) than the educational or home-care children ($F = 4.69$, $df = 2, 216$, $p = .01$).[21]

The mother-trained children surpassed the control group on the standardized WISC–R vocabulary test, which is an indicator of verbal cognitive performance. This finding is significant, particularly in view of research showing more limited vocabulary among children from lower SES families in Turkey (Kağıtçıbaşı & Savasir, 1988; Savasir et al. 1992; Savasir & Sahin, 1988; Semin, 1975) and in the world (Bernstein, 1974; Laosa, 1984; Leseman, 1993). Also chapters 2 and 3 discussed the importance of vocabulary and language proficiency for school performance. In a two-way analysis of variance, the mother-trained group of children obtained a significantly higher mean score (45.62) than the control group (41.92) on this test (over a range of 0–68, the standard deviations being 10.23 and 13.39, respectively). The main effect for mother training was significant at the .033 level ($F = 4.63$, $df = 2, 216$).

Early care context also produced a significant main effect at the .009 level ($F = 4.78$, $df = 2, 216$), with the educational day-care group scoring highest (47.06), followed by the custodial group (43.22), and the home-care group (40.11). An interaction effect was also obtained, with mother training making a greater difference for the custodial day-care and home-care groups than for the educational day-care group. Again, a ceiling effect may be the case for the latter group, whereas those starting from a lower level of performance (custodial and home groups) benefited more from the mother training intervention.

[21]Retentions are not reflected in grades, because the grades of the year failed are deleted.

TABLE 8.5
Adolescent's Academic Orientation

Child Variables	Trained N = 83		Not Trained N = 134			
	Mean	SD	Mean	SD	t	p
Could child be best in class if studies hard?	4.58	.64	4.38	.81	1.98	.025
Having nothing better to do as a reason for going to school	1.63	1.01	1.99	1.22	-2.22	.015
Parent's wishes as a reason for going to school	2.39	1.31	2.87	1.46	-2.45	.01
How pleased child is with school success	3.64	.86	3.41	.92	1.83	.035
How pleased teachers are with child's school success	3.63	.74	3.44	.86	1.79	.04
How much preschool preparation helped	4.41	.68	4.15	.95	2.07	.02
How long preschool preparation helped?	5.23	1.90	4.31	2.12	3.01	.001

Adolescents' Academic Orientation

The effects of intervention are also seen in adolescents' academic orientation, their self-esteem regarding academic performance, and their retrospective assessment of how well prepared they were for school at school entry (Table 5).

As seen in Table 5, the experimental group of adolescents (whose mothers had been trained), compared with the control group, were more pleased with their school success and thought their teachers were pleased with them; they also felt they could be the best in class if they studied hard. Negative or external pressure reasons for going to school (having nothing better to do or parents' wishes) were endorsed more by the control group. Thus, positive orientation to education and self-esteem appear to be concomitant with good academic performance.

The mother-trained children were also perceived by their parents in a more positive light regarding academic orientation than were the control children. Thus, the experimental group of children were perceived by their fathers as more motivated to succeed in school, compared with the controls (4.00 vs. 3.26; t =

3.03, $p = .003$), and by their mothers as actually having greater school success (3.54 vs. 3.32; $t = 1.8$, $p = .04$).

Preschool context made a difference mainly in terms of a negative effect from the custodial day-care experience. The custodial group perceived their parents ($F = 3.67$, $df = 2, 214$, $p = .027$) and their teachers ($F = 3,53$, $df = 2, 214$, $p = .031$) as being less pleased with their school performance than educational day-care and home-care children.

As for school preparation, many more of the experimental group felt they were prepared when they started school, compared with the control group (97% vs. 77%; $\chi^2 = 15.1$, $p = .0001$). It is to be noted; that all types of preparation were referred to in the question, including day care (two thirds of both the experimental and control groups had attended day care). Among those adolescents who felt they were prepared for school, the mother-trained ones, as compared with the controls, believed their preparation helped them more in school (4.42 vs. 4.15; $t = 2.07$, $p = .02$), and that it helped them for longer (5.2 years vs. 4.3 years; $t = 3.01$, $p = .002$). Thus, the home intervention was perceived retrospectively as helpful by the adolescents.

Preschool context also had an effect on retrospective assessment of school preparedness. Home-care children, compared with those in educational or custodial care, were much less likely to think they had been prepared for school (32 % vs. 96% and 93%, respectively; $\chi^2 = 27.42$, $df = 2$, $p = .0000$).

Socioemotional Development and Social Integration of the Adolescent

The experimental group (mother-trained) fared better than the control group in some indicators of socioemotional development and social integration (Table 6).

The mother-trained adolescents demonstrated greater autonomy, as reflected in making their own decisions. They also gave evidence of better social integration and social adjustment, in terms of their ideas being accepted by friends, mothers' approval of their friends, and having had less trouble with the law (Table 6). Juvenile delinquency is rare among these young adolescents, most of whom have intact families, nevertheless the few who had trouble with the law (6%) were all from the control group.

As for preschool context, again the negative effects of custodial care are apparent. Adolescents with a custodial day-care experience tend to have less self-confidence than others. For example, they rate themselves as less intelligent than their classmates ($F = 3.68$, $df = 2, 214$, $p = .027$), and have a near-significant tendency to have less confidence in their ability to cope with different situations ($F = 2.4$, $df = 2, 214$, $p = .093$). With regard to juvenile delinquency, six of the eight adolescents who had been in trouble with the law were from the custodial

TABLE 8.6
Adolescent's Social Integration and Autonomy

Child Variables		Trained N = 83		Not Trained N = 134			
		Mean	SD	Mean	SD	t	p
Are children's ideas accepted by friends?		3.74	.64	3.54	.71	2.06	.02
Children make their own decisions		3.54	.83	3.32	.96	1.73	.045

Mother Variables		%	f	%	f	X^2	p
Did child ever have	YES	0	0	6	8		
trouble with the police?	NO	100	100	94	126	3.69	.05
What mother thinks of child's friends:							
Approve highly		56	46	38	51	9.02	.03
Approve somewhat		31	26	33	45		
Not sure		8	7	21	28		
Does not approve		5	4	7	10		

care group; the other two had been in home care; none were from an educational day-care background. Though the numbers are too small for statistical significance, the pattern is suggestive.

Compared with the fourth-year findings, where the socioemotional outcomes were not very clear-cut, the long-range effects appear more notable.

Adolescents' Perception of the Mother

Adolescents' retrospective perception of their mothers demonstrates what our mother enrichment program accomplished (Table 7). The adolescents whose mothers had been trained perceived them to be more nurturant and more responsive than the control group. Specifically, the former group perceived their mothers to talk with them, to console them, to help them, to be interested in them and to appreciate them more, and to spank them less than the latter (Table 7). Obviously, the trained mothers manifested a different style of parenting. This was probably the key difference between the human environments of the two groups of children.

TABLE 8.7
Adolescent's Perception of Mother

	Trained N = 83		Not Trained N = 134			
Variables	Mean	SD	Mean	SD	t	p
Mother liked to talk with child when little	3.89	.96	3.61	1.06	1.99	.025
Mother used to spank child when little	2.00	.96	2.32	1.07	-2.25	.015
Mother used to console child when little	4.26	.82	3.93	1.00	2.52	.005
Mother used to appreciate child when little	3.94	.84	3.69	.89	1.99	.025
Mother was interested in what child did	4.22	.87	4.00	.90	1.75	.040
Mother used to help child when little	4.20	.79	4.00	.91	1.69	.045

Parents' Perception of Child and Family Relations

Responses of mothers and fathers to the questions in interviews provide further evidence to substantiate the findings obtained from the adolescents. They imply that the changes in the mothers meant changes in family emotional atmosphere and family relations, with corresponding changes in children already described. Significant differences between the two groups emerged in many basic family variables, parent–child interaction, and perception of children by the parents. Thus in the experimental group, better parent–child communication, better adjustment of the child in the family, less physical punishment, and closer and better family relations were reported by both mothers and fathers (Table 8).

The differences between the mother-trained and control groups emerge in terms of both 5-point single variables (interview items) and the Likert scales formed to measure parental communication with the child and family adjustment of the child. An index measuring woman's status also differentiated the experimental and control groups. This is the same measure used in the fourth year of the original study. It consists of communication, shared decision making, and role sharing between the spouses. The higher intrafamily status enjoyed by the trained mothers after the intervention (in the fourth year) is found to continue 7

TABLE 8.8

Parent's Perception of Child and Family Relations

Mother Scales	Trained N = 83		Not Trained N = 134			
	Mean	SD	Mean	SD	t	p
Communication with child	14.33	1.60	13.50	2.08	3.11	.001
Family adjustment of child	28.78	3.32	27.69	4.28	1.95	.026
Woman's status	13.64	2.38	12.91	2.33	2.18	.015
Mother Variables						
Is the child quarrelsome?	1.49	.65	1.71	.84	-1.99	.025
Is the child sassy?	1.45	.57	1.66	.88	-1.95	.026
Was the child spanked or beaten?	1.59	.73	1.92	.97	-2.64	.004
Does the child talk about problems with mother?	3.54	.72	3.17	.91	3.16	.001
How well mother understands the child?	3.75	.44	3.58	.68	2.07	.02
How good are relations in the family	4.35	.61	4.08	.75	2.80	.003
How close are family members?	4.46	.63	4.22	.88	2.11	.02
Father Variables						
Was the child spanked or beaten?	1.17	.38	1.62	.72	-3.38	.000
Does the child talk about problems with father?	2.91	1.04	2.48	1.03	2.02	.025

years later. This is an important finding attesting to enduring favorable position of the woman in the family as a result of mother training.

Parents' Academic Orientation/Perception

A final category of findings have to do with parental orientations/expectations regarding the child's educational status (student role, educational attainment, etc.) (Table 9).

Both mothers' and fathers' educational expectations for their children are found to be higher in the mother-trained than in the control group. Additionally, fathers in the mother-trained group report greater interest in what is going on in

TABLE 8.9
Parent's Academic Orientation/Perception

		Trained N = 83		Not Trained N = 134			
Father Variables		Mean	SD	Mean	SD	t	p
Father's educational expectations for child		4.59	.80	4.03	1.04	2.33	.01
Father's interest in what is going on in school		3.19	.71	2.84	.85	2.08	.02
Mother Variables							
Mother's educational expectation for child		4.27	1.15	3.66	1.28	2.56	.005
How much preschool preparation helped?		4.27	1.09	3.67	1.26	3.22	.001
Environmental Stimulation Index		11.69	2.26	11.03	2.50	1.98	.025
		%	f	%	f	x^2	p
Does help with home-work exist in family?	YES	89	73	76	94		
	NO	11	9	24	29	4.37	.04
Was child prepared starting school?	YES	100	83	65	87		
	NO	0	0	35	47	35.12	.000

school. All of the trained mothers think that the child had been prepared for school at the start, compared with only 65% of the control mothers. They also believed this preparation had been helpful, confirming further their children's independent assessments. Thus the mother-training program is seen in retrospect by both mothers and children as valuable school preparation.

Two measures in Table 8 provide an indication of the existence of support at home for the child's student role, which is indirectly related to parents' academic orientation. One of these is the existence of help with the child's homework at home. The other is the environmental stimulation index. This index was also used in the original intervention study and includes father's and mother's education, mother's language skills, the frequency of buying newspapers and magazines, and the presence of books at home. On both of these indicators, the mother-trained group fared better than the control group, reflecting a home environment more likely to promote educational achievement.

In closing the presentation of the findings, I would like to note that only some of the analyses conducted have been included here. The intention has been to provide a general description of the findings of the study. Specifically, the multivariate analyses of both the fourth-year and the follow-up data have not been presented. This is because they go beyond the scope of this chapter, which aims to present a case study of a policy-relevant intervention research. In general, the multivariate analyses further substantiated the results presented in this chapter; they are presented elsewhere.[22]

DISCUSSION OF THE FINDINGS

Relative Effects of the Two Interventions

When we started the original study, we were interested in studying both center-based (child-focused) and home-based (mother-focused) early enrichment. That is why we studied the effects of both context (educational, custodial day care, and home care) and mother training. Our original view was that having both an educationally oriented day-care experience and a supportive, stimulating home environment (through mother training) would provide optimal enrichment. We considered this combination to constitute "a comprehensive preschool education" and called our work the "Comprehensive Preschool Education Project" (Kağıtçıbaşı et al., 1988).

Our fourth-year results indeed showed that children who had both an educational day-care experience and mother training outperformed the others in almost all the measures of cognitive development (Table 2) and school achievement. Although the main finding was that the effects of the educational day care and of mother training were both positive, their combined effect was additive, not multiplicative. In other words, a significant interaction between them was not obtained. Indeed, as indicated before, often the more deprived custodial-care and home-care children benefited more from the mother training. Thus, the fourth-year results showed that because of ceiling effects in the cognitive gains of the educational day-care children, mother training did not contribute much more to them. Therefore, the two interventions (educational day care and mother training) appeared as possible alternatives rather than necessarily being complementary to one another. This led us to look more carefully into the relative effects of day-care context (center-based) and mother training (home-based) interventions, particularly in the follow-up study.

---

[22]It is to be noted that the absolute differences between the experimental and the control groups reported in this chapter are often not very large, though statistically significant. Obviously, there is a great deal of unaccounted variance in a longitudinal study covering 10 years. Nevertheless, the overall pattern of differences between the two groups is clear.

Another factor prompting us to look into the relative affectiveness of the center-based and the home-based interventions, ingrained in our original research design, is the recent debate in early childhood care and development (ECCE) research on the relative effectiveness of these two approaches. This debate and the several issues involved in it were discussed in the previous chapter. It is rather difficult to reach conclusive results regarding the relative effectiveness of the center-based and home-based approaches because these approaches may not be mutually exclusive. As pointed out before, often there is parent involvement in center-based (child-focused) approaches, and there can be a direct child-focused orientation in a home-based intervention.

The latter was the case in our project. Nevertheless, our research design allows us to examine the relative effectiveness of the two types of interventions we had in our original study. I have described the defining characteristics of each, and they need to be considered in terms of these characteristics.

Taking up the fourth-year results, and examining cognitive-school achievement outcomes, which are more clear-cut than the socioemotional outcomes, we find that both interventions are effective. In specific terms, the children with educational day-care experience showed a significantly superior performance on 23 measures and a positive though nonsignificant trend on 5. By contrast, the custodial group was superior on only 3 measures, and the home-care group never had the highest score. Likewise, the mother-trained group was superior to the nontrained group on 12 measures and showed a nonsignificant positive trend on 15, whereas the nontrained group was in no way superior to the mother-trained group.

Indeed, both are effective, and if anything, the gains from the educational day care are even more notable in terms of being reflected in a greater number of significant differences. In view of this, it is interesting that when we move from the fourth-year to the long-term effects, something of a reversal in the relative effectiveness of the two types of intervention emerges. More of the gains from mother training are sustained compared with those from educational day care. This is found to be the case for both school attainment, school achievement, and academic orientation, on the one hand, and for socioemotional development and social adjustment/integration, on the other. Only in vocabulary (WISC–R) were there significant main effects for both mother training and day-care context, with the educational day-care group scoring the highest. Even the custodial day-care group fared better in this measure than the home-care group. As indicated earlier, however, even here the mother-trained children in both custodial and home-care groups performed better than the non-mother-trained children, as shown by the interaction effect.

The dissipation of gains over the long-term from educational day care is in line with other research findings reviewed in the last chapter regarding the situation where parental involvement is lacking or minimal (as in our study for the nontrained group). It is possible that despite their clear superiority to the custodial day-care centers, the educational centers in our study may not have been of a sufficiently high quality to exert much long-term influence. This might have been the case even though we chose the three highest quality centers in Istanbul catering to the children of the working classes. In fact, some research does provide evidence for long-term effects from high quality center-based programs (e.g., Berrueta-Clement et al, 1984), which also entailed some parent involvement, even if not substantial.

It is to be noted, nevertheless, that the educational day-care centers in our study were of a sufficiently good quality to have substantial short-term effects (in the fourth year). It is indeed the obtained difference between the short- and long-term effects of educational day-care that is problematic. Although we have to allow for the possibility that an even higher quality educational day care might have produced a broader range of long-term effects, we are left with the question of whether it is realistic. Particularly in developing countries, it is unlikely to achieve such high quality in large numbers of day-care centers catering to the children of the poor, as evidenced by our experience in Istanbul and as noted in the literature (Myers, 1992). Thus the policy implications call for greater attention to be paid to more contextual approaches involving the caretakers rather than complete dependence on center-based care.

In this context, the relative ineffectiveness of custodial care also in the longer time perspective is a reason for concern. In too many cases day care for the children of the poor, especially in the Majority World, tends to be custodial care. Far from being beneficial for children's overall development, such custodial care can do harm, as evidenced by our long-term results (adolescents with custodial day-care background had more grade retentions; perceived their parents and teachers to be less satisfied with their school performance; had lower self-concepts; and displayed more delinquency). This is probably due, at least in part, to the authoritarian-restrictive orientation commonly found in custodial day-care centers (Bekman, 1993; Myers, 1992). Therefore, just "more day-care," as often demanded by the public (especially women's groups), is not a solution unless the quality of care is seriously attended to. This issue is discussed further in the next chapter. I now want to turn to a further discussion of the long-term effects of mother training.

Effects of Project Intervention (Mother Training)

The theoretical assumptions underlying our expectations are supported by the results of the follow-up study. Indeed, a virtuous circle was apparently set into action by mother training, which has proven itself to be self-sustaining. This is notable in view of the fact that the follow-up data were collected 7 years after the end of the intervention, and there had been no contact with the families in the interim period. The mothers (and children) were apparently empowered by the intervention so that they could perpetuate the gains from the program on their own. Our contextual-interactional approach undoubtedly had a lot to do with this. It was not single individuals who had been the target of intervention, but rather individuals in interaction with one another (or human interactions in the family context). It was because the children's environment was changed that their gains could be lasting.

It is also to be noted that the gains were not only in the cognitive realm or school-related performance. They were also in family relations, including the parent–child and spousal relations. As already explained, the mother enrichment program (group discussions) focused on improving mothers' communication skills (listening to others, expressing own feelings rather than being judgmental of others, developing sensitivity to others' needs as well as to one's own), basically in interacting with their children. However, in group discussions the theme often expanded to cover communications with others, especially with the spouse, an area where many women had more problems than in communicating with their children. The impact is seen 7 years later in better family relations and greater well-being of mothers and children (e.g., in higher self-esteem, greater autonomy and better social adjustment of children, and higher intrafamily status of the mothers vis-à-vis their husbands).

It was the combination of our whole-child approach and contextual–interactional approach that produced the obtained effects in such a wide range of developmental realms and touching on the whole family. There is a consistency of positive findings relating to the project intervention (mother training); in no measure did the nontrained group show a more favorable outcome. This was the case covering a wide scope, from adolescents' school attainment to social integration, from vocabulary competence to harmonious family relations.

It is to be noted that the positive long-term effects of mother training in several spheres emerged with different types of assessments used. Specifically, both self-report measures (interviews with mothers, adolescents and fathers) and also objective outcome measures (school attainment, primary school achievement) and tests (the vocabulary sub-test of the WISC–R) provided consistent evidence of the superiority of the mother-trained group. Furthermore, the long-term effectiveness of mother training was evident in both child outcomes and mother outcomes, as well as better family outcomes.

School attainment, as I discussed before, is of key importance for this group of people for whom access to continued education is the road to social mobility. In turn, primary school achievement is an important factor in determining whether a child from a poor family will go on to middle school or leave education for work. The superiority of the mother-trained group in both school attainment and primary school performance, therefore, constitutes objective outcomes with significant policy implications. The superior vocabulary competence of the mother-trained group is another important objective outcome, indicative of a higher level of cognitive competence.

As for self-reports obtained through the interviews, it must be admitted that they constitute less robust evidence, being open to subjective evaluations and social desirability response biases. Despite these weaknesses, which were relevant for *all* the respondents to some degree, the systematic intergroup differences in self-reports are notable. Especially noteworthy are the convergences between adolescents' and parents' responses. Some positive disposition on the part of the trained mothers toward the project in general might have been a factor influencing their responses, though the interviewers were not familiar to the mothers and 7 years had passed since the intervention. This could not have been a factor for the fathers or the children, however, who were not directly targeted by the project intervention. So, confirming responses from fathers and children, alongside mothers' responses, may be seen to constitute evidence for real changes in the experimental group over time.

On the basis of these long-term results, it may be proposed that a contextual–interactional approach to early enrichment has potential for promoting "human development," particularly in the Majority World. Especially if a multipurpose approach is undertaken, it promises to have wide-ranging beneficial effects. It is to be noted that such approaches also tend to be cost-effective, as they do not involve institutional investments and professional employment. Especially if a group-based, rather than an individual-based (home-visiting) approach is used, costs decrease further.

A proper cost-effectiveness analysis was not carried out for the Turkish Early Enrichment Project. Nevertheless, there is every indication that it was not at all a costly undertaking, even though it did not use a solely group orientation but a combination of group and individual-oriented training. In the more recent applications we have shifted to a complete group orientation in mother training both to decrease costs further and also because we found the group setting to be a factor facilitating change, as I discussed earlier. The use of paraprofessionals rather than professionals was another important factor decreasing costs. It also provided some training and employment opportunities to previously nonworking women (mothers' aides and group leaders).

The Turkish Early Enrichment Project has been presented as an example of a theoretically informed applied research that has policy implications. Those implications have, in fact, materialized as public service. The mother training program is now in actual use in many urban and rural areas in Turkey through the adult education centers of the Ministry of Education. I would like to present next these applications deriving from the Turkish Early Enrichment Project.

APPLICATIONS

Even before the completion of the original 4-year study of the Turkish Early enrichment Project, interest in the mother training program started to emerge on the basis of preliminary reports. A first initiative was taken by some of the mothers participating in the mother training program who encouraged us to prepare a television program "to reach more mothers and children" and who volunteered to take part in this undertaking. An 11-session series was prepared of the "mother enrichment program" component in the form of small group discussions (of the mothers in the program). It was shown on the then-single-channel state television and was well-received. Partial and full applications of the mother training program were then carried out as public service mainly in Istanbul. These applications involved funding by various groups, such as parent–teacher associations, women's groups, and private business. They also entailed training of more paraprofessionals and revision and improvement of the program content.

After the initial phase of limited applications, the main developments started with the cooperation of the Turkish Ministry of Education and UNICEF. This was mainly in response to the evidence from our follow-up study demonstrating beneficial long-term effects of the mother training program. The mother enrichment program component was first adopted into the adult education programs of the ministry to train child minders, and the training manual was published by UNICEF. Then when it became apparent that the whole mother training program could find widespread application through the Ministry of Education Adult Education infrastructure, we undertook to devise a new cognitive training program to replace HIPPY. We also changed the whole program into a 25-week program (from the previous 60-week one), concentrating on the year immediately preceding school entry. Regular individual home visits were discarded, and a complete group orientation was adopted with weekly (rather than fortnightly) group meetings to conduct both the cognitive training program and the mother enrichment program.

Thus, the program was made less demanding in terms of mothers' time (1 instead of 2 years) and was made less costly. However, these adjustments did not decrease the quality, mainly because all training is now being done by the well-trained group leaders with higher formal education (rather than depending on less educated mothers' aides who conducted the training in fortnightly home visits). Nevertheless, this has not increased the costs, because the Ministry of Education adult education teachers are trained as group leaders. In most cases, this means upgrading and optimized use of already existing personnel and facilities. Thus, the absolute costs are minimal. Close supervision and regular upgrading of the personnel and the materials insure quality. Two recent evaluation studies, one with the children and one with the mothers (Ayçiçeği, 1993; Ercan, 1993) provide evidence of significant benefits from the program.

An important development is the establishment of the Mother–Child Education Foundation in 1993, supported by a private Turkish bank. This foundation aims to expand the program to reach "children all over the country." The numbers of mothers and children reached are increasing greatly. The program is now operating in most of the Ministry of Education adult education centers in Istanbul and Ankara, as well as in more than 20 other provinces in Turkey, including some of the least developed areas. Municipal centers under the Ministry of State for Women, Family, and Children are also joining in as another outlet for the program.

The Turkish Early Enrichment Project and the applications deriving from it have influenced educational policy and have helped formulate new policy in Turkey. These recent policy-relevant developments are presented in the next chapter.

9 Search for Integration and Policy Relevance

This book has covered wide ground. On the one hand, I examined the theoretical issues involved in human development, family, and culture interfaces; on the other hand, I delved into applications designed to induce change. I attempted to bridge the gap between theory and application by presenting the Turkish Early Enrichment Project as a case in point. This final chapter further attempts to verify my theoretical formulations of the development of the self and of human competence in the (changing) family in terms of the results of this project. In turn, I use these theoretical conceptualizations and research results as guidelines for drawing policy-relevant conclusions.

In providing a synopsis and integration of the main points discussed in the previous chapters, I follow more or less the same order as in the presentation of the chapters. An analysis of some critical issues and their policy implications will then be undertaken.

SUMMARY AND CRITICAL ISSUES

From the very start, I laid out some priorities in my orientation to psychology, namely, an involvement with interpersonal relations and social relevance. Then a contextual–developmental–functional approach was used in establishing the linkages between the self, family, and society, on the one hand, and between theory and application, on the other. Furthermore, this approach was located within a cultural and cross-cultural perspective. This is a synoptic characterization of the general theoretical orientation used in this book.

Human development and the self were examined in context with this theoretical orientation. First, context was analyzed as a source of meaning, involving societal and parental beliefs, goals, and values regarding children. The functional underpinnings of these aspects of context emerged as important. Then socialization for competence and the self were examined within family and culture. The development of cognitive competence and of the self formed the core topics in this book from both a theoretical and an applied perspective. They are subject to far-reaching cultural influences.

In particular, the distinction between the relational self and the separated self, along the (inter)dependence–independence dimension constitutes a key to an understanding of the functional links between culture, family, and the self and of family change through socioeconomic development. I distinguished between three different human/family patterns and proposed a general shift toward the model of emotional interdependence. This reflects a different type of convergence than what is commonly assumed by modernization views.

The next step was a consideration of the role of psychology in promoting human development at both the individual and societal levels. Issues such as setting comparative standards versus relativism, nature–nurture underpinnings, and the social–political implications of psychological research came to the fore. I then picked up early childhood care and education as an area of induced change and examined the research application issues involved. Finally, the Turkish Early Enrichment Project was presented as a case study of induced change.

Thus, part I dealt mainly with theoretical issues regarding the family, human development, and the self in cultural context. Part II examined induced change and the role of psychology, focusing on early enrichment. Throughout the discussions, several important questions and issues emerged. I would like to dwell on some of them here in an attempt to integrate the material presented in the different chapters. In particular I try to relate theoretical considerations in the first part with the applied work in the second, especially the Turkish Early Enrichment Project.

Critical Issues Underlying Intervention

A key question that emerged in this book is whether there is an optimal fit between societal values/practices and children's "developmental trajectories." This is a legitimate question if we do not subscribe to a rampant relativism. It is answered necessarily affirmatively by an extreme functionalist–deterministic–relativistic stance in the sense that whatever a society needs, it values and practices, and therefore by definition, the outcome of this practice (e.g., child-rearing) fits optimally with society's prerogatives.

There are some serious problems with this view. First of all, there is never full control or consensus in any society, and deviance exists everywhere. Therefore there is no such thing as a perfect fit between societal values/practices and behavioral outcomes. Second, even though functional analysis is enlightening, it has its limitations. If it is used in a deterministic fashion, it can deteriorate into a circular teleological reasoning and can end up assuming a static, nonchanging society. This assumption is obviously false in the face of constant ongoing change in all societies. Through societal change, what used to be a functional, optimal fit can turn into a dysfunctional relationship; this needs to be corrected.

This latter assertion is based on the assumption that decisions—such as what is optimal, what is not; what is correct, what is not; and what is good, what is not—*can* be made. It brings up the related issues of standards/relativism and the role of psychology in inducing change, which have been discussed at length in this book.

The general stand I take on this issue is that the original question, whether the fit between societal values/practices and children's developmental trajectories is optimal, is a legitimate question and that psychology has accumulated adequate knowledge and expertise to answer it. However, to do so, psychology must be prepared to establish some basic standards of human development while at the same time being sensitive to culture. This may appear as contradiction in terms, but it is not, as has been argued in this book. A culturally sensitive stance does not mean the uniqueness of each culture or the impossibility of comparative standards. What it means is that assessment (evaluation) is done correctly, by utilizing culturally valid and relevant standards of shared attributes that can be applied in a comparative way. Thus, a balance is called for between an "emic" and an "etic" orientation, in line with the "derived etic" concept benefiting from both (Berry, 1989; Berry et al., 1992), as discussed earlier.

This stand underlies intervention research in general. It is quite clear in the area of the promotion of cognitive competence where certain standards such as "school preparedness" and school achievement can be used. These standards are applied in both specific realms of intervention, such as in enhancing preliteracy and prenumeracy skills, and also in the outcome measures used in evaluation. They are based on the psychological knowledge about the development of cognitive competence, school requirements, and school-related achievement criteria.

Though less clear than cognitive/school-related indicators, indicators of healthy socioemotional development can also be established. To give the example of the Turkish Early Enrichment Project, these indicators were based mainly on the theoretical views discussed in chapters 4 and 5 regarding the two basic human needs of autonomy and relatedness and the human/family model of emotional interdependence integrating them. Specifically, as we were dealing in the case of Turkey with a culture of relatedness, with a high value put on relatedness and closely knit human bonds, this basic human need for relatedness was considered well met. But the other basic need, need for autonomy, was considered not adequately recognized and fulfilled. This was in fact found to be the case from the initial baseline assessments of mothers' childrearing orientations, valuing relatedness, and disapproving autonomy. It was also evidenced by other Turkish research (Eksi, 1982; Fisek, 1991; Gectan, 1973). Thus a main goal of the intervention in the socioemotional realm was the acceptance of autonomy in childrearing and the resultant promotion of autonomy in children.

Another related issue emerging in this book is the role of psychology in the face of less-than-optimal fit between cultural values/practices and children's developmental trajectories. I have made it clear that psychology has a role in inducing change where needed, in addition to analyzing, understanding, and explaining the situation. This is obviously implicated by any intervention research. The further issue of how to bring about change, or the most effective strategy to be used, is an empirical question.

The contextual approach, stressed throughout this book, informed our choices regarding this issue in the Turkish Early Enrichment Project. The main intervention introduced in the project had to do with changing the family context of the child, focusing on the mother. Thus, we applied a home-based early enrichment intervention together with and in comparison to a center-based intervention that was already under way. The general approach utilized in the intervention introduced by the project was one of "empowerment" rather than ameliorating "deficiency."

This is another issue of both theoretical and applied significance. Not subscribing to a "deficiency" model does not imply that the existing conditions are optimal for the development of children. If this were so, there would be no need for intervention. It rather means that the agent of change builds on the existing strengths in changing the conditions to promote optimal development. Empowerment refers, in effect, to strengthening what is adaptive in order to change what is maladaptive. Again, this kind of approach requires that the psychologist, first of all, accepts a role as an agent of change and, second, is willing to make decisions based on scientific evidence of what is to change. In other words, some standards (norms/criteria) of optimal development need to be accepted.

Obviously, some risks are taken in making such decisions. However, as discussed before, these risks can be decreased if an effort is made to better understand the "realities" of the situation, aspirations of the people concerned, and so on. Furthermore, not making any decisions and not getting involved also carries risks in the sense that this may entail, in effect, a "decision by indecision" in perpetuating the status quo.

Also important is the quidance of sound theory, supported by research evidence. The intervention of the Turkish Early Enrichment Project was informed by the theory of family change I have developed, as well as by general theory and research in developmental psychology discussed before, which was culturally relevant. There was an attempt to combine cultural contextualism with universal standards (as discussed in chapters 2, 3, 5, 6). The changing lifestyles of mostly formerly rural families whose children were to attend urban schools was the socioeconomic context of the intervention. Based on these considerations, some decisions of induced change were made in the Turkish Early Enrichment Project, focusing on changing maternal orientations/behavior and introducing new elements into it. They were designed to promote better mother–child interactions for greater cognitive competence (and school achievement) and more healthy socioemotional development of the child. They included such specific induced changes as increased verbalization, more effective communication, responsiveness, perspective taking of the mother; more induction and authoritative (rather than authoritarian) discipline; better acceptance of the child and greater appreciation of his autonomy by the mother; more supportive parenting; higher educational aspirations; and carrying out a systematic program of school preparation with the child.

They were based on psychological knowledge regarding age-specific cognitive development and school preparedness, on the one hand, and the human/family model of emotional interdependence (chapter 5), on the other. The research and theory I discussed in part I are relevant here. For example, the main goal of mother training was to induce the kind of stimulating parental orientation called "parental modernity" by Goodnow (1988), which was found to contribute to children's cognitive development and school success (chapters 2 and 3). Another goal was to instill autonomy into the development of the related self, balancing the needs for agency and communion (chapters 4 and 5).

As mentioned before, these goals were considered fitting with the "emotional interdependence" family model, which is proposed to lead to the synthesis of the autonomous–relational self. There may be an objection that rather than moving toward such a synthesis of the interdependent and independent developmental pathways, what we have done was to induce independence (individualism). As seen from the findings of the Turkish Early Enrichment Project, relational orientations were not weakened while a more positive orientation toward autonomy emerged among some of the mothers. This is a different change than one toward complete individualism/separation. It may be argued that these are the beginnings of a move toward a synthesis of autonomy and relatedness.

A contextual orientation was used in inducing change. Group discussion (group dynamics in general) was utilized as the instrument of change. K. Lewin's early work (1951, 1958), though not adequately appreciated today, clearly showed the facilitation by group processes of attitude and behavior change.[23] The same facilitating effects were seen in our project. In regularly meeting small groups, individuals identify with the group and internalize its norms as their own, because they are its active participants. Thus, they feel the responsibility for carrying out group decisions; this seems to be a process that facilitates attitude and behavior change. Furthermore, because the group members feel the group support even when they are not in the group, they are empowered to resist

---

[23]Group process is used effectively in many applied areas, ranging from group therapy to sensitivity training in management. However, it does not figure in an important way in current social psychology given the latter's heavy individual cognitive focus.

others' possible opposition better than if they were carrying out their own individual decisions alone. This appears to underlie group effects being sustained over time.

A culture-sensitive approach also favored a group process. In the traditional Turkish culture, women's kin and neighborhood groups serve an important support function (Aswad, 1974; Benedict, 1974; Kiray, 1981; Olson, 1982). Thus, utilizing such a familiar social structure meant building on an existing cultural strength. Indeed, women's support networks have been observed to be important in many cultural contexts, ranging from patriarchal Mediterranean societies with limited sharing of activities between males and females (Peristiany, 1976) to female-headed Black families in the United States (Coll, 1990; Garbarino, 1990; Harrison et al., 1990; Stevens, 1988). Thus, Slaughter (1983) claimed that group discussion is a more culturally consonant intervention approach than individual home visits for low income Black mothers. In any "culture of relatedness" with closely knit human bonds (as in Turkish society) it makes good sense to capitalize on groups as support mechanisms and as agents of change.

Finally, group training is more cost-effective than individual training. In terms of investment of time, personnel, and service (training) per person, the group setting is clearly more economical than targeting persons individually. For all these reasons, a group orientation was utilized in the Turkish Early Enrichment Project. Thus, *contextuality* characterized our main theoretical and methodological approach in this project at two different levels, both in dealing with the development of the child in family context (through the mother) and also in dealing with the mother in group—micro and mesosystems, respectively, in Bronfenbrenner's terms (1979).

Our contextual orientation, in working with the mother, also entailed an induced change in the conceptualization of the mother's role. Among lower SES groups, rural people, and ethnic minorities occupying marginal positions in urban society, the commonly held definition of parenting involves loving and caring but does not include preparing the child for school; this contrasts with the middle-class definitions, which include the latter (chapters 2 and 3). As a great deal of research (Coll, 1990; Goodnow, 1988; Laosa, 1980, 1984; R. A. LeVine & White, 1986; Slaughter, 1988), shows the latter more comprehensive definition of parenthood to be more favorable for the child's school preparedness and school performance, we introduced it in our intervention. In fact, cognitively oriented mother-focused intervention assumes this parent-as-teacher role.

The Turkish Early Enrichment Project applications and results demonstrate that cultural definitions of parenthood can change and can even be brought about through intervention. Our long-term findings also showed that such change can be favorable for children's developmental trajectories.

Together with changes in the definitions of parental roles, there were also changes in conceptions of ("competent" and "good") children by parents. As discussed in chapters 3 and 4, where a relational conceptualization of the self and closely knit human bonds are prevalent (in the "culture of relatedness"), a "social definition of intelligence" prevails. Here a compliant and socially responsible child is highly valued. The first-year baseline assessments of the Turkish Early Enrichment Project also showed this. The project intervention stressing cognitive competence and autonomy, however, expanded this conceptualization to include these latter elements. The change was apparent, for example, in more of the trained mothers accepting autonomy of their children, expecting their children to do school-related activities on their own, and aspiring for higher levels of education and educational achievement for their children, compared with the nontrained mothers.

Such "new" values, however, did not seem to replace values of relatedness but to be *added* to them, as evidenced by the continued stress put on relatedness by the trained mothers. These results provide some evidence for the validity of the human/family model of emotional interdependence (chapter 5). They also demonstrate that such a model of human relations can be induced through intervention.

This discussion of the critical issues and their reflections in the Turkish Early Enrichment Project shows that many of the theoretical considerations covered in part I were of relevance for the applications covered in part II. Also, the general contextual–developmental–functional approach that I adopted in linking human development/self, family, and society also underlay our project.

PSYCHOLOGY AND SOCIAL POLICY

In what directions do these discussions lead? When we ask this question, we come to policy implications. There is much to be said about the policy relevance of the material covered here. However, I would first like to examine the relation between psychology and social policy.

Unlike other social scientists such as political scientists, sociologists, and economists, psychologists have not been typically much involved with social (public) policy. In the United States, where psychology is well recognized and well established, it has some tradition of social involvement, mainly as a mental health profession. Nevertheless, even in the United States it has not realized its potential as an agent of change in the "public interest" (M. B. Smith 1990).[24] In

---

[24]There are some signs that this may be changing, especially in the United States where the American Psychological Association (APA) and some of its committees are involved in the current U. S. national health care reform (*APA Monitor*, 25 (1), 1994). A recent issue of the *American Psychologist* (49 (2), 1944) reviews psychology's involvement with the Head Start from its beginnings and its renewed commitment to the current efforts to strengthen Head Start. A recent issue of *Psychology International* (published by the International Affairs Office of the APA, 5 (1), 1994) describes a new involvement with international human rights issues.

other countries and particularly in the Majority World, psychology has typically had much less policy involvement. This is not surprising given the individual focus in psychological analysis and a lack of interest in general issues of societal development, as discussed before. I have argued in this book that this has to change and psychology has to carry social as well as scientific responsibility. Policy relevance of research and theory is the key here. According to Bronfenbrenner (1979), "Basic science needs public policy even more than public policy needs basic science. Moreover, what is required is not merely a complementary relation between these two domains but their functional integration" (p. 8). And M. B. Smith (1991) noted that "the contribution of psychology is not limited to reporting conclusive research data (data are seldom if ever conclusive); it is also and maybe more importantly the redefining of policy questions by raising awareness of unconsidered possibilities or by reconceptualizing familiar dilemmas" (p. xviii).

Public policy has an impact on human conditions and human behavior that psychology studies. In turn, policies often reflect ideologies, cultural values, and social–structural characteristics of a society. Thus,they form an important aspect of the context in which human development and human behavior takes place. Yet, policies can and should be based on scientific knowledge and should be modifiable to serve changing human needs.

Many examples can be given of both cultural/ideological basis of policies and also their influence on human conditions. For example, in the social welfare states of the Nordic countries of Europe it is considered the responsibility of the state to provide early childhood care and education (ECCE) to all children. In Sweden every child is "entitled" to ECCE after the end of parental leave from about age 1 (Kağıtçıbaşı et al. 1994; Kamerman, 1991). This type of a social welfare ideology leads to a cogent child-care policy with universal coverage. The universal availability of high quality child care, in turn, serves as a factor contributing to women's labor force participation, which in Sweden reaches 85% (the highest in the world). This contrasts with, for example, the situation in the United States where child care is not considered as a societal responsibility but as "essentially an individual and private problem" (Huston, 1991, p. 306); the result is a lack of comprehensive child-care policies (Kamerman, 1991; Kamerman & Kahn, 1989).

Another example is the student allowances in the Netherlands. Every young person age 18 or above who is a student gets an allowance from the State for up to 6 years (if in good standing). And, if students live on their own, rather than with their family, they receive an appreciably greater amount of allowance. This policy certainly reflects an individualistic cultural value system, and it may serve as a centrifugal factor encouraging the separation of the young person from the family. Indeed, the whole social security system in most western European countries is individual based. Thus, a recent Council of Europe Study Group on "the Interaction Between the Providers of Family Services" (Kağıtçıbaşı et al.,

1994) noted that even the so-called family services in Europe are basically services to individuals. So much so that in some cases it is more advantageous (financially) to live alone than to cohabit. Again, the reflections of the "culture of separateness" are clear, further reinforcing separateness.

These examples, particularly when viewed from a global cross-cultural perspective, point to the mutual influences and functional integration between cultural values, policies, and human conditions. The scientific study of these conditions, therefore, must take policy into consideration. Any applied research inducing change needs to attend to the policy implications. Thus, psychology should assume a place next to other social sciences in addressing policy issues. It should study social policy–human behavior–human condition interfaces; it should work to inform social policies; and it should undertake to help establish or change policies in order to enhance human well-being.

POLICY RELEVANCE

I now discuss briefly some of the main policy implications of the material I have covered in this book, and particularly of the Turkish Early Enrichment Project. I examine policy relevance both in general terms and also with regard to specific applications.

Policies to Enhance Early Human Development

Probably the single most important policy implication of the deliberations in parts I and II of this book is the necessity of addressing early human development and investing in ECCE. This does not necessarily imply a deterministic view of early years as a "critical period." There is indeed evidence pointing to the resilience of children who turn out to function normally after early deprivation (Brim & Kagan, 1980; see also Tizard, 1991, for a review). Nevertheless, there are limits to resilience from adverse conditions. For example, chronic and severe protein-calorie malnutrition, particularly during the first years of life when there is rapid growth of the brain and the body, can result in permanent mental and physical damage or even death; the same is found to be true for the deficiency of micronutrients (specifically, iodine, iron, and vitamin A) (Evans & Shah, 1994; Pollitt et al., 1993; World Bank, 1993). Though I have not dealt with malnutrition in this book, it is a reminder that there are limits to recovery from severe adversity.

Furthermore, whether recovery or resilience occurs is itself influenced by the immediate environment of the child. As discussed earlier (chapter 7), there is an interaction between the (environmental) care/psychosocial stimulation and nutrition to produce so-called positive deviance. The children who survive, even thrive, in adverse conditions do so with the support of a caring and stimulating environment with closely knit human bonds (Brazelton, 1982; Carvioto, 1981; Kotchabhakdi et al., 1987; Levinger, 1992; Myers, 1992; Weiss & Jacobs, 1988; Werner & R. S. Smith, 1982; Zeitlin, 1991; Zeitlin et al., 1990). Even the deleterious effects of undernutrition on mental development can be ameliorated by "appropriate stimulation in the home" (L. Eisenberg, 1982, p. 63).

All this evidence calls for policies to focus on early human development and especially to enhance the environmental support provided to the child. The synergy between nutrition, health, and psychosocial aspects of development needs to be recognized. As parents get better informed about children's multiple needs and multifaceted development, they can better contribute to this complex process.

Investing in ECCE to promote more healthy human development is justified on many grounds. Myers (1992) listed a number of them. First and foremost among these is the basic human rights argument of children being "entitled to grow and develop to their full potential," as spelled out in the Declaration of the Rights of the Child, adopted unanimously in 1959 by the United Nations General Assembly. Thirty years later, in 1989, a Convention on the Rights of the Child was ratified, urging the signatories to ensure child survival and development and to provide services for the care of children. Indeed, this is adequate justification for any policy aiming to promote early human well-being. Nevertheless, as we are far from this ideal, often more specific justifications are needed to enact policies to invest in ECCE. They cover wide ground from scientific arguments (about the importance of early years for long-term effects) to economic ones (of long-term benefits to society from increased production and cost savings); from social equity reasons (to provide a fair start to disadvantaged children) to programmatic ones (increasing the efficiency of women's programs, e.g., by combining them with ECCE programs).

Policies enhancing early development also have direct educational impact, through increased "school preparedness." This is, in turn, another basic human right—the right to education (Article 26 of the Universal Declaration of Human Rights). Thus, to allow arrested development and lack of schooling to disable millions of young children when it could be prevented is a violation of basic human rights. Recent increased efforts to invest in alternative models of ECCE in the Majority World (Myers, 1992) are steps in the right direction. The recent resurgence of interest and increased investment in the Head Start program in the United States (Kassenbaum, 1994; Zigler & Styfco, 1994) also point to a growing recognition of the need to focus on early human development in the context of increasing poverty within some technological societies.

Holistic, Multipurpose Policies

A great deal of discussion in this book about the importance of the environment has implications for a holistic, contextual policy orientation to early human development and ECCE. The weight of the evidence from ECCE and intervention research, covered in chapter 7, and from the Turkish Early Enrichment Project points to the greater effectiveness of a contextual–holistic, rather than an individual-focused, approach to intervention. Parental/caregiver involvement appears to be the key here.

As this issue was discussed in chapters 7 and 8, I do not dwell on it further here. Note that this does not mean child-focused approaches are ineffective. An effective intervention with long-term benefits, the Perry Preschool Project (Berrueta-Clement et al., 1984; Schweinhart & Weikert, 1980), was a child-focused study, though it did have some parent involvement. The point is that a contextual approach is bound to contribute to greater gains as it supports the environment together with the child. This would be especially the case where the environment, for any reason, is not providing the child the amount (and quality) of support that it potentially could.

A contextual/holistic policy is particularly useful in targeting multiple goals. Thus, multipurpose programs—addressing for example, health, nutrition, development, and school readiness needs of children, as well as needs of mothers (e.g., health, family planning, income generation, etc.)—tend to create greater motivation and participation to be cost-effective, and to have expanding effects. For example, the Turkish Early Enrichment Project, combining ECCE with adult education, was cost-effective and had enduring effects. It also had nutrition, health, and family planning components. Mothers were provided information on all these topics designed to increase their awareness and knowledge as well as to help them get the services they needed. Such broad coverage of needs serves multiple purposes.

The previous points are particularly relevant for the Majority World, where unmet multiple-intersecting needs abound and resources are limited. Multipurpose policies that are family and community based, while targeting ECCE, have the potential to set into action mutually reinforcing and self-perpetuating virtuous cycles of development.

In a recent analysis of commonalities among successful intervention programs for children in poverty in the United States, Schorr (1991) pointed to a number of characteristics. Among them, she noted that "successful programs *see the child in the context of family and the family in the context of its surroundings*" (italics in orignial; p. 267). Thus, successful programs, even if they start out focusing on the child or on the parent, evolve into *two-generational* programs—some even three generational (Zigler & Styfco, 1994). Furthermore, successful programs are also found to "emphasize the importance of *relationships*" (with the recipients) in "a *flexible* structure with *coherent, integrated broad spectrum of services, adapted to the needs of the people they serve*" (emphasis in the original) (Schorr, 1991, pp. 267–269). This discussion comes to show that comprehensive policies supporting multipurpose programs are needed and promise to be effective everywhere, not only in the Majority World.

In many cases, child-care programs, particularly in the Majority World, are based on the goal of providing custodial care for the children of working mothers (Huston, 1991; Myers, 1992; Phillips, 1991). This is often what is demanded. Yet, ECCE program evaluations (chapter 7) and particularly the follow-up results of the Turkish Early Enrichment Project (chapter 8) show that custodial care is inadequate at best and can even be detrimental to the overall development of children. Thus, even policies focusing on supporting women's employment have to adopt child development goals to benefit all concerned. This calls for multi-purpose policies as well as for policies aiming at "quality care."

There are implications of the latter for center-based and home/community-based approaches. Particularly in the Majority World, center-based care for children of the working class tends to easily deteriorate into custodial care, as we found in Istanbul. Yet, center-based care, even starting in infancy, can be of high quality, with demonstrated long-term benefits, as evidenced by research in Sweden (Andersson, 1992). This comes to show that if child-care policies stress "quality" and "developmental goals" sufficiently, different types of programs (center or home/community-based) can be beneficial.

Nevertheless, the fact of the matter is that Sweden has the highest quality of care in the world (Kamerman, 1991), and particularly in the Majority World, this level of care appears a very remote possibility. Therefore, especially when the home conditions are not conducive to the optimal development of the child, not much sustained benefit can be expected from center-based approaches. Accordingly, a general policy implication might be that when the home provides the early stimulation and support the child needs (as in many middle class contexts), center-based ECCE would be satisfactory; however, if not, then a contextual approach, involving parents/family would be in order.

Another policy implication and challenge has to do with the potential for wide-scale implementation of ECCE programs. The more cost-effective approaches are more likely to evolve into large-scale policies and applications. Nonformal, group-oriented, home- and community-based programs are more promising, particularly in the Majority World, to "go to scale," though low-cost center-based programs have the potential to increase in coverage as well (Myers, 1992).

Policy Implications of the Model of Emotional Interdependence

There are also policy implications of the human/family model of emotional interdependence. I have noted a shift toward this model in the Majority World with socioeconomic development. This is because in the urban, more developed contexts in the Majority World, with universal schooling and increased social welfare, the economic and old-age security value of children decrease, and their economic costs increase. This process of change decreases material dependence on children and grown-up offspring. This, in turn, allows for autonomy to enter into childrearing, as complete interdependence is not the goal any longer.

However, this process is sometimes too slow to take place and cultural lags can occur. Thus even when material interdependence in the family decreases with changing socioeconomic conditions, expectations of complete obedience from children and rejection of autonomy can persist as cultural values. Such persistence of authoritarian parenting could be dysfunctional in more developed urban contexts of the Majority World where individual decision making and autonomy of the growing person are adaptive in changing lifestyles.

Educational policies are implicated here that could encourage and facilitate changes in child care and education. For example, in schools and particularly in adult education programs, autonomy can be introduced as a goal, together with relatedness. With decreased material dependencies autonomy of the growing child in the changing family should not be threatening to the family integrity any longer. Therefore, such an induced change need not encounter great resistance. Thus, the family model of emotional interdependence that produces the autonomous-related self has specific policy/program implications, as used in the Mother Enrichment Program of the Turkish Early Enrichment Project.

Other aspects of family change entailed in the model of emotional interdependence also have relevance for policy. A very important one is the change in the intrafamily status of the woman. Increased education and urbanization, decreased fertility, decreased importance of patrilineage, and decreased son preference go with increased woman's status. Social and educational policies upholding women's status and well-being can further facilitate this process of change. This was done, for example, in a small way, through an empowerment program (mother enrichment program) in the Turkish Early Enrichment Project.

Similarly, family planning programs designed to decrease fertility would further help promote a higher intrafamily status of the woman. In many societies woman's status is negatively associated with fertility (Kağıtçıbaşı, 1982a). High fertility is further associated with poor health of both women and children. Thus, educational programs on family planning, nutrition, and health, as for example integrated in our mother enrichment program, promote women's well-being and higher intrafamily status.

Thus, different aspects of the model of emotional interdependence have implications for policies. Some of these were reflected in the general approach and the specific programs used in the Turkish Early Enrichment Project, going beyond the cognitive enrichment program of school preparation.

Policy Impact

Just as policies engender programs, successful programs that find wide applications can also impact policy. For example, the Turkish Early Enrichment Project and the applications deriving from it have influenced educational policy and have helped formulate new policy in Turkey. ECCE was conceptualized traditionally only as formal preschools, with the resultant grossly inadequate coverage (7%) (chapter 7). With the example of the Turkish Early Enrichment Project as an alternative nonformal model of ECCE, this narrow definition of the field has been expanded to include a new policy of integrating ECCE into the widespread adult education services, in addition to the preschools. The project has also helped to form cooperation among agencies and government bodies that normally do not work together but provide noncoordinated piecemeal services, noted to be a real problem for service provision (Huston, 1991; Myers, 1992; Schorr, 1991). Thus two different ministries, a private foundation (Mother–Child Education Foundation), an international NGO (UNICEF), and universities are involved in a joint effort to expand the Mother–Child Education Program in Turkey.

This is an example of how scientific research can inform and impact policy. This work has also helped increase the recognition and prestige of psychology in public opinion and among policy makers in Turkey as an important scientific discipline that is relevant for development. As discussed earlier (chapter 6), in many parts of the Majority World social development lags behind economic development mainly because development is still conceived mainly in economic/technological terms. Culturally appropriate and relevant psychological research can go a long way in bridging this gap, especially with regard to initiating new programs and policies.

CONCLUSIONS

This book has examined and related some basic theoretical and applied issues. From a theoretical perspective, two parallel developmental trajectories—the development of the self (and of human relations), on the one hand, and the development of human competence, on the other—have formed focal topics of study. Family has become of key importance in engendering culturally varying characteristics of the self and of self–other relations. Family change, in turn, assumed significance in mediating between social change and the individual. Family and childrearing are also found to impact the development of cognitive competence. The role of cultural/parental values, beliefs, and behaviors emerged as influential, particularly in early years.

The powerful impact of the context, as mediated by the family, is evident in these two basic spheres of human development—that of the self and that of cognitive competence. Given the centrality of the early environment and particularly of the family for the previous two developmental spheres, the implications for induced change also point toward the early environment and the family.

From an applied perspective, the field of early childhood care and education (ECCE) was taken up as an area of induced change. This field is quite fitting with a focus on the early environment and the family, especially when viewed from a contextual orientation, rather than an individualistic one. The weight of the evidence points to a contextual approach in early intervention, particularly in adverse socioeconomic conditions where there is less-than-adequate family support for human development.

In line with the theoretical considerations regarding the two parallel developmental processes—of the self and of cognitive competence—specific interventions were pursued in the Turkish Early Enrichment Project. These were basically introducing autonomy into a family culture of relatedness and cognitive emphasis into a social-relational orientation to childrearing. One goal was to create a new synthesis in line with the theoretical human/family model of emotional interdependence, considered more optimal for human development than the models of independence and (total) interdependence. Another one was to expand the conceptualization of parenting and of the good (and competent) child to also include cognitive components in addition to social–relational ones.

Particularly the long-term benefits from the project point to the family as an appropriate level at which an intervention can be effective. This is in line with similar policy recommendations regarding "societies with a strong collectivist orientation" (D. Sinha & Kao, 1988, p. 25) and views considering family support and education programs to be a middle ground for family policy (Weiss, 1988). The results obtained call for efforts to support the family and to build on its existing strengths for promoting more optimal human development. It should be noted that this is not at all a call for conservative family ideology. Indeed, the family model of (total) interdependence, which typically carries a conservative world view, suppressing individual autonomy for the common good, is undergoing change with social change and development. The emerging model of emotional interdependence promises to uphold individual autonomy *within* relatedness—engendering the development of the "autonomous-related self."

The United Nations has named 1994 the Year of the Family. This is an opportune time to look into the potentials of the family for the promotion of human well-being, ranging from nutrition and health to cognitive development, from individual accomplishment to emotional support. Psychology has much to offer to an understanding of the mechanisms involved and to contribute to their better functioning.

Inducing change, as for example in intervention research, carries a weight of responsibility. This is particularly problematic when the knowledge base from which to act is not well established. This is one of the reasons underlying the hesitation of psychologists to get involved in policy-relevant issues. Indeed, there is "a tension between action and research in any area of applied scholarship" (Huston, 1991, p. 307). On the one hand, we have accumulated knowledge on which to act, and problems cannot wait for solutions indefinitely. On the other hand, rushing into policy decisions without sound knowledge can be wasteful and even harmful. This is why research (science) and action (policy) have to be in a mutually reinforcing complementary relationship.

We should also keep in mind, however, that policies are enacted because there are human problems requiring solutions, whether or not psychologists are involved. When psychologists (or other social scientists) do not get involved, policies are made by others, such as politicians; and when not informed by scientific knowledge, they turn out to be less than adequate. Therefore, notwithstanding the need to improve our insufficient database and our theories, we have to take on the heavy responsibility to get involved in action. This is a role that psychology may be getting ready to assume if it aspires to contribute to human well-being, not only at the level of the individual, but also globally.

References

Adair, J. G. (1992). Empirical studies of indigenization and development of the discipline in developing countries. In S. Iwawaki, Y. Kashima, & K. Leung (Eds.), *Innovations in cross-cultural psychology* (pp. 62–74). Lisse: Swets & Zeitlinger.

Adorno, T. W., Frenkel-Brunswik, E., Levinson, D. J., & Sanford, R. N. (1950). *The authoritarian personality.* New York: Harper.

Agarwal, R., & Misra, G. (1986). A factor analytical study of achievement goals and means: An Indian view. *International Journal of Psychology, 21,* 717–731.

Allport, G. W. (1937). *Personality: a psychological interpretation.* New York: Henry Holt.

Allport, G. W. (1959). The historical background of modern social psychology. In G. Lindzey (Ed.). *Handbook of social psychology* (Vol. 1, pp. 3–56). Reading, MA: Addison-Wesley.

Anandalaksmy, S. (1994). *The girl child and the family: An action research study.* Department of Women and Child Development, Ministry of Human Resources Development, India.

Anandalaksmy, S., & Bajaj, M. (1981). Childhood in the weavers' community in Varanasi: socialization for adult roles. In D. Sinha (Ed.), *Socialization of the Indian Child* (pp. 31–38). New Delhi: Concept Publishing Company.

Anastasi, A. (1958). Heredity, environment, and the question "How?" *Psychological Review, 65,* 197–208.

Anastasi, A. (1992). A century of psychological science. *American Psychologist, 47,* 842–843.

Anderson, R. C., & Freebody, P. (1981). Vocabulary knowledge. In J. T. Guthrie (Ed.), *Comprehension and Teaching: Research Reviews.* Newark, NJ: IRA.

Andersson, B. E. (1992). Effects of day-care on cognitive and socioemotional competence of 13-year-old Swedish schoolchildren. *Child Development, 63,* 20–36.

Angyal, A. (1951). A theoretical model for personality studies. *Journal of Personality, 20,* 131–142.

Applegate, J. L., Burleson, B. R., & Delia, J. G. (1992). Reflection enhancing parenting as an antecedent to children's social-cognitive and communicative development. In I. E. Sigel, A. V. McGillicuddy DeLisi, & J. J. Goodnow (Eds.), *Parental belief systems* (pp. 3–40). Hillsdale, NJ: Lawrence Erlbaum Associates.

Aries, P. (1962). *Centuries of childhood: A social history of family life* (R. Baldick, Trans.). New York: Knopf.

Aries, P. (1980). Two successive motivations for the declining birth rate in the West. *Population and Development Review, 6,* 645–650.

Aswad, B. (1974). Visiting patterns among women of the elite in a small Turkish city. *Anthropological Quarterly, 47,* 9–27.

Ataman, J., & Epir, S. (1972). Socio economic status and classificatory behavior among Turkish children. In L.J.C. Cronbach & P.J.D. Drenth (Eds.), *Mental test and and cultural adaptation.* (pp. 329–337). The Hague: Mouton.

Ayçiçeği, A. (1993). *The effects of the mother training program.* Unpublished master's thesis, Boğazîçi University, Istanbul.

Azmitia, M. (1988). Peer interaction and problem solving: When are two heads better than one? *Child Development, 59,* 87–96.

Azuma, H. (1984). Secondary control as a heterogeneous category. *American Psychologist, 39,* 970–971.

Azuma, H. (1986). Why study child development in Japan? In H. Stevenson, H. Azuma, & K. Hakuta (Eds.). *Child development and education in Japan* (pp. 3–12). New York: Freeman.

Bakan, D. (1966). *The duality of human existence.* Chicago: Rand McNally.

Bakan, D. (1968). *Disease, pain, and sacrifice.* Chicago: University of Chicago Press.

Baldwin, J. M. (1895). *Mental development in the child and the race.* New York: Macmillan.

Baldwin, J. M. (1909). *Darwin and the humanities.* Baltimore: Review Publishing.

Baltes, P. B. (1987). Theoretical propositions of life-span developmental psychology: On the dynamics between growth and decline. *Developmental Psychology, 23,* 611–626.

Baltes, P. B., & Brim, O. (Eds.). (1979). *Life span development and behavior* (Vol. 2). New York: Academic Press.

Baltes, P. B., Reese, H. W., & Lipsitt, L. P. (1980). Life-span developmental psychology. *Annual review of psychology, 31,* 65–110.

Bandura, A. (1962). Social learning through imitation. In M. R. Jones (Ed.), *Nebraska symposium on motivation* (Vol. 10, pp. 211–271). Lincoln, NE: University of Nebraska Press.

Bandura, A. (1977). *Social learning theory.* Englewood Cliffs, NJ: Prentice-Hall.

Bandura, A. (1986). *Social foundations of thought and action.* London: Allen & Unwin.

Barciauskas, R. C., & Hull, D. B. (1989). *Loving and working: Reweaving women's public and private lives.* Bloomington, IN: Meyer–Stone Books.

Barker, R. G. (1968). *Ecological psychology.* Stanford, CA: Stanford University Press.

Barnett, W. S. (1985). The Perry Preschool Program and its long-term effects: A benefit–cost analysis. Ypsilanti, MI: High/Scope Educational Research Foundation: *Early Childhood Policy Papers.*

Barry, H., Bacon, M., & Child, I. (1957). A cross-cultural survey of some sex differences in socialization. *Journal of Abnormal and Social Psychology, 55,* 327–332.

Barry, H., Child, I., & Bacon, M. (1959). Relation of child training to subsistence economy. *American Anthropologist, 61,* 31–63.

Basaran, F. A. (1974). *Psiko-sosyal gelişim* [Psycho-social development]. Ankara, Turkey: Ankara University Press.

Batson, C. D. (1990). How social an animal? *American Psychologist, 45,* 336–346.

Baumeister, R. F. (1986). *Identity: Cultural change and the struggle for self.* New York: Oxford University Press.

Baumeister, R. F. (1991). *Meanings of life.* New York: Guilford.

Baumrind, D. (1971). Current patterns of parental authority. *Developmental Psychology Monographs, 4* (1, Pt. 2).

Baumrind, D. (1980). New directions in socialization research. *American Psychologist, 35,* 639–652.

Baumrind, D. (1989). Rearing competent children. In W. Damon (Ed.), *Child development today and tomorrow* (pp. 349–378). San Francisco: Jossey-Bass.

Befu, H. (1986). The social and cultural background of child development in Japan and the United

States. In H. Stevenson, H. Azuma, & K. Hakuta (Eds.), *Child development and education in Japan* (pp. 13–25). New York: Freeman.

Bekman, S. (1990). Alternative to the available: Home based vs. centre based programs. *Early Childhood Development and Care, 58*, 109–119.

Bekman, S. (1993). The preschool education system in Turkey revisited. *OMEP International Journal of Early childhood, 25*, 13–19.

Bellah, R. N., Madsen, R., Sullivan, W. M., Swidler, A., & Tipton, S. M. (1985). *Habits of the heart: Individualism and commitment in American life*. Berkeley: University of California Press.

Belsky, J., & Pensky, E. (1988). Developmental history, personality, and family relationships: Toward an emergent family system. In R. A. Hinde & J.S.-Hinde (Eds.), *Relationships within families* (pp. 193–217). Oxford, England: Clarendon.

Bendix, R. (1967). Tradition and modernity reconsidered. *Comparative studies in society and history, 9*, 292–346.

Benedict, P. (1974). The Kabul Günü: Structured visiting in an Anatolian provincial town. *Anthropological Quarterly, 47*, 28–47.

Benedict, R. (1934). *Patterns of culture*. New York: Mentor.

Benedict, R. (1970). Patterns of the good culture. *Psychology Today, 4*, 53–55.

Bennett, J. M. (1993). Jomtien revisited: A plea for a differentiated approach. In L. Eldering & P. Leseman (Eds.), *Early intervention and culture* (pp. 11–19). Netherlands, The Hague: UNESCO.

Bennett, J. (1984). The tie that binds: Peasant marriage and families in late Medieval England. *Journal of Interdisciplinary History, 15*, 111–129.

Berger, B., & Berger, P. L. (1984). *The war over the family*. New York: Anchor.

Berger, P. L., & Luckmann, T. (1967). *The social construction of reality*. New York: Doubleday.

Berman, J. J. (Ed.). (1990). *Cross-cultural perspectives: Nebraska symposium on motivation 1989*. Lincoln: University of Nebraska Press.

Bernstein, B. (1974). *Class, codes, and control: Theoretical studies toward a sociology of language* (rev. ed.). New York: Shocken.

Berrueta-Clement, J. R., Schweinhart, L. L., Barnett, W., Epstein, A., & Weikart, D. (1984). *Changed lives: The effects of the Perry Preschool Programme on youths through age 19*. Ypsilanti, MI: High/Scope Press.

Berry, J. W. (1969). On cross-cultural comparability. *International Journal of Psychology, 4*, 119–128.

Berry, J. W. (1976). *Human ecology and cognitive style: Comparative studies in cultural and psychological adaptation*. New York: Sage/Halsted.

Berry, J. W. (1979). A cultural ecology of social behaviour. In L. Berkowitz (Ed.), *Advances in experimental social psychology* (Vol. 12, pp. 177–206). New York: Academic Press.

Berry, J. W. (1980). Ecological analyses for cross-cultural psychology. In N. Warren (Ed.), *Studies in cross-cultural psychology* (Vol. 2, pp. 157–189). New York: Academic Press.

Berry, J. W. (1984). Toward a universal psychology of cognitive competence. *International Journal Of Psychology, 19*, 335–361.

Berry, J. W. (1985). Cultural psychology and ethnic psychology: A comparative analysis. In I. Reyes-Lagunes & Y. Poortinga (Eds.), *From a different perspective* (pp. 3–15). Lisse: Swets & Zeitlinger.

Berry, J. W. (1989). Imposed etics–emics-derived etics: The operationalization of a compelling idea. *International Journal of Psychology, 24*, 721–735.

Berry, J. W. (1990). Cultural variations in cognitive style. In S. Wapner (Ed.), *Bio-psycho-social factors in cognitive style* (pp. 289–308). Hillsdale, NJ: Lawrence Erlbaum Associates.

Berry, J. W., & Bennett, J. A. (1992). Cree conceptions of cognitive competence. *International Journal of Psychology, 27*, 73–88.

Berry, J. W., & Dasen, P. R. (Eds.) (1974). *Culture and cognition: Readings in cross-cutural psychology*. London: Methuen & Co Ltd.

Berry, J. W., Irvine, S. H., & Hunt, E. B. (Eds.). (1988). *Indigenous cognition: Functioning in cultural context*. Dordrecht: Nijhoff.

Berry, J. W., Poortinga, Y. H., Seagall, M. H., & Dasen, P. R. (1992). *Cross-cultural psychology: Research and applications*. Cambridge, England: Cambridge University Press.

Bertalanffy, L. von. (1968). *General systems theory*. New York: Braziller.

Bisht, S., & Sinha, D. (1981). Socialization, family and psychological differentiation. In D. Sinha (Ed.), *Socialization of the Indian child* (pp. 41–54). New Delhi: Concept.

Boas, F. (1911). *The mind of primitive man*. New York: Macmillan.

Bock, P. K. (1988). *Rethinking psychological anthropology: Continuity and change in the study of human actions*. New York: Freeman.

Bond, M. H. (Ed.). (1986). *The psychology of the Chinese people*. Hong Kong: Oxford University Press.

Bond, M. H. (Ed.). (1988). *The cross-cultural challenge to social psychology*. Newbury Park, CA: Sage.

Bond, M. H., & Cheung, T. S. (1983). The spontaneous self-concept of college students in Hong Kong, Japan, and the United States. *Journal of Cross-Cultural Psychology, 14*, 153–171.

Bornstein, M. H. (1984). Cross-cultural developmental psychology. In M. H. Bornstein & M. E. Lamb (Eds.), *Developmental psychology: An advanced textbook* (pp. 231–281). London: Lawrence Erlbaum Associates.

Bornstein, M. H. (1989). Between caretakers and their young: Two modes of interaction and their consequences for cognitive growth. In M. H. Bornstein & J. S. Bruner (Eds.), *Interaction in human development* (pp. 197–214). Hillsdale, NJ: Lawrence Erlbaum Associates.

Bornstein, M. H. (1991). *Cultural approaches to parenting*. Hillsdale, NJ: Lawrence Erlbaum Associates.

Bornstein, M. H., & Bruner, J. S. (Eds.). (1989). *Interaction in human development*. Hillsdale, NJ: Lawrence Erlbaum Associates.

Bornstein, M. H., Tal, J., & Tamis-LeMonda, C. (1991). Parenting in cross-cultural perspective: The United States, France and Japan. In M. H. Bornstein (Ed.), *Cultural approaches to parenting* (pp. 69–89). London: Lawrence Erlbaum Associates.

Bornstein, M. H., & Tamis-LeMonda, C. (1990). Activities and interactions of mothers and their first born infants in the first 6 months of life. *Child Development, 61*, 1206–1217.

Bornstein, M. H., Tamis-LeMonda, C. S., Tal, J., Ludemann, P., Toda S., Rahn, C. W., Pecheux, M. G., Azuma, H., & Vardi, D. (1992). Maternal responsiveness to infants in three societies: The United States, France, and Japan. *Child Development, 63*, 808–821.

Boszormenyi-Nagy, I., & Spark, G. (1973). *Invisible loyalties: Reciprocity in intergenerational family therapy*. New York: Harper & Row.

Boyden, J., (1990). Childhood and the policy makers: A comparative perspective on the globalization of childhood. In A. James & A. Prout (Eds.), *Constructing and reconstructing childhood* (pp. 184–215). New York: Palmer Press.

Bradburn, N. M. (1963). *N* achievement and father dominance in Turkey. *Journal of Abnormal and Social Psychology, 67*, 464–468.

Brazelton, B. T. (1982). Early intervention: What does it mean? In H. E. Fitzgerald (Ed.), *Theory and research in behavioral pediatrics* (pp. 1–34). New York: Plenum.

Brim, O. G., & Kagan, J. (Eds.). (1980). *Constancy and change in human development*. Cambridge, MA: Harvard University Press.

Brislin, R. W. (1983). Cross-cultural research in psychology. *Annual Review of Psychology, 34*, 363–400.

Brislin, R. W. (1993). *Culture's influence on behavior*. Fort Worth, TX: Harcourt Brace Jovanovich.

Britton, E. (1976). The peasant family in 14th-century England. *Peasant Studies, 5*, 20–27.

Bronfenbrenner, U. (1974). *Is early intervention effective?* Unpublished Report for Department of Health Education and Welfare, Washington DC.

Bronfenbrenner, U. (1979). *The ecology of human development: Experiments by nature and design.* Cambridge, MA: Harvard University Press.

Bronfenbrenner, U. (1986). Ecology of the family as a context for human development: Research perspectives. *Developmental Psychology, 22* (6), 723–742.

Bronfenbrenner, U., & Ceci, S. J. (1993). Heredity, environment, and the question "how?"—A first approximation. In R. Plomin & G. E. McClearn (Eds.), *Nature–nurture* (pp. 313–324). Washington, DC: American Psychological Association.

Bronfenbrenner, U., & Weiss, H. B. (1983). Beyond policies without people: An ecological perspective on child and family policy. In E. F. Zigler, S. L. Kagan, & E. Klugman (Eds.), *Children, families and government: Perspectives on American social policy* (pp. 393–414). New York: Cambridge University Press.

Bruner, J. S., & Bornstein, M. H. (1989). *Interaction in human development.* Hillsdale, NJ: Lawrence Erlbaum Associates.

Brunswik, R. (1955). Representative design and probabilistic theory. *Psychological Review, 62,* 236–242.

Bulatao, R. A. (1979). *On the nature of the transition in the value of children.* Honolulu, Hawaii: East–West Population Institute.

Caldwell, J. C. (1977). Towards a restatement of demographic transition theory. In J. C. Caldwell (Ed.), *The persistence of high fertility* (pp. 25–122). Canberra: Australian National University.

Caldwell, J. C. (1979). "Education as a factor in mortality decline: An examination of Nigerian data." *Population Studies, 33,* 395–413.

Caldwell, J. C. (1980). "Mass education as a determinant of the timing of fertility decline." *Population and development Review, 6*(2), 225–256.

Campbell, D. T. (1975). On the conflicts between biological and social evolution and between psychology and moral tradition. *American Psychologist, 30,* 1103–1126.

Carraher, T. N., Schliemann, A. D., & Carraher, D. W. (1988). Mathematical concepts in everyday life. In G. B. Saxe & M. Gearhart (Eds.), *Children's mathematics: New directions in child development* (pp. 71–87). San Francisco: Jossey-Bass.

Carvioto, J. (1981). *Nutrition, stimulation, mental development and learning.* W. O. Atwater Memorial Lecture presented at the 12th International Congress of Nutrition, San Diego, CA.

Cashmore, J. A., & Goodnow, J. J. (1986). Influences on Australian parents' values: Ethnicity versus socioeconomic status. *Journal of Cross Cultural Psychology, 17,* 441–454.

Caudill, W. A., & Frost, L. (1973). A comparison of maternal care and infant behavior in Japanese-American, American and Japanese families. In W. P. Lebra (Ed.), *Mental health research in Asia and the Pacific.* Honolulu: University Press of Hawaii.

Caudill, W. A., & Schooler, C. (1973). Child behavior and child rearing in Japan and the United States: An interim report. *Journal of Nervous and Mental Disease, 157,* 323–338.

Chamoux, M. N. (1986). Apprendre autrement: Aspects des pédagogies dites informelles chex les Indiens du Méxique [A different type of learning: Aspects of informal pedagogy among Mexican Indians]. In P. Rossel (Ed.), *Demain l'artisanat?* [Tomorrow's handicraft?]. Paris: Cahiers IUED.

Chao, R. K. (1995). Chinese and European-American mothers' views about the role of parenting upon children's school success. *Journal Cross-Cultural Psychology* (in print).

Childs, C. P., & Greenfield, P. M. (1980). Informal modes of learning and teaching: The case of Zinacantoco weaving. In N. Warren (Ed.), *Studies in cross-cultural psychology* (Vol. 2, pp. 269–316). London: Academic Press.

Chodorow, N. (1974). Family structure and feminine personality. In M. Z. Rosaldo & L. Lamphere (Eds.), *Women, culture and society* (pp. 43–66). Stanford, CA: Stanford University Press.

Chodorow, N. (1978). *The reproduction of mothering: Psychoanalysis and the sociology of gender.* Berkeley: University of California Press.

Chodorow, N. (1989). *Feminism and psychoanalytic theory.* New Haven, CT: Yale University Press.

Choi, S. H. (1992). Communicative socialization processes: Korea and Canada. In S. Iwawaki, Y. Kashima, & K. Leung (Eds.), *Innovations in cross-cultural psychology* (pp. 103–121). Lisse: Swets & Zeitlinger.

Christie, R., & Jahoda, M. (1954). *Studies in the scope and method of "the Authoritarian Personality."* Glencoe, IL: Free Press.

Cicirelli, V. G., Evans, J. W., & Schiller, J. S. (1969). *The impact of Head Start: An evaluation of the effects of Head Start on children's cognitive and affective development.* Washington, DC: Westinghouse Learning Corporation, Ohio University.

Cochrane, S., & Mehra, K. (1983). Socioeconomic determinants of infant and child mortality in developing countries. In O. A. Wagner (Ed.), *Child development and international development: Research-policy interfaces* (pp. 27–44). San Francisco: Jossey-Bass.

Cohler, B., & Geyer, S. (1982). Psychological autonomy and interdependence within the family. In F. Walsh (Ed.), *Normal family processes* (pp. 196–227). New York: Guilford.

Cohler, B., & Grunebaum, H. (1981). *Mothers, grandmothers, and daughters: Personality and child-care in three generation families.* New York: Wiley.

Cole, M., Hood, L., & McDermott, R. P. (1978). Concept of ecological validity: Their differing implications for comparative cognitive research. *Quarterly Newsletter of the Institute for Comparative Human Development, 2,* 34–37.

Cole, M., Sharp, D., & Lave, C. (1976). The cognitive consequences of education: Some empirical evidence and theoretical misgivings. *Urban Review, 9,* 218–233.

Coleman, J. S. (1990). *Foundations of social theory.* Cambridge, MA: Harvard University Press.

Coll, C.T.G. (1990). Developmental outcome of minority infants: A process-oriented look into our beginnings. *Child Development, 61,* 270–289.

Consortium for Longitudinal Studies (1983). *As the twig is bent: Lasting effects of preschool programs.* Hillsdale, NJ: Lawrence Erlbaum Associates.

Connolly, K. (1985). Can there be a psychology for the Third World? *Bulletin of the British Psychological Society, 38,* 249–257.

Consultative Group on Early Childhood Care and Development (1986). *Measuring early childhood development: A review of instruments and measures.* New York: UNICEF.

Copple, C., Cline, M., & Smith, A. (1987). *Paths to the future: Long term effects of Head Start in Philadelphia school district.* Washington, DC: U.S. Department of Health and Human Services.

Cotterell, J. L. (1986). Work and community influences on the quality of child rearing. *Child Development, 57,* 362–374.

Cousins, S. (1989). Culture and selfhood in Japan and the U. S. *Journal of Personality and Social Psychology, 56,* 124–131.

Cowan, P. A., Field, D., Hansen, D. A., Skolnick, A., & Swanson, G. E. (Eds.). (1993). *Family, self, and society.* Hillsdale, NJ: Lawrence Erlbaum Associates.

Cronbach, L. J. (1957). The two disciplines of scientific psychology. *American Psychologist, 12,* 671–684.

Curran, V. H. (Ed.). (1984). *Nigerian children: Developmental perspectives.* London: Routledge & Kegan Paul.

Cushman, P. (1990). Why the self is empty: Toward a historically situated psychology. *American Psychologist, 45,* 599–611.

Dalal, A. K. (1990). India: Psychology in Asia and the Pacific. In G. Shouksmith & E. A. Shouksmith (Eds.), *Status reports on teaching research in eleven countries.* Bangkok: UNESCO.

Damon, W. (Ed.). (1989). *Child development today and tomorrow.* San Francisco: Jossey-Bass.

D'Andrade, R. G., & Strauss, C. (Eds.). (1992). *Human motives and cultural models.* Cambridge, England: Cambridge University Press.

Darroch, R., Meyer, P. A., & Singarimbun, M. (1981). *Two are not enough: The value of children to Javanese and Sundanese parents.* Honolulu: East-West Population Institute.

Dasen, P. R. (1984). The cross-cultural study of intelligence: Piaget and the Baoule. *International Journal of Psychology, 19*, 407–434.

Dasen, P. R. (1988a). Developpement psychologique et activités quotidiennes ches des enfants Africains [Psychological development and daily activities of African children]. *Enfance, 41*, 3–24.

Dasen, P. R. (1988b). Cultures et développement cognitif: La recherche et ses applications [Cultures and cognitive development: Research and its applications]. In R. Bureau & D. de Saivre (Eds.), *Apprentissages et cultures: Les manières d'apprendre (Colloque de Cerisy)* [Apprenticeship and culture: ways of learning (Cerisy Colloquim) (pp. 123–141). Paris: Karthala.

Dasen, P. R., Berry, J. W., & Sartorius, N. (Eds.), (1988). *Health and cross-cultural psychology: Toward applications*. London: Sage.

Dasen, P. R., & Jahoda, G. (1986). Cross-cultural human development. *International Journal of Behavioral Development, 9*, 413–416.

Dawson, J.L.M. (1967). Traditional versus Western attitudes in West Africa: The construction, validation and application of a measuring device. *British Journal of Social and Clinical Psychology, 6*, 81–96.

De Silva, M., Nikapota, A., & Vidyasagara (1988). "Advocacy and opportunity: Planning for child mental health in Sri Lanka." *Health, Policy and Planning, 3*, 302–307.

Deutsch, M. (1962). Cooperation and trust: Some theoretical notes. In M. R. Jones (Ed.), *Nebraska symposium on motivation*. Lincoln, NE: University of Nebraska Press.

De Vos, G. (1968). Achievement and innovation in culture and personality. In E. Norbeck, D. Price-Williams, & E. W. McCord (Eds.), *The study of personality* (pp. 348–370). New York: Holt, Rinehart & Winston.

De Vos, G. (1985). Dimensions of the self in Japanese culture. In M. G. De Vos & F.L.K. Hsu (Eds.), *Culture and self*. New York: Tavistock.

Diaz-Guerrero, R. (1991). Historic-sociocultural premises (HSCPs) and global change. *International Journal of Psychology, 26*(5), 665–673.

Doi, T. (1973). *Anatomy of dependence*. Tokyo: Kodansha International.

Doi, L. A. (1974). Amae: A Key concept for understanding Japanese personality structure. In R. A. LeVine (Ed.), *Culture and personality* (pp. 307–314).

Doob, L. W. (1967). Scales for assaying psychological modernization in Africa. *Public Opinion Quarterly, 31*, 414–421.

Dornbusch, S. M., Ritter, P. L., Leiderman, P. H., Roberts, O. F., & Fraleigh, M. J. (1987). The relation of parenting style to adolescent school performance. *Child Development, 58*, 1244–1257.

Drenth, P.J.D. (1991). *Scientific and social responsibility: A dilemma for the psychologist as a scientist*. Paper presented at the Second European Congress, Budapest.

Duben, A. (1982). The significance of family and kinship in urban Turkey. In Ç. Kağıtçıbaşı (Ed.), *Sex, roles, family and community in Turkey* (pp. 73–99). Bloomington: Indiana University Press.

DuBois, C. (1944). *The people of Alor*. New York: Harper & Row.

Dym, B. (1988). Ecological perspectives on change in families. In H. B. Weiss & F. H. Jacobs (Eds.), *Evaluating family programs* (pp. 477–496). New York: Aldine.

Eckensberger, L. (1979). A metamethodological evaluation of psychological theories from a cross-cultural perspective. In L. Eckensberger, W. Lonner, & Y. H. Poortinga (Eds.), *Cross-cultural contributions to psychology* (pp. 255–275). Lisse: Swets & Zeitlinger.

Eckensberger, L. (1990). On the necessity of the culture concept in psychology: A view from cross-cultural psychology. In F.J.R. van de Vijver & G.J.M. Hutschemaekers (Eds.), *The investigation of culture* (pp. 153–177). Tilburg: Tilburg University Press.

Eisenberg, L. (1982). Conceptual issues on biobehavioral interactions. In D. L. Parron & L. Eisenberg (Eds.), *Infants at risk for developmental dysfunction* (pp. 57–68). Washington, DC: National Academy of Sciences, Institute of Medicine.

Eksi, A. (1982). *Gençlerimiz ve sorunlari* [Our youth and their problems]. Istanbul: Istanbul University Publication, 2790.

Ekstrand, L. H., & Ekstrand, G. (1987). Children's perceptions of norms and sanctions in two cultures. In Ç. Kağıtçıbaşı (Ed.), *Growth and progress in cross-cultural psychology* (pp. 171–180). Lisse: Swets & Zeitlinger.

Eldering, L., & Kloprogge, F. (Eds.). (1989). *Different cultures same school*. Lisse: Swets & Zeitlinger.

Eldering, L., & Vedder, P. (1993). Culture-sensitive home intervention: The Dutch Hippy experiment. In L. Eldering & P. Leseman (Eds.), *Early intervention and culture* (pp. 231–252). Paris: UNESCO.

Eliram, T., & Schwarzwald, J. (1987). Social orientation among Israeli youth. *Journal of Cross-Cultural Psychology, 18,* 31–44.

Engle, P. L. (1986). *The intersecting needs of working mothers and their young children: 1980 to 1985*. Unpublished manuscript, California Polytechnic State University, CA.

Enriquez, V. G. (1988). The structure of Philippine social values: Towards integrating indigenous values and appropriate technology. In D. Sinha & H.S.R. Kao (Eds.), *Social values and development: Asian perspectives* (pp. 124–148). Newbury Park, CA: Sage.

Enriquez, G. E. (1990). *Indigenous psychology*. Philippines: New Horizons Press.

Ercan, S. (1993). *The short-term effects of the Home Intervention Program on the cognitive development of childeren*. Unpublished Master's Thesis. Istanbul: Bogazici University.

Erelçin, F. G. (1988). *Collectivistic norms in Turkey: Tendency to give and receive support*. Unpublished master's thesis, Boğaziçi University, Istanbul.

Etzioni, A. (1993). *Spirit of community. Rights, responsibilities and the communitarian agenda*. New York: Crown.

Evans, J. L., & Myers, R. G. (1985). *Improving program actions to meet the intersecting needs of women and children in developing countries: A policy and program review*. The Consultative Group on Early Childhood Care and Development, Ypsilanti, MI: High/Scope Educational Research Foundation.

Evans, J. L., & Shah, P. M. (1994). *Child care programmes as an entry point for maternal and child health components of primary health care*. Geneva: World Health Organisation.

Fawcett, J. T. (1983). Perceptions of the Value of Children: Satisfactions and costs. In R. Bulatao, R. D. Lee, P. E. Hollerbach, & J. Bongaarts (Eds.), *Determinants of fertility in developing countries* (Vol. 1, pp. 347–369). Washington, DC: National Academy Press.

Featherman, D. L., & Lerner, R. M. (1985). Ontogenesis and sociogenesis: Problematics for theory and research about development and socialization across the lifespan. *American Sociological Review, 50,* 659–676.

Festinger, L. (1954). A theory of social comparison processes. *Human Relations, 8,* 117–140.

Fisek, G. O. (1991). A cross-cultural examination of proximity and hierarchy as dimensions of family structure. *Family Process, 30,* 121–133.

Forgas, J. P., & Bond, M. H. (1985). Cultural influences on the perception of interaction episodes. *Personality and Social Psychology Bulletin, 11,* 75–88.

Fu, V. R., Hinkle, D. E., & Hanna, M. A. (1986). A three-generational study of the development of individual dependence and family interdependence. *Genetic, Social and General Psychology Monographs, 112* (2), 153–171.

Fujinaga, T. (1991). *Development of personality among Japanese Children*. Paper presented at the International Society for the Study of Behavioural Development, Workshop on Asian Perspectives of Psychology, Ann Arbor, MI.

Furstenberg, F. F., Jr. (1966). Industrialization and the American family: A look backward. *American Sociological Review, 31,* 326–337.

Gabrenya, W. K., Wang, Y., & Latane, B. (1985). Social loafing on an optimizing task: Cross-cultural differences among Chinese and Americans. *Journal of Cross-Cultural Psychology, 16,* 223–242.

Gaines, A. D. (1984). Cultural definitions, behavior and the person in American psychiatry. In A. J. Marsella & G. M. White (Eds.), *Cultural conceptions of mental health and therapy* (pp. 167–192). Dordrecht: D. Reidel.

Garbarino, J. (1990). The human ecology of early risk. In S. J. Meisels & J. P. Shonkoff (Eds.), *Handbook of early childhood intervention* (pp. 78–96). Cambridge, England: Cambridge University Press.

Garber, H., & Heber, R. (1983). Modification of predicted cognitive development in high-risk children through early intervention. In M. K. Oetterman & R. J. Sternberg (Eds.), *How much can intelligence be increased?* (pp. 121–137). Norwood, NJ: Ablex.

Gay, J., & Cole, M. (1967). *The new mathematics and an old culture.* New York: Holt, Rinehart & Winston.

Gectan, E. (1973). *Toplumumuz bireylerinde kimlik kavraml* [Identity in the individuals of our society]. Ankara, Turkey: Ankara University, Faculty of Education Publication.

Geertz, C. (1975). On the nature of anthropological understanding. *American Scientist, 63,* 47–53.

Gellner, E. (1992). *Postmodernism, reason and religion.* London: Routledge & Kegan Paul.

Georgas, J. (1989). Changing family values in Greece: From collectivistic to individualistic. *Journal of Cross-Cultural Psychology, 20,* 80–91.

Gerard, H. B., & Rabbie, J. M. (1961). Fear and social comparison. *Journal of Abnormal and Social Psychology, 62,* 586–592.

Gergen, K. J. (1973). Social psychology as history. *Journal of Personality and Social Psychology, 26*(2), 309–320.

Gergen, K. J. (1985). Social constructionist inquiry: Context and implications. In K. J. Gergen & K. E. Davis (Eds.), *The social construction of the person.* New York: Springer-Verlag.

Gergen, K. J. (1991). *The saturated self: Dilemmas of identity in contemporary life.* New York: Basic Books.

Gergen, K. J., & Davis, K. E. (Eds.). (1985). *The social construction of the person.* New York: Springer-Verlag.

Gillespie, J. M., & Allport, G. W. (1955). *Youth's outlook on the future: A cross national study.* Garden City, NY: Doubleday.

Gilligan, C. (1982). *In a different voice.* Cambridge, MA: Harvard University Press.

Goodnow, J. J. (1984). Parents' ideas about parenting and development: A review of issues and recent work. In M. E. Lamb, A. L. Brown & B. Rogoff (Eds.), *Advances in developmental psychology* (Vol. 3, pp. 193–242). Hillsdale, NJ: Lawrence Erlbaum Associates.

Goodnow, J. J. (1985). Change and variation in ideas about childhood and parenting. In I. E. Sigel (Ed.), *Parental belief systems* (pp. 235–270). Hillsdale, NJ: Lawrence Erlbaum Associates.

Goodnow, J. J. (1988). Parents' ideas, actions, and feeling: Models and methods from developmental and social psychology. *Child development, 59,* 286–320.

Gorer, G., & Rickman, J. (1949). *The people of great Russia.* New York: Norton.

Gottfried, A., & Gottfried, A. (1984). Home environment and cognitive development in young children of middle socioeconomic status families. In A. Gottfried (Ed.), *Home environment and early cognitive development* (pp. 57–116). New York: Academic Press.

Gottlieb, G. (1991). Experimental canalization of behavioral development. *Developmental Psychology, 27,* 4–13.

Gray, S., Ramsey, B., & Klaus, R. (1983). The early training project 1962–1980. In The Consortium for Longitudional Studies (Ed.), *As the twig is bent.* (pp. 33–70). Hillsdale, NJ: Lawrence Erlbaum Associates.

Greenfield, P. M. (1994). Independence and interdependence as developmental scripts: implications for theory, research and practice. In P. M. Greenfield & R. R. Cocking (Eds.), *Cross-cultural roots of minority child development.* (pp. 1–40). Hillsdale, NJ: Lawrence Erlbaum Associates.

Greenfield, P. M., & Cocking, R. R. (Eds.). (1994). *Cross-cultural roots of minority child development*. Hillsdale, NJ: Lawrence Erlbaum Associates.

Greenfield, P. M., & Lave, J. (1982). Cognitive aspects of informal education. In D. Wagner & H. Stevenson (Eds.), *Cultural perspectives on child development* (pp. 181–207). San Francisco: Freeman.

Greenwald, A. G., & Pratkanis, A. R. (1984). The self. In R. S. Wyer & T. K. Srull (Eds.), *Handbook of social cognition* (Vol. 3, pp. 129–178). Hillsdale, NJ: Lawrence Erlbaum Associates.

Grotevant, H. D. (1989). Child development within the family context. In W. Damon (Ed.), *Child development today and tomorrow* (pp. 34–51). San Francisco: Jossey-Bass.

Gusfield, J. R. (1967). Tradition and modernity: Misplaced polarities in the study of social change. *American Journal of Sociology, 73*, 351–362.

Guerin, P. J. (1976). Family therapy: The first 25 years. In P. J. Guerin (Ed.), *Family therapy: Theory and practice* (pp. 2–22). New York: Gardner.

Guisinger, S., & Blatt, S. J. (1994). Individuality and relatedness: Evolution of a fundamental dialectic. *American Psychologist, 49*, 104–111.

Gupta, G. C. (1992). *Ecology, cognition, metacognition and mind*. New Delhi, India: B. R. Publishing.

Gutierrez, J., Sameroff, A. J., & Karrer, B. M. (1988). Acculturation and SES effects on Mexican-American parents' concepts of development. *Child Development, 59*, 250–255.

Haglund, E. (1982). The problem of the match: Cognitive transition between early childhood and primary school: Nigeria. *Journal of Developing Areas, 17*, 77–92.

Halpern, R. (1990). Community based early intervention. In S. J. Meisels & J. P. Shonkoff (Eds.), *Handbook of early childhood intervention* (pp. 469–498). Cambridge, England: Cambridge University Press.

Hanawalt, A. A. (1986). *The ties that bound: Peasant families in medieval England*. New York: Oxford University Press.

Harkness, S. (1992). Parental ethnotheories in action. In I. E. Sigel, A. V. Mc.Gillicuddy-DeLisi, & J. J. Goodnow (Eds.), *Parental belief systems* (pp. 373–391). Hillsdale, NJ: Lawrence Erlbaum Associates.

Harkness, S., & Super, C. (1993). The developmental Niche: Implications for children's literacy development. In L. Eldering & P. Leseman (Eds.), *Early intervention and culture* (pp. 115–132). Paris: UNESCO.

Harrison A. D., Wilson, M. N., Pine, C. J., Chan, S. R., & Buriel, R. (1990). Family Ecologies of ethnic minority children. *Child Development, 61*, 347–362.

Hartman, H. (1958). *Ego psychology and the problem of adaptation* (D. Rapaport, Trans.). New York: International Universities Press. (Original work published 1939)

Hatano, G. (1982). Cognitive consequences of practice in culture specific procedural skills. *Quarterly Newsletter of the Laboratory of Comparative Human Cognition 4*(1), 15–18.

Hayashi, C., & Suzuki, T. (1984). Changes in belief systems, quality of life issues and social conditions over 25 years in post-war Japan. *Annals of the Institute of Statistical Mathematics, 36*, 135–161.

Hebbeler, K. (1985). An old and a new question on the effects of early education for children from low income families. *Educational Evaluation and Policy Analysis, 7*, 207–216.

Heelas, P., & Lock, A. (Eds.). (1981). *Indigenous psychologies: The anthropology of the self*. London: Academic Press.

Helling, G. A. (1966). *The Turkish village as a social system*. Los Angeles, CA: Occidental College.

Hendrix, L. (1985). Economy and child training reexamined. *Ethos, 13*, 246–261.

Heron, A., & Kroeger, E. (1981). Introduction to developmental psychology. In H. C. Triandis & A. Heron (Eds.), *Handbook of cross-cultural psychology* (Vol. 4, pp. 1–15). Boston: Allyn & Bacon.

Herskovits, M. J. (1948). *Man and his works: The science of cultural anthropology*. New York: Knopf.

Hess, R. D., & Shipman, V. C. (1965). Early experience and the socialization of cognitive modes in children. *Child Development, 36*, 869–888.

Himes, J. R., Landers, C., & Leslie, J. (1992). *Women, work and child care*. Florence, Italy: Innocenti, UNICEF.

Hoffman, L. W. (1987). The value of children to parents and childrearing patterns. In Ç. Kağıtçıbaşı (Ed.), *Growth and progress in cross-cultural psychology* (pp. 159–170). Lisse: Swets & Zeitlinger.

Hoffman, L. W. (1988). Cross-cultural differences in childrearing goals. *New Directions for Child Development, 40*, 99–122.

Hoffman, M. L. (1977). Moral internalization: Current theory and research. In L. Berkowitz (Ed.), *Advances in experimental social psychology* (pp. 85–133). New York: Academic Press.

Hoffmann, F. L. (1989). Developmental issues, college students and the 1990s. *Journal of College Student Psychotherapy, 4*, 3–12.

Hofstede, G. (1980). *Culture's consequences*. Beverly Hills, CA: Sage.

Hogan, R. (1975). Theoretical egocentrism and the problem of compliance. *American Psychologist, 30*, 533–540.

Holtzman, W. H., Diaz-Guerrero, R., & Swartz, J. D. (1975). *Personality development in two cultures: A cross-cultural longitudinal study of school children in Mexico and the United States*. Austin: University of Texas Press.

Horowitz, F. D. (1993). The need for a comprehensive new environmentalism. In R. Plomin & G.E.C. McClearn (Eds.), *Nature–nurture* (pp. 341–354). Washington, DC: American Psychological Association.

Hoselitz, B. (1965). *Economics and the idea of mankind*. New York: Columbia University Press.

Hsu, F.L.K. (Ed.). (1972). *Psychological anthropology*. (2nd ed:). Cambridge, MA: Schenkman.

Hsu, F.L.K. (1985). The self in cross-cultural perspective. In A. J. Marsella, G. DeVos, & F.L.K. Hsu (Eds.), *Culture and self: Asian and Western perspectives* (pp. 24–55). New York: Tavistock.

Huesmann, L. R., Eron, L. D., Lefkowitz, M. N., & Walder, L. O. (1983). *The stability of aggression over time and generation*. Paper presented at the meeting of the society for Research in Child Development, Detroit, MI.

Hurrelman, K. (1988). *Social structure and personality development: The individual as a productive processor of reality*. New York: Cambridge University Press.

Huston, A. C. (1991). Antecedents, consequences, and possible solutions for poverty among children. In A. C. Huston (Ed.), *Children in poverty: Child development and public policy* (pp. 282–315). Cambridge, England: Cambridge University Press.

Huynh, C. T. (1979). *The concept of endogenous development centered on man*. Paris: UNESCO.

Imamoğlu, E. O. (1987). An interdependence model of human development. In Ç. Kağıtçıbaşı (Ed.), *Growth and progress* (pp. 138–145). Lisse: Swets & Zeitlinger.

Inglehart, R. (1991). Changing human goals and values: A proposal for a study of global change. In K. Pawlik (Ed.), *Perception and assessment of global environmental conditions and change* (Page c, Rep. No. 1).

Inkeles, A. (1969). Making men modern. On the causes and consequences of individual change in six developing countries. *American Journal of Sociology, 75*, 208–225.

Inkeles, A. (1977). Understanding and misunderstanding individual modernity. *Journal of Cross Cultural Psychology, 8*, 135–176.

Inkeles, A., & Levinson, D. J. (1954). The study of modal personality and socio-cultural systems. In G. Lindzey (Ed.), *Handbook of social psychology* (Vol. 2, pp. 977–1020). Reading, MA: Addison-Wesley.

Inkeles, A., & Smith, D. H. (1974). *Becoming modern: Individual changes in six developing countries*. Cambridge, MA: Harvard University Press.

Irvine, S. H. (1966). Towards a rational for testing abilities and attainments in Africa. *British Journal of Educational Psychology, 36*, 24–32.

Irvine, S. H. (1970). Affect and construct—a cross-cultural check on theories of intelligence. *Journal of Social Psychology, 80*, 23–30.

Ito, K. L. (1985). Affective bonds: Hawaiian interrelationships of self. In G. M. White & J. Kirkpatrick (Eds.), *Person, self, and experience: Exploring Pacific ethnopsychologies* (pp. 301–311). Berkeley: University of California Press.

Iwawaki, S. (1986). Achievement motivation and socialization. In S. E. Newstead, S. M. Irvine, & P. L. Dann (Eds.), *Human assessment: Cognition and motivation*. Boston: Martinus Nijhoff.

Jahoda, G. (1975). Applying cross-cultural psychology to the Third World. In J. W. Berry & W. J. Lonner (Eds.), *Applied cross-cultural psychology* (pp. 3–7). Lisse: Swets & Zeitlinger.

Jahoda, G. (1977). In pursuit of the emic-etic distinction: Can we ever capture it? In Y. H. Poortinga (Ed.), *Basic problems in cross-cultural psychology* (pp. 55–63). Lisse: Swets & Zeitlinger.

Jahoda, G. (1983). The cross-cultural emperor's conceptual clothes: The emic–etic issue revisited. In J. B. Deregowski, S. Dziurawiec, & R. A. Annis (Eds.), *Expiscations in cross-cultural psychology* (pp. 19–38). Lisse: Swets & Zeitlinger.

Jahoda, G. (1986). A cross-cultural perspective on developmental psychology. *International Journal of Behavioral Development, 9*, 417–437.

Jahoda, G., & Dasen, P. R. (Eds.). (1986). *International Journal of Behavioral Development, 9*(4), 413–416.

James, A., & Prout, A. (1970). *Constructing and reconstructing childhood*. Lewes: Falmer Press.

Jansen, H.A.M. (1987). The development of communal living in the Netherlands. In L. Shamgar-Handelman & R. Palomba (Eds.), *Alternative patterns of family life in modern societies*. Rome: Collana Monografie.

Jarrett, R. L. (1993). *Voices from below: The value of ethnographic research for informing public policy*. Paper presented at the Biennial Meeting of the Society for Research in Child Development, New Orleans.

Jolly, R. (1988). Deprivation in the child's environment: Seeking advantage in adversity. *Canadian Journal of Public Health Supplement*, 20.

Kagan, J. (1984). *Nature of the child*. New York: Basic Books.

Kağıtçıbaşı, Ç. (1970). Social norms and authoritarianism: A Turkish-American comparison. *Journal of Personality and Social Psychology, 16*, 444–451.

Kağıtçıbaşı, Ç. (1973a). Early childhood education and intervention. *UNESCO: Child, Family, Community*. Paris: UNESCO.

Kağıtçıbaşı, Ç. (1973b). Psychological aspects of modernization in Turkey. *Journal of Cross-Cultural Psychology, 4*, 157–174.

Kağıtçıbaşı, C. (1981). Early childhood education and intervention. *UNESCO: Child, Family, Community*.

Kağıtçıbaşı, Ç. (1982a). *The changing value of children in Turkey* (Publ. No. 60-E). Honolulu: East–West Center.

Kağıtçıbaşı, Ç. (1982b). Sex roles, value of children and fertility in Turkey. In Ç. Kağıtçıbaşı (Ed.), *Sex roles, family and community in Turkey* (pp. 151–180). Bloomington, IN: Indiana University Press.

Kağıtçıbaşı, Ç. (1982c). Old-age security value of children: Cross-national socio-economic evidence. *Journal of Cross-Cultural Psychology, 13*, 29–42.

Kağıtçıbaşı, Ç. (1984). Socialization in traditional society: A challenge to psychology. *International Journal of Psychology, 19*, 145–157.

Kağıtçıbaşı, Ç. (1985a). Culture of separateness-culture of relatedness. In C. Klopp (Ed.), *1984*

Vision and Reality. Papers in Comparative Studies (Vol. 4, pp. 91–99). Columbus, OH: Ohio State University.

Kağıtçıbaşı, Ç. (1985b). A Model of family change through development: The Turkish family in comparative perspective. In R. Lagunes & Y. H. Poortinga (Eds.), *From a different perspective: Studies of behavior across cultures* (pp. 120–135). Lisse: Swets & Zeitlinger.

Kağıtçıbaşı, Ç. (1986). Status of women in Turkey: Cross-cultural perspectives. *International Journal of Middle East Studies, 18,* 485–499.

Kağıtçıbaşı, Ç. (1987a). Child rearing in Turkey: Implications for immigration an intervention. In L. Eldering & F. Kloprogge (Eds.), *Different cultures, same school* (pp. 137–152). Lisse: Swets & Zeitlinger.

Kağıtçıbaşı, Ç. (1987b). Individual and group loyalties. In Ç. Kağıtçıbaşı (Ed.), *Growth and progress in cross-cultural psychology* (pp. 94–103). Lisse: Swets & Zeitlinger.

Kağıtçıbaşı, Ç. (1990). Family and socialization in cross-cultural perspective: A model of change. In J. Berman (Ed.), *Cross-cultural perspectives: Nebraska symposium on motivation, 1989* (pp. 135–200). Lincoln, NE: Nebraska University Press.

Kağıtçıbaşı, Ç. (1991a). Decreasing infant mortality as a global demographic change: A challenge to psychology. *International Journal of Psychology, 26,* 649–664.

Kağıtçıbaşı, Ç. (1991b). The early enrichment project in Turkey. *UNESCO–UNICEF–WFP Notes Comments . . .* (No. 193). Paris: UNESCO.

Kağıtçıbaşı, Ç. (1992a). Linking the indigenous and universalist orientations. In S. Iwawaki, Y. Kashima, & K. Leung (Eds.), *Innovations in cross-cultural psychology* (pp. 29–37). Lisse: Swets & Zeitlinger.

Kağıtçıbaşı, Ç. (1992b). Research on parenting and child development in cross-cultural perspective. In M. Rosenzweig (Ed.), *International psychological science* (pp. 137–160). Washington, DC: APA.

Kağıtçıbaşı, Ç. (1994a). A critical appraisal of individualism-collectivism: Toward a new formulation. In U. Kim, H. Triandis, Ç. Kağıtçıbaşı, S-C. Choi, & G. Yoon (Eds.), *Individualism and Collectivism: Theory, Method and Applications* (pp. 52–65). Beverly Hills, CA: Sage.

Kağıtçıbaşı, Ç. (1994b). Human development and societal development. In Bouvy, A-M, v. d. Vijver, F.J.R., Boski, P. (Eds.), *Journeys in cross-cultural psychology* (pp. 3–24). Lisse: Swets & Zeitlinger.

Kağıtçıbaşı, C. (1995). Individualism and collectivism. In J. W. Berry, M. H. Segall, & ß C. Kağıtçıbaşı (Eds.), *Handbook of cross-cultural psychology*, 2nd Ed.

Kağıtçıbaşı, Ç., Benedek, L., Dubois, A., Carney, C., Jallinoja, A., & Vlaardingerbroek, P. (1994). *The interaction between the providers of family services.* Strasbourg: Council of Europe.

Kağıtçıbaşı, Ç. & Berry, J. W. (1989). Cross-cultural psychology: Current research and trends. *Annual Review of Psychology, 40,* 493–531.

Kağıtçıbaşı, C., & Savasir, I. (1988). Human abilities in the eastern mediterranean. In S. H. Irvine & J. W. Berry (Eds.), *Human abilities in cultural context* (pp. 232–262). Cambridge; Cambridge University Press.

Kağıtçıbaşı, Ç., Sunar, D., & Bekman, S. (1988). *Comprehensive preschool education project: Final Report.* Ottawa: International Development Research Centre.

Kahl, J. A. (1968). *The measurement of modernism: Study of values in Brazil and Mexico.* Austin: University of Texas Press.

Kakar, S. (1978). *The inner world: A psychoanalytic study of childhood and society in India.* Oxford, England: Oxford University Press.

Kamerman, S. B. (1991). Child care policies and programs: An international overview. *Journal of Social Issues, 47,* 179–196.

Kamerman, S. B., & Kahn, A. J. (1989). Family policy: Has the United States learned from Europe? *Policy Studies Review, 8,* 581–598.

Kao, H.S.R., & Hong, N. S. (1988). Minimal 'self' and Chinese work behavior: Psychology of the grass-roots. In D. Sinha & H.S.R. Kao (Eds.), *Social values and development: Asian perspectives* (pp. 254–272). London: Sage.

Kapp, W. K. (1963). *Hindu culture, economic development and economic planning in India.* Bombay: Asia Publishing House.

Kardiner, A., & Linton, R. (1945). *The individual and his society.* New York: Columbia University Press.

Kashima, Y., Siegel, M., Tanaka, K., & Isaka, H. (1988). Universalism in lay conceptions of distributive justice: A cross-cultural examination. *International Journal of Psychology, 23,* 51–64.

Kashima, Y., & Triandis, H. C. (1986). The self-serving bias in attributions as a coping strategy: A cross-cultural study. *Journal of Cross-Cultural Psychology, 17,* 83–97.

Kassebaum, N. L. (1994). Head start: Only the best for America's children. *American Psychologist, 49,* 123–126.

Kaur, B., & Saraswathi, T. S. (1992). New directions in human development and family studies: Research, policy, and programme interfaces. *International Journal of Psychology, 27,* 333–349.

Keller, H., Schölmerich, A., & Eibl-Eibesfeldt, I. (1988). Communication patterns in adult–infant interactions in western and non-western cultures. *Journal of cross-cultural psychology, 19,* 427–445.

Keniston, K. (1985). The myth of family independence. In J. M. Henslin (Ed.), *Marriage and family in a changing society* (2nd ed., pp. 27–33). New York: Free Press.

Kessen, W. (1991). The American child and other cultural inventions. In M. Woodhead, P. Light, & R. Carr (Eds.), *Growing up in a changing society* (pp. 37–53). London: Routledge & Kegan Paul.

Kim, U., & Berry, J. W. (1993). *Indigenous psychologies: Research and experience in cultural context.* Newbury Park, CA: Sage.

Kim, U., Triandis, H. C., Kağıtçıbaşı, Ç. Choi, S-C., & Yoon, G. (Eds.). (1944). *Individualism and collectivism: Theory method applications.* Newbury Park, CA: Sage.

King, K., & Myers, R. (1983). *Preventing school failure: The relationship between preschool and primary education.* Ottawa, Canada: International Development Research Center.

Kiray, M. B. (1981). The women of small town. In N. Abadan-Unat (Ed.), *Women in Turkish society* (pp. 259–274). Leiden: Brill.

Kirkpatrick, J., & White, G. M. (1985). Exploring ethnopsychologies. In G. M. White & J. Kirkpatrick (Eds.), *Person, self and experience: Exploring Pacific ethnopsychologies.* Berkeley: University of California Press.

Klaus, R. A., & Gray, S. W. (1968). The early training project for disadvantaged children. *Monographs of the Society for Research in Child Development, 33* (4, Serial No. 120).

Kluckhohn, C. (1957). *Mirror for man.* New York: Premier Books.

Kohlberg, L. (1981). From *is* to *ought*: How to commit the naturalistic fallacy and get away with it in the study of moral development. In L. Kohlberg (Ed.), *Essays on moral development: The philosophy of moral development* (Vol. 1, pp. 101–189). San Francisco: Harper & Row.

Kohn, M. L. (1969). *Class and conformity: A study in values.* New York: Dorsey.

Kohut, H. (1977). *The restoration of the self.* New York: International Universities Press.

Kohut, H. (1984). *How does analysis cure?* Chicago: University of Chicago Press.

Kojima, H. (1984). A significant stride toward the comparative study of control. *American Psychologist, 39,* 972–973.

Koppitz, E. M. (1968). *Psychological evaluation of children's human figure drawings.* New York: Grune & Stratton.

Kornadt, H. J. (1987). The aggression motive and personality development: Japan and Germany. In F. Halish & J. Kuhl (Eds.), *Motivation, intention and volition.* Berlin: Springer-Verlag.

Kotchabhakdi, N. J., Winichagoon, P., Smitasiri, S., Dhanamitta, S., & Valya-Sevi, A.

(1987). The integration of psychosocial components in nutrition education in northeastern Thai villages. *Asia Pacific Journal of Public Health, 2,* 16–25.

Kroeber, A. L., & Kluckhohn, C. (1952). *Culture, part III: Papers of the Peabody Museum of Harvard University.* Cambridge, MA: Harvard.

Kuhn, D., & Brannock, J. (1977). Development of the isolation of variables scheme in experimental and "natural experiment" context. *Developmental Psychology, 13,* 9–14.

Kuhn, M. H., & McPartland, T. S. (1954). An empirical investigation of self-attitudes. *American Sociological Review, 19,* 68–76.

Kvale, S. (Ed.). (1992). *Psychology and postmodernism.* London: Sage.

Laboratory of Comparative Human Cognition (LCHC) (1983). Culture and cognitive development. In Kessen W. (Ed.), *Handbook of child psychology* (14th. ed., Vol. 1, pp. 295–356). New York: Wiley.

Lakoff, G., & Johnson, M. (1980). *Metaphors we live by.* Chicago: University of Chicago Press.

Lambert, W. E. (1987). The fate of old-country values in a new land: A cross-national study of childrearing. *Canadian Psychology, 28* (1), 9–20.

Lamborn, S. D., Mounts, N. S., Steinberg, L., & Dornbusch, S. M. (1991). Patterns of competence and adjustment among adolescents from authoritative, authoritarian, indulgent, and neglectful families. *Child Development, 62,* 1049–1065.

Landers, C. (1992). *Measuring the development of young children: A comparative review of screening and assessment techniques.* New York: UN/C: Consultative Group on Early Childhood Care and Development.

Landers, C., & Kağıtçıbaşı, Ç. (1990). *Measuring the psychosocial development of young children.* Florence: Innocenti/UNICEF.

Laosa, L. M. (1978). Maternal teaching strategies in Chicano families of varied educational and socioeconomic levels. *Child development, 49,* 1129–1135.

Laosa, L. M. (1980). Maternal teaching strategies in Chicano and Anglo-American families: The influence of culture and education on maternal behavior. *Child Development, 51,* 759–765.

Laosa, L. M. (1982). Families as facilitators of children's intellectual development at 3 years of age. In L. M. Laosa, & I. E. Sigel (Eds.), *Families as learning environments for children* (pp. 1–45). New York: Plenum.

Laosa, L. M. (1984). Ethnic, socioeconomic, and home language influences upon early performance on measures of abilities. *Journal of Educational Psychology, 76,* 1178–1198.

Laosa, L. M., & Sigel I. E. (1982). *Families as learning environments for childeren.* New York: Plenum Press.

Larsen, J. M., & Leigh, G. K. (1977). *Early childhood self-concept index: Test manual and technical report.* Provo, UT: Department of Child Development and Family Relations, Brigham Young University.

Lasch, C. (1978). *The culture of narcissism.* New York: Norton.

Lasch, C. (1984). *The minimal self: Psychic survival in troubled times.* New York: Norton.

Laslett, P. (1971). *The world we have lost.* New York: Scribner's.

Laslett, P. (1977). Characteristics of the Western family considered over time. In P. Laslett (Ed.), *Family and illicit love in earlier generations.* London: Cambridge University Press.

Lau, S., & Cheung, P. C. (1987). Relations between Chinese adolescents' perception of parental control and organization and their perception of parental warmth. *Developmental Psychology, 23,* 726–729.

Lau, S., Lew, W.J.F., Hau, K. T., Cheung, P. C., & Berndt, T. J. (1990). Relations among perceived parental control, warmth, indulgence, and family harmony of Chinese in Mainland China. *Developmental Psychology, 26,* 674–677.

Lave, J. (1977). Tailor-made experiments and evaluating the intellectual consequences of apprenticeship training. *Quarterly Newsletter of the Institute for Comparative Human Development, 1,* 1–3.

202 REFERENCES

Lazar, I., Darlington, R. B., Murray, H. W., & Snipper, A. S. (1982). Lasting effects of early education: A report from the consortium for longitudinal studies. *Monographs of Society for Research in Child Development*, (33, Serial No. 120).

Leahy, R. L. (1990). The development of concepts of economic and social inequality. In V. C. McLoyd & C. A. Flanagan (Eds.), *Economic stress: Effects on family life and child development* (pp. 107–120). San Francisco: Jossey-Bass.

Lebra, T. S. (1976). *Japanese patterns of behavior.* Honolulu: University of Hawaii Press.

Lenero-Otero, L. (Eds.). (1977). *Beyond the nuclear family model: Cross-cultural perspectives,* Newbury Park, CA: Sage.

Lerner, J.V.A. (1983). "Goodness of fit" model of the role of temperament in psyhosocial adaptation in early adolescents. *Journal of Genetic Psychology, 143,* 149–157.

Lerner, R. M. (1982). Children and adolescents as producers of their own development. *Developmental Review, 2,* 342–370.

Lerner, R. M. (1989). Developmental contextualism and the lifespan view of person–context interaction. In M. H. Bornstein and J. S. Bruner (Eds.), *Interaction in human development* (pp. 217–243). Hillsdale, NJ: Lawrence Erlbaum Associates.

Lerner, R. M., & Busch-Rossnagel, N. A. (1981). *Individuals as producers of their development: A life span perspective.* New York: Academic Press.

Lerner, R. M., Hultsch, D. F., & Dixon, R. A. (1983). Contextualism and the character of developmental psychology in the 1970s. *Annals of the New York Academy of Sciences, 412,* 101–128.

Leseman, P. (1993). How parents provide young children with access to literacy. In L. Eldering & P. Leseman (Eds.), *Early intervention and culture* (pp. 149–172). The Hague: UNESCO.

Lesthaeghe, R. (1980). On the social control of human reproduction. *Population and Development Review, 6,* 527–548.

Lesthaeghe, R. (1983). A century of demographic and cultural change in Western Europe: An exploration of underlying dimensions. *Population and Development Review, 9*(3), 411–437.

Lesthaeghe, R., & Surkyn, J. (1988). Cultural dynamics and economic theories of fertility change. *Population and Development Review, 14*(1), 1–47.

Leung, K. (1987). Some determinants of reactions to procedural models for conflict resolution. A cross national study. *Journal of Personality and Social Psychology, 53,* 898–908.

Levenstein, P., O'Hara, J., & Madden, J. (1983). The mother–child home program of the verbal interaction project. In Consortium for Longitudinal Studies (Ed.), *As the twig is bent* (pp. 237–264). New York: Lawrence Erlbaum Associates.

LeVine, R. A. (1974). Parental goals: A cross-cultural view. *Teachers' College Record, 76,* 226–239.

LeVine, R. A. (1983). Fertility and child development: An anthropological approach. In D. A. Wagner (Ed.), *Child development and international development: Research-policy interfaces* (pp. 45–56). San Francisco: Jossey-Bass.

LeVine, R. A. (1988). Human parental care: Universal goals, cultural strategies, individual behavior. *New Directions in Child Development, 40,* 37–50.

LeVine, R. A. (1989). Cultural environments in child development. In N. Damon (Ed.), *Child development today and tomorrow.* San Francisco: Jossey-Bass.

LeVine, R. A., & LeVine, B. (1966). *Nyansongo: A Gusii community in Kenya.* New York: Wiley.

LeVine, R. A., & White, M. I. (1986). *Human conditions: The cultural basis of educational development.* London: Routledge & Kegan Paul.

LeVine, R. A., & White, M. I. (1991). Revolution in parenthood. In M. Woodhead, P. Light, & R. Carr (Eds.), *Growing up in a changing society* (pp. 5–25). London: Routledge & Kegan Paul.

Levinger, B. (1992). *Promoting child quality: Issues, trends and strategies.* Washington, DC: Academy for Educational Development.

Lévy-Bruhl, L. (1910). *Les fonctions mentales dans les sociétés inférieures* [How natives think]. Paris: Alcan.

Lévy-Bruhl, L. (1922). *Mentalité primitive*. [Primitive mentality]. Paris: Alcan.

Lewin, K. (1951). *Field theory in social science*. New York: Harper.

Lewin, L. (1958). Group decision and social change. In E. E. Maccoby, T. M. Newcomb, & E. L. Hartley (Eds.), *Readings in social psychology* (pp. 197–211). New York: Holt, Rinehart & Winston.

Lightfoot, C., & Valsiner, J. (1992). Parental belief systems under the influence: Social guidance of the construction of personal cultures. In I. E. Sigel, A. McGillicuddy, & J. Goodnow (Eds.), *Parental belief systems* (pp. 393–414). Hillsdale, NJ: Lawrence Erlbaum Associates.

Lin, C-Y. C., & Fu, V. R. (1990). A comparison of child-rearing practices among Chinese, immigrant Chinese, and Caucasian-American parents. *Child Development, 61,* 429–433.

Lindzey, G. (1961). *Projective techniques and cross-cultural research*. New York: Appleton-Century-Crofts.

Lombard, A. (1981). *Success begins at home*. Lexington, MA: Heath.

Lonner, W. J. (1980). The search for psychological universals. In H. C. Triandis & W. W. Lambert (Eds.), *Handbook of cross-cultural psychology* (Vol. 1, pp. 143–204). Boston: Allyn & Bacon.

Lonner, W. J. (1989). The introductory psychology text and cross-cultural psychology. Beyond Ekman, Whorf, and Biased I. Q. tests. In D. M. Keats, D. Munro, & L. Mann (Eds.), *Heterogeneity in cross-cultural psychology* (pp. 4–22). Lisse: Swets & Zeitlinger.

Lonner, W. J., & Malpass, R. S. (Eds.). (1994). *Psychology and culture*. Boston: Allyn & Bacon.

Lykes, M. B. (1985). Gender and individualistic vs. collectivistic bases for nations about the self. *Journal of Personality, 53,* 356–383.

Maccoby, E. E. (1992). The role of parents in the socialization of children: An historical overview. *Developmental Psychology, 28,* 1006–1017.

MacDonald, K. (1986). Developmental models and early experience. *International Journal of Behavioral Development, 9,* 175–190.

MacFarlane, A. (1978). *The origins of English individualism*. Oxford, England: Blackwell.

Macro (1993). *Ailede cocuk eğitimi araştirmasi* [Child training in the family]. Istanbul:

Mahler, M. (1972). On the first three phases of the separation-individuation process. *International Journal of Psychoanalysis, 53,* 333–338.

Mahler, M., Pine, F., & Bergman, A. (1975). *The psychological birth of the human infant*. New York: Basic Books.

Marin, G. (1985). The preference for equity when judging the attractiveness and fairness of an allocator: The role of familiarity and culture. *Journal of Social Psychology, 125,* 543–549.

Markus, H. R., & Kitayama, S. (1991). Culture and the self: Implications for cognition, emotion, and motivation. *Psychological Review, 98*(2), 224–253.

Markus, H. R., & Kitayama, S. (1992). The what, why and how of cultural psychology: A Review on Shweder's "Thinking through cultures." *Psychological Inquiry, 3*(4), 357–364.

Marsella, A. J., DeVos, G., & Hsu, F.L.K. (Eds.). (1985). *Culture and self: Asian and Western perspectives*. New York: Tavistock.

Marsella, A. J., & White, G. M. (Eds.). (1984). *Cultural conceptions of mental health and therapy*. Boston: Reider.

Masters, J. C. (1984). Psychology, research and social policy. *American Psychologist, 31,* 851–862.

Matsumoto, D. (1994). *People: Psychology from a cultural perspective*. Pacific Grove, CA: Brooks/Cole.

Mazrui, A. (1968). From social Darwinism to current theories of modernization. *World Politics, 21,* 69–83.

McClelland, D. C. (1971). *Motivational trend in society*. New York: General Learning Press.

McClelland, D. C., Atkinson, J. W., Clark, R. A., & Lowell, E. L. (1953). *The achievement motive*. New York: Appleton-Century-Crofts.

McClelland, D. C., & Winter, D. G. (1969). *Motivating economic achievement*. New York: Free Press.

McDonald, K. (1986). Developmental models and early experience. *International Journal of Behavioral Development, 9*, 175–190.

McGillicuddy-De Lisi, A. V. (1982). The relationship between parents' beliefs about development and family constellation, socio-economic status and parents' teaching strategies. In L. M. Laosa & I. E. Sigel (Eds.), *Families as learning environments for children* (pp. 261–299). New York: Plenum.

McGillicuddy-De Lisi, A. V., Sigel, I. E., & Johnson, J. E. (1982). The family as a system of mutual influences: Parental beliefs, distancing behaviors, and children's representational thinking. In M. Lewis & L. A. Rosenblum (Eds.), *The child and its family* (pp. 91–106). New York: Plenum.

McGoldrick, M., & Carter, E. A. (1982). The family life cycle. In F. Walsh (Ed.), *Normal family processes*. New York: Guilford.

McKey, R. H., Condelli, L., Ganson, H., Barret, B. J., McConkey, C., & Plantz, M. C. (1985). *The impact of Head Start on children, families and communities*. Washington, DC: Final Report of the Head Start Evaluation, Synthesis and Utilization Project.

McLoyd, V. C. (1990). The impact of economic hardship on black families and children: Psychological distress, parenting, and socioemotional development. *Child Development, 61*, 311–346.

McLoyd, V. C., & Wilson, L. (1990). Maternal behavior, social support, and economic conditions as predictors of distress in children. In V. C. McLoyd & C. Flanagan (Eds.), *Economic stress: Effects on family life and child development* (pp. 49–70). San Francisco: Jossey-Bass.

McNally, S., Eisenberg, N., & Harris, J. D. (1991). Consistency and change in maternal child-rearing practices and values: A longitudinal study. *Child Development, 62*, 190–198.

Mead, G. H. (1934). *Mind, self, and society*. Chicago: University of Chicago Press.

Mead, M. (1928). *Coming of age in Samoa*. New York: Morrow.

Meisels, S. J., & Shonhoff, J. P. (Eds.). (1990). *Handbook of early childhood intervention*. Cambridge, England: Cambridge University Press.

Miller, J. G. (1984). Culture and the development of everyday social explanation. *Journal of Personality and Social Psychology, 46*, 961–978.

Miller, J. G., Bersoff, D. M., & Harwood, R. L. (1990). Perceptions of social responsibilities in India and the United States: Moral imperatives or personal decisions? *Journal of Personality and Social Psychology, 58*, 33–47.

Miller, S. A. (1988). Parents' beliefs about children's cognitive development. *Child Development, 59*, 259–285.

Min, Kan Feng. (1994). *Empowering Women Through Formal Education*. The Hague: CESO

Minturn, L., & Hitchcock, J. T. (1966). *The Rajputs of Khalapur, India* (Six Cultures Series, Vol. 3). New York: Wiley.

Minturn, L., & Lambert, W. W. (1964). *Mothers of six cultures*. New York: Wiley.

Minuchin, S. (1974). *Families and family therapy*. Cambridge, MA: Harvard University Press.

Misra, G. & Gergen, K. J. (1993). On the place of culture in psychological science. *International Journal of Psychology, 28*, 225–243.

Misra, G., & Agarwal, R. (1985). The meaning of achievement: Implications for a cross-cultural theory of achievement motivation. In I. R. Lagunes & Ype H. Poortinga (Eds.), *From a different perspective: Studies of behavior across cultures* (pp. 250–226). Lisse: Swets & Zeitlinger.

Mogey, J. (1991). Families: Intergenerational and generational connections-conceptual approaches to kinship and culture. *Marriage and Family Review, 16*, 47–66.

Moghaddam, F. M. (1990). Modulative and generative orientations in psychology: Implications for psychology in the three worlds. *Journal of Social Issues, 1*, 21–41.

Moghaddam, F. M., & Taylor, D. M. (1986). What constitutes an "appropriate psychology" for the developing world? *International Journal of Psychology, 21*, 253–267.

Moghaddam, F. M., Taylor, D. M., & Wright, S. C. (1993). *Social psychology in cross-cultural perspective*. New York: Freeman.

Moock, P., & Leslie, J. (1986). Childhood malnutrition and schooling in the Terai region of Nepal. *Journal of Development Economics*, 33–52.

Moos, R. H., & Moos, B. S. (1981). *Family environment scale manual*. Palo Alto, CA: Consulting Psychologists' Press.

Morsbach, H. (1980). Major psychological factors influencing Japanese interpersonal relations. In N. Warren (Ed.), *Studies in cross-cultural psychology* (Vol. 2, pp. 317–344). London: Academic Press.

Mosley, W. H., & Chen, L. C. (1984). An analytic framework for the study of child survival in developing countries. In W. H. Mosley & L. C. Chen (Eds.), Child Survival strategies for research. *Population and Development Review, 10*, (suppl.), 25–45.

Mulhall, S., & Swift, A. (1982). *Liberals & Communaitarians*. UK: Blackwell Publishers.

Mundy-Castle, A. (1974). Social and technological intelligence in Western and non-Western cultures. In S. Pilowsky (Ed.), *Cultures in collision*. Adelaide: Australian National Association of Mental Health.

Munroe, R. L., & Munroe, R. H. (1975). *Cross-cultural human development*. Monterey, CA: Brooks/Cole.

Munroe, R. L., Munroe, R. H., & Shimmin, H. (1984). Children's work in four cultures: Determinants and Consequences *American Anthropologist, 86*, 342–348.

Munroe, R. L., Munroe, R. H., & Whiting, B. B. (Eds.). (1981). *Handbook of cross-cultural human development*. New York: Garland.

Myers, R. (1992). *The 12 who survive*. London: Routledge.

Naidu, R. K. (1983). *A developing program of stress research*. Paper presented at the seminar on Stress, Anxiety and Mental Health. Allahabad, Dec. 1983.

Neki, J. S. (1976). An examination of the cultural relativism of dependence as a dynamic of social and therapeutic relationships. *British Journal of Medical Psychology, 49*, 1–10.

Nikapota, A. D. (1990). *Case study for Sri Lanka—child development in primary care*. Paper presented at the Innocenti Technical Workshop on Psychosocial Development, Florence, Italy.

Novikoff, A. B. (1945). The concept of integrative levels of biology. *Science, 62*, 209–215.

Nsamenang, A. B. (1992). *Human development in cultural context: A third world perspective*. Newbury Park, CA: Sage.

Nsamenang, A. B. (1993). Psychology in Sub-Saharan Africa. *Psychology and Developing Societies, 5*, 171–184.

Nunes, T. (1992). *The environment of the child*. The Bernard van Leer Foundation: Occasional Paper No. 5, The Hague.

Nunes, T. (1993). Psychology in Latin America: The case of Brazil. *Psychology and Developing societies, 5*, 123–134.

Nunes, T., Schliemann, A. D., & Carraher, D. W. (1993). *Street mathematics and school mathematics*. New York: Cambridge University Press.

Ogbu, J. (1988). Cultural diversity and human development. *New Directions for child Development, 42*, 11–28.

Ogbu, J. U. (1990). Cultural model, identity, and literacy. In J. W. Stigler, R. A. Shweder, & G. Herdt (Eds.), *Cultural psychology: Essays on comparative human development* (pp. 520–541). Cambridge, England: Cambridge University Press.

Ohuche, R. O., & Otaala, B. (Eds.). (1981). *The African child and his environment*. Oxford, England: Pergamon Press.

Okagaki, L., & Sternberg, R. J. (1993). Parental beliefs and children's school performance. *Child Development, 64*, 36–56.

Okman, F. (1982). *The determinants of cognitive style: An investigation on adolescents* (in Turkish). Unpublished thesis, Boğaziçi University, Istanbul, Turkey.

Olmsted, P. P., & Weikart, D. P. (1989). *How nations serve young children: Profiles of child care and education in 14 countries*. Ypsilanti, MI: High/Scope Press.

Olmsted, P. P., & Weikart, D. P. (Eds.). (1994). *Families Speak: Early childhood care and education in 11 countries*. Ypsilanti, MI: High/Scope Press.

Oloko, B. A. (1994). Children's street work in urban Nigeria: Dilemma of modernizing tradition. In P. M. Greenfield & R. R. Cocking (Eds.), *Cross-cultural roots of minority child development* (pp.197–224). Hillsdale, NJ: Lawrence Erlbaum Associates.

Olson, E. (1982). Duofocal family structure and an alternative model of husband–wife relationship. In Ç. Kağıtçıbaşı (Ed.), *Sex roles, family and community in Turkey* (pp. 33–72). Bloomington: Indiana University Press.

Oppong, C. (Ed.). (1980). *Child development in African contexts: A collection of readings*. London: Allen & Unwin.

Osterweil, Z., & Nagano, K. N. (1991). Maternal views on autonomy: Japan and Israel. *Journal of Cross-Cultural Psychology, 22*, 363–375.

Oyama, S. (1985). *The ontogeny of information*. Cambridge, England: Cambridge University Press.

Pandey, J. (Ed.). (1988). *Psychology in India: The state-of-the-art* (Vols. 1–3). New Delhi: Sage.

Panel (1973a). The experience of separation–individuation in infancy and its reverberations through the course of life: 1. Infancy and childhood. *Journal of the American Psychoanalytic Association, 21*, 135–154.

Panel (1973b). The experience of separation–individuation in infancy and its reverberations through the course of life: 2. Adolescence and maturity. *Journal of the American Psychoanalitic Association, 21*, 155–167.

Papousek, H., & Papousek, M. (1991). Innate and cultural guidance of infants' integrative competencies: China, The United States, and Germany. In M. H. Bornstein (Ed.), *Cultural approaches to parenting* (pp. 23–44). Hillsdale, NJ: Lawrence Erlbaum Associates.

Patterson, G. R., & Dishion, T. J. (1988). Multilevel family process models: traits, interactions, and relationships. In R. A. Hinde & J. Hinde (Eds.), *Relationships within families* (pp. 283–310). Oxford, England: Clarendon.

Peisner, E. S. (1989). To spare or not to spare the rod. In J. Valsiner (Ed.), *Child development in cultural context* (pp. 111–141). Toronto: Hogrefe.

Pepitone, A. (1987). The role of culture in theories of social psychology. In Ç. Kağıtçıbaşı (Ed.), *Growth and progress in cross-cultural psychology* (pp. 12–22). Lisse: Swets & Zeitlinger.

Peristiany, J. C. (1976). *Mediterranean family structures*. London: Cambridge University Press.

Phalet, K., & Claeys, W. (1993). A comparative study of Turkish and Belgian youth. *Journal of Cross-Cultural Psychology, 24*, 319–343.

Phillips, D. A. (1991). With a little help: Children in poverty and child care. In A. C. Huston (Ed.), *Children in poverty: Child development and public policy* (pp. 158–189). Cambridge, MA: Cambridge University Press.

Plomin, R. (1989). Environment and genes: Determinants of behavior. *American Psychologist, 44*, 105–111.

Plomin, R., & McClearn, G. E. (Eds.). (1993). *Nature, nurture and psychology*. Washington, DC: American Psychological Association Publications.

Podmore, V. N., & St. George, R. (1986). New Zealand Maori and European mothers and their 3-year-old children: Interactive behaviors in pre-school settings. *Journal of Applied Developmental Psychology, 7*, 373–382.

Pollitt, R., Gorman, K. S., Engle, P. L., Martorell, R., & Rivera, J. (1993). Early supplementary feeding and cognition. *Monographs of the Society for Research in Child Development, 58*, 7.

Pollitt, E., & Metallinos-Katsaras, E. (1990). Iron deficiency and behavior: Constructs, methods and validity of the findings. In Wurtman and Wurtman (Eds.), *Nutrition and the brain: Vol. 8. Behavioral effects of metals, and their biochemical mechanisms* (pp. 101–146). New York: Raven.

Pomerlau, A., Malcuit, G., & Sabatier, C. (1991). Child-rearing practices and parental beliefs in three cultural groups of Montreal: Quebeçois, Vietnamese, Haitian. In M. Bornstein (Ed.), *Cultural approaches to parenting* (pp. 56–68). London: Lawrence Erlbaum Associates.

Poortinga, Y. H. (1992). Towards a conceptualization of culture for psychology. In S. Iwawaki, Y. Kashima, & K. Leung (Eds.), *Innovations in cross-cultural psychology* (pp. 3–17). Lisse: Swets & Zeitlinger.

Poortinga, Y. H., Van de Vijver, F.J.R., Joe, R. C., & Van de Koppel, J.M.H. (1987). Peeling the onion called culture: A sypnosis. In Ç. Kağıtçıbaşı (Ed.), *Growth and progress in cross-cultural psychology* (pp. 22–34). Lisse: Swets & Zeitlinger.

Price-Williams, D. (1980). Toward the idea of a cultural psychology: A superordinate theme for study. *Journal of Cross-Cultural Psychology, 11,* 75–88.

Provence, S., & Naylor, A. (1983). *Working with disadvantaged parents and their children: Scientific and practice issues.* New Haven, CT: Yale University Press.

Ramey, C. T., & Campbell, F. A. (1991). Poverty, early childhood education, and academic competence: The abecedarian experiment. In A. C. Huston (Ed.), *Children in poverty: Child development and public policy* (pp. 190–221). London: Cambridge University Press.

Ramey, C. T., Yeates, K. O., & Short, E. T. (1984). The plasticity of intellectual development: Insights from preventive intervention. *Child Development, 55,* 1913–1925.

Rank, O. (1929). *The trauma of birth.* New York: Knopf.

Rank, O. (1945). *Will therapy and Truth and reality.* New York: Knopf.

Razí, Z. (1993). The myth of the immutable English family. *Past and Present: A Journal of Historical Studies, 140,* 3–44.

Rogoff, B. (1981). Schooling and the development of cognitive skills. In H. C. Triandis & A. Heron (Eds.), *Handbook of cross-cultural psychology: Vol. 4. Developmental psychology* (pp. 233–294). Boston: Allyn & Bacon.

Rogoff, B. (1990). *Apprenticeship in thinking.* New York: Oxford University Press.

Rogoff, B., Gauvain, M., & Ellis, S. (1984). Development viewed in its cultural context. In M. H. Bornstein & M. E. Lamb (Eds.), *Developmental psychology: An advanced textbook* (pp. 533–571). London: Lawrence Erlbaum Associates.

Rogoff, B., & Lave, L. (1984). *Everyday cognition: Its development in social context.* Cambridge, MA: Harvard University Press.

Rogoff, B., Mistry, J., Göncü, A., & Mosier, C. (1991). Cultural variation in the role relations of toddlers and their families. In M. H. Bornstein (Ed.), *Cultural approaches to parenting* (pp. 173–183). London: Lawrence Erlbaum Associates.

Rogoff, B., & Morelli, G. (1989). Perspectives on children's development from cultural psychology. *American Psychologist, 44*(2), 343–348.

Rohner, R. (1980). *Handbook for the study of parental acceptance and rejection* (3rd ed.) Storrs, CT: University of Connecticut.

Rohner, R. (1984). Toward a conception of culture for cross-cultural psychology. *Journal of Cross-Cultural Psychology, 15,* 111–138.

Rohner, R. P., & Pettengill, S. M. (1985). Perceived parental acceptance-rejection and parental control among Korean adolescents. *Child Development, 56,* 524–528.

Rohner, R. P., & Rohner, E. C. (1978). Unpublished research data. Center for the Study of Parental Acceptance and Rejection, University of Connecticut.

Roland, A. (1988). *In search of self in India and Japan.* Princeton, NJ: Princeton University Press.

Roopnarine, J. L., & Talukder, E. (1990). Characteristics of holding, patterns of play, and social behaviors between parents and infants in New Delhi, India. *Developmental Psychology, 26,* 667–673.

Rosen, B. C. (1962). Socialization and achievement motivation in Brazil. *American Sociological Review, 27,* 612–624.

Rotenberg, M. (1977). Alienating-individualism and reciprocal-individualism: A cross-cultural conceptualisation. *Journal of Humanistic Psychology, 3,* 3–17.

Rotter, J. B. (1966). Generalized expectancies for internal versus external control of reinforcement. *Psychological Monographs, 80,* 1–28.

Royce, J. M., Darlington, R. B., & Murray, H. W. (1983). Pooled analysis: Ginding across studies. In Consortium for Longitudional Studies, *As the twig is bent* (pp.411–460). London: Lawrence Erlbaum Associates.

Saal, C. D. (1987). Alternative forms of living and housing. In L. Shamgar-Handelman & R. Palomba (Eds.), *Alternative patterns of family life in modern societies.* Rome: Collana Monografie.

Saavedra, J. M. (1980). Effects of perceived parental warmth and control on the self-evaluation of Puerto Rican adolescent males. *Behavior Science Research, 15,* 41–45.

Sabatier, C. (1986). La mère et son bébé: Variations culturelles: Analyse critique de la littérature [Mother and her baby: Cultural variations: Critical analysis of literature]. *Journal of International Psychology, 21,* 513–553.

Sameroff, A. J., & Fiese, B. H. (1992). Family representations of development. In I. E. Sigel, A. V. McGillicuddy-DeLisi, & J. J. Goodnow (Eds.), *Parental belief systems* (pp. 347–369). Hillsdale, NJ: Lawrence Erlbaum Associates.

Sameroff, A. J., Seifer, R., Barocas, B., Zax, M., & Greenspan, S. (1987). IQ scores of 4-year-old children: Social environmental risk factors. *Pediatrics, 79,* 343–350.

Sampson, E. E. (1977). Psychology and the American ideal. *Journal of Personality and Social Psychology, 35,* 767–782.

Sampson, E. E. (1985). The decentralization of identity: Towards a revised concept of personal and social order. *American Psychologist, 40,* 1203–1211.

Sampson, E. E. (1987). Individuation and domination: Undermining the social bond. In Ç. Kağıtçıbaşı (Ed.), *Growth and progress in cross-cultural psychology* (pp. 84–93). Lisse: Swets & Zeitlinger.

Sampson, E. E. (1988). The debate on individualism: Indigenous psychologies of the individual and their role in personal and societal functioning. *American Psychologist, 43,* 15–22.

Sampson, E. E. (1989). The challenge of social change for psychology: Globalization and psychology's theory of the person. *American Psychologist, 44,* 914–921.

Santerre, R. (1973). *Pedagogie Musulmane d'Afrique noire* [Muslim schooling in black Africa]. Montréal: Les Presses de l'Université de Montréal.

Sarason, S. B. (1981). *Psychology misdirected.* New York: Free Press.

Sarason, S. B. (1988). *The making of an American psychologist: An autobiography.* San Francisco: Jossey-Bass.

Saraswathi, T. S., & Dutta, R. (1987). *Developmental psychology in India, 1975–1986: An annotated bibliography.* New Delhi: Sage.

Saraswathi, T. S., & Kaur, B. (1993). *Human development and family studies in India.* New Delhi: Sage.

Savaşir, I., & Şahin, N. (1988). *Weschler çocuk zekâ ölçeği (WISC–R)* [Weschler Intelligence Scale for Children]. Ankara: Milli Egitim Basimevi.

Savasir, I., Sezgin, N., & Erol, N. (1992). 0–6 Yaş Cocuklari icin gelişim tarama envanteri gelistirilmesi. [Devising a developmental screening inventory for 0–6 year old children]. *Türk Psikiyatri Dergisi, 3,* 33–38.

Scarr, S. (1992). Developmental theories for the 1990s. *Child development, 63,* 1–19.

Schorr, L. B. (1991). Effective programs for children growing up in concentrated poverty. In A. C. Huston (Ed.), *Children in poverty: Child development and public policy* (pp. 260–281). Cambridge, England: Cambridge University Press.

Schwartz, B. (1986). *The battle for human nature.* New York: Norton.

Schwartz, S. H. (1992). Universals in the content and structure of values: Theoretical advances and empirical tests in 20 countries. In M. Zanna (Ed.), *Advances in experimental social psychology* (Vol. 25, pp. 1–65). Orlando, FL: Academic Press.

Schwartz, S. H., & Bilsky, W. (1987). Toward a psychological structure of human values. *Journal of Personality and social Psychology, 53,* 550–562.

Schwartz, S. H., & Bilsky, W. (1990). Toward a theory of the universal content and structure of values: Extensions and cross-cultural replications. *Journal of Personality and Social Psychology, 58,* 878–891.

Schwartz, T. (1981). The acquisition of culture. *Ethos, 9,* 4–17.

Schweinhart, L. J., Barnes, H. V., Weikart, D. P., Barnett, W. S., & Epstein, A. S. (1994). *Significant Benefits: The High/Scope Perry Preschool Study Through Age 27.* Ypsilanti, MI: High/Scope Press.

Schweinhart, L. J., & Weikart, D. P. (1980). *Young children grow-up* (Monograph no. 7). Ypsilanti, MI: High/Scope Press.

Scribner, S., & Cole, M. (1981). *The psychology of literacy.* Cambridge, MA: Harvard University Press.

Segall, M. H. (1983). On the search for the independent variable in cross-cultural psychology. In S. H. Irvine & J. W. Berry (Eds.), *Human assessment and cultural factors* (pp. 127–138). New York: Plenum.

Segall, M. H. (1984). More than we need to know about culture, but are afraid not to ask. *Journal of Cross-Cultural Psychology, 15,* 153–162.

Segall, M. H. (1986). Culture and behavior: Psychology in global perspective. *Annual Review of Psychology, 37,* 523–564.

Segall, M. H., Dasen, P. R., Berry, J. W., & Poortinga, Y. H. (1990). *Human behavior in global perspective.* New York: Pergamon.

Seitz, V., & Provence, S. (1990). Caregiver-focused models of early intervention. In S. J. Meisels & J. P. Shonkoff (Eds.), *Handbook of early childhood intervention* (pp. 400–427). New York: Cambridge University Press.

Seitz, V., Rosenbaum, L. K., & Apfel, N. H. (1985). Effects of family support intervention: A 10-year follow-up. *Child Development, 56,* 376–391.

Selman, R. L. (1989). Fostering intimacy and autonomy. In W. Damon (Ed.), *Child development today and tomorrow* (pp. 409–436). San Francisco: Jossey-Bass.

Semin, R. (1975). Failure in school

Serpell, R. (1977). Strategies for investigating intelligence in its cultural context. *Quarterly Newsletter, Institute for Comparative Human Development, 3,* 11–15.

Serpell, R. (1979). How specific are perceptual skills? A cross-cultural study of pattern reproduction. *British Journal of Psychology. 70,* 365–380.

Serpell, R. (1993). *Significance of schooling.* Cambridge, England: Cambridge University Press.

Seshadri, S., & Gopaldas, T. (1989). Impact of iron supplementation on cognitive functions in preschool and school-aged children: The Indian experience. *American Journal of Clinical Nutrition,* Supplement.

Shand, N. (1985). Culture's influence in Japanese and American maternal role perception and confidence. *Psychiatry, 48,* 52–67.

Shwalb, D. W., Shwalb, B. J., & Murata, K. (1991). Individualistic striving and group dynamics of fifth and eighth grade Japanese boys. *Journal of Cross-Cultural Psychology, 22,* 347–361.

Shweder, R. A. (1984). Anthropology's romantic rebellion against the enlightenment, or there is more to the thinking than reason and evidence. In R. A. Shweder & R. A. LeVine (Eds.), *Culture theory: Essays on mind, self, and emotion.* (pp. 1–27). Cambridge: Cambridge University Press.

Shweder, R. A. (1990). Cultural psychology—What is it? In J. W. Stigler, R. A. Shweder & G. Herdt (Eds.), *Cultural psychology: Essays on comparative human development* (pp. 1–43). Cambridge, England: Cambridge University Press.

Shweder, R. A. (1991). *Thinking through cultures: Expeditions in cultural psychology.* Cambridge, MA: Harvard University Press.

Shweder, R. A., & Bourne, E. J. (1984). Does the concept of the person vary cross-culturally? In

R. A. Shweder & R. A. LeVine (Eds.), *Culture theory: Essays on mind, self and emotion* (pp. 158–199). Cambridge, England: Cambridge University Press.

Shweder, R. A., & LeVine, R. (1984). *Culture theory.* New York: Cambridge University Press.

Shweder, R. A., Mahapatra, M., & Miller, J. G. (1987). Culture and moral development. In J. Kagan & S. Lamb (Eds.), *The emergence of morality in young children* (pp. 1–90). Chicago: University of Chicago Press.

Shweder, R. A., & Sullivan, M. A. (1993). Cultural Psychology: Who needs it? *Annual Review of Psychology, 44,* 497–523.

Sigel, I. E. (1985). A conceptual analysis of beliefs. In I. E. Sigel (Ed.), *Parental belief systems* (pp. 345–371). Hillsdale, NJ: Lawrence Erlbaum Associates.

Sigel, I. E. (1992). The belief–behavior connection: A resolvable dilemma? In I. E. Sigel, A. McGillicuddy-Delisi, & J. J. Goodnow (Eds.), *Parental belief systems* (pp. 433–456). Hillsdale, NJ: Lawrence Erlbaum Associates.

Sigel, I. E., McGillicuddy-Delisi, A., & Goodnow, J. (1992). *Parental belief systems.* Hillsdale, NJ: Lawrence Erlbaum Associates.

Sigman, M., & Wachs, T. D. (1991). Structure, continuity, and nutritional correlates of caregiver behavior patterns in Kenya and Egypt. In M. H. Bornstein (Ed.), *Cultural Approaches to Parenting* (pp. 123–136). NJ: Lawrence Erlbaum Associates.

Silverman, L. H., & Weinberger, J. (1985). Mommy and I are one: Implications for psychotherapy. *American Psychologist, 40*(12), 1296–1308.

Simons, R. L., Whitbeck, L. B., Conger, R. D., & Chyi, I. W. (1991). Intergenerational transmission of harsh parenting. *Developmental Psychology, 27,* 159–171.

Sinha, D. (Ed.). (1981). *Socialization of the Indian child.* New Delhi: Naurang Rai.

Sinha, D. (1983). Cross-cultural psychology: A view from the Third World. In J. B. Deregowski, S. Dziuraviec, & R. C. Annis (Eds.), *Expiscations in cross-cultural psychology* (pp. 3–17). Lisse: Swets & Zeitlinger.

Sinha, D. (1986). *Psychology in a third world country: The Indian experience.* New Delhi: Sage.

Sinha, D. (1988). The family scenario in a developing country and its implications for mental health: The case of India. In P. R. Dasen, J. W. Berry, & N. Sartorious (Eds.), *Health and cross-cultural psychology: Toward applications* (pp. 48–70). Newbury Park, CA: Sage.

Sinha, D. (1989). Cross-cultural psychology and the process of indigenisation: A second view from the Third World. In D. M. Keats, D. M. Munro, & L. Mann (Eds.), *Heterogeneity in cross-cultural psychology* (pp. 24–40). Lisse: Swets & Zeitlinger.

Sinha, D. (1992). Appropriate indigenous psychology in India: A search for new identity. In S. Iwawaki, Y. Kashima, & K. Leung (Eds.), *Innovations in cross-cultural psychology* (pp. 38–48). Lisse: Swets & Zeitlinger.

Sinha, D., & Kao, H.S.R. (1988). *Social values and development: Asian perspectives.* Newbury Park, CA: Sage.

Sinha, D., & Tripathi, R. C. (1994). Individualism in a collectivist culture: A case of coexistence of opposites. In U. Kim, H. C. Triandis, Ç. Kağıtçıbaşı, S-C. Choi, & G. Yoon (Eds.), *Individualism and collectivism: Theory, Method and Applications* (pp. 123–136). Newbury Park, CA: Sage.

Sinha, J.B.P. (1985). Collectivism, social energy, and development in India. In I. R. Lagunes & Y. H. Poortinga (Eds.), *From a different perspective: Studies of behavior across cultures* (pp. 120–135). Lisse: Swets & Zeitlinger.

Sinha, J.B.P. (1988). Reorganizing values for development. In D. Sinha & S. R. Kao (Eds.), *Social values and development: Asian perspectives.* New Delhi: Sage.

Sinha, J.B.P. (1993). The bulk and the front of psychology in India. *Psychology and Developing Societies, 5,* 135–150.

Sinha, S. R. (1985). Maternal strategies for regulating children's behavior. *Journal of Cross Cultural Psychology, 16,* 27–40.

Slaughter, D. T. (1983). Early intervention and its effects upon maternal and child development. *Monographs of the Society for Research in Child Development, 48.*

Slaughter, D. T. (1988). Black children, schooling, and educational interventions. In D. T. Slaughter (Ed.), *Black children and poverty: A developmental perspective* (pp. 109–116). San Francisco: Jossey-Bass.

Slobin, D. I. (1972). Children and language: They learn the same way all around the world. *Psychology Today, 6,* 71–74, 82.

Smilansky, M. (1979). *Priorities in education: Preschool evidence and conclusions* (World Bank Staff Working Paper, No. 323). Washington, DC: World Bank.

Smith, M. B. (1968). Competence and socialization. In J. A. Clausen (Ed.), *Socialization and Society* (pp. 270–320). Boston: Little, Brown.

Smith, M. B. (1978). Perspectives on selfhood. *American Psychologist, 33,* 1053–1063.

Smith, M. B. (1990). Psychology in the public interest: What have we done? What can we do? *American Psychologist, 45,* 530–536.

Smith, M. B. (1991). *Values, self, and society.* New Brunswick, NJ: Transaction Publishers.

Smith, M. B. (1994). Selfhood at risk: Post-modern perils and the perils of post-modernism. *American Psychologist, 49,* 405–411.

Smith, P. B., & Bond, M. H. (1993). *Social psychology across cultures.* Hartfordshire, England: Harvester Wheatsheaf.

Smith, R. M. (1979). Kin and neighbours in a 13th-century Suffolk community. *Journal of Family History, 4,* 79089.

Snow, C. E. (1991). The theoretical basis for relationships between language and literacy in development. *Journal of Research in Childhood Education, 6,* 5–10.

Snow, C. E. (1993). Linguistic development as related to literacy. In L. Eldering & P. Leseman (Eds.), *Early intervention and culture* (pp. 133–148). Netherlands: UNESCO.

Sockalingam, S., Zeitlin, M., & Satoto, C. N. (1990). *Study to encourage positive indigenous caretaking behaviour in improving child nutrition and health.* Paper available from the Consultative Group on Early Child Care and Development, New York.

Spence, J. T. (1985). Achievement American style. *American Psychologist, 12,* 1285–1295.

Staub, S., & Green, P. (Eds.). (1992). *Psychology and social responsibility: Facing global challenges.* New York: New York University Press.

Steinberg, L., Elmen, J. D., & Mounts, N. S. (1989). Authoritative parenting, psychosocial maturity, and academic success among adolescents. *Child Development, 60,* 1424–1436.

Stevens, J. H. (1988). Social support, locus of control and parenting in three low-income groups of mothers: Black teenagers, black adults, and white adults. *Child Development, 59,* 635–642.

Stevenson, H., Azuma, H, & Hakuta, K. (Eds.). (1986). *Child development and education in Japan.* New York: Freeman.

Stigler, J. W., Shweder, R. A., & Herdt, G. (1990). *Cultural psychology.* Cambridge, England: Cambridge University Press.

Suina, J. H., & Smolkin, L. B. (1994). From natal culture to school culture to dominant society culture: Supporting transitions for Pueblo Indian students. In P. M. Greenfield & R. R. Cocking (Eds.), *Cross-cultural roots of minority child development* (pp. 115–132). Hillsdale, NJ: Lawrence Erlbaum Associates.

Sun, L. K. (1991). Contemporary Chinese culture: Structure and emotionality. *Australian Journal of Chinese Affairs, 26,* 1–41.

Super, C. M. (1981). Behavioral development in infancy. In R. H. Munroe, R. L. Munroe, & B. B. Whiting (Eds.), *Handbook of cross-cultural human development.* New York: Garland.

Super, C. M. (1983). Cultural variation in the meaning and uses of children's "intelligence". In J. Deregowski, S. Dziuraviec, & R. Annis (Eds.), *Expiscations in cross-cultural psychology* (pp. 199–212). Lisse: Swets & Zeitlinger.

Super, C. M., & Harkness, S. (1986). The developmental niche: A conceptualization at the interface of child and culture. *International Journal of Behavioral Development, 9,* 545–570.

Suvannathat, C., Bhanthumnavin, D., Bhuapirom, L., & Keats, D. M. (1985). *Handbook of Asian child development and child rearing practices.* Bangkok: Behavioral Science Research Institute.

Suzuki, T. (1984). Ways of life and social milieus in Japan and the United States: A comparative study. *Behaviormetrika, 15,* 77–108.

Swaminathan, I. (1986). *Coordinators Notebook, 2,* 16. New York: The Consultative Group on Early Childhood Care and Development.

Szapocznik, J., & Kurtines, W. M. (1993). Family psychology and cultural diversity. *American Psychologist, 48,* 400–407.

Tajfel, H. (1972). "Experiments in a vacuum." In J. Israel & H. Tajfel (Eds.), *The context of social psychology: A critical assessment* (pp. 66–119). London: Academic Press.

Taylor, C. (1989). *Sources of the self: The making of the modern identity.* Cambridge, MA: Harvard University Press.

Teasdale, G. R., & Teasdale, J. I. (1992). Culture and curriculum: Dilemmas in the schooling of Australian Aboriginal children. In S. Iwawaki, Y. Kashima, & K. Leung (Eds.), *Innovations in cross-cultural psychology* (pp. 442–457). Lisse: Swets & Zeitlinger.

Thadani, V. N. (1978). The logic of sentiment: The family and social change. *Population and Development Review, 4*(3), 457–499.

Thorton, A. (1984). Modernization and family change. In *Social change and family policies. Proceedings of the 20th International CFR Seminar.* Melbourne: Australian Institute of Family Studies.

Thorton, A., & Fricke, T. E. (1987). Social change and the family: Comparative perspectives from the West, China, and South Asia. *Sociological Forum, 2,* 746–779.

Tizard, B. (1991). Working mothers and the care of young children. In M. Woodhead, P. Light, & R. Caar (Eds.), *Growing up in a changing society* (pp. 61–77). London: Routledge & Kegan Paul.

Toennies, F. (1957). *Community and society.* (C.P. Loomis, translator) East Lansing: Michigan State Press.

Triandis, H. C. (1972). *The analysis of subjective culture.* New York: Wiley.

Triandis, H. C. (1978). Some universals of social behavior. *Personality and Social Psychology Bulletin, 4,* 1–16.

Triandis, H. C. (1988). Collectivism and individualism: A reconceptualization of a basic concept in cross-cultural psychology. In G. K. Verma & C. Bagley (Eds.), *Personality, attitudes, and cognitions* (pp. 60–95). London: Macmillan.

Triandis, H. C. (1989). The self and social behavior in differing cultural contexts. *Psychological Review, 96,* 506–520.

Triandis, H. C. (1990). Cross-cultural studies of individualism and collectivism. In J. J. Berman (Ed.), *Cross-cultural perspectives: Nebraska symposium on motivation* (pp. 41–134). Lincoln, NE: University of Nebraska Press.

Triandis, H. C. (1994). *Culture and social behavior.* New York: McGraw-Hill.

Triandis, H. C. (1995). *Individualism and collectivism.* Boulder, CO: Westview.

Triandis, H. C., Leung, K., Villareal, M. V., & Clack, F. L. (1985). Allocentric versus idiocentric tendencies: Convergent and discriminant validation. *Journal of Research in Personality, 19,* 395–415.

Triandis, H. C., Malpass, R., & Davidson, A. R. (1973). Psychology and culture. *Annual Review of Psychology, 24,* 355–378.

Triandis, H. C., McCusker, C., & Hui, C. H. (1990). Multimethod probes of individualism and collectivism. *Journal of Personality and Social Psychology, 59,* 1006–1020.

Trickett, P. K., & Susman, E. J. (1988). Parental perceptions of childrearing practices in physically abusive and nonabusive families. *Developmental Psychology, 24,* 270–276.

Tripathi, R. C. (1988). Aligning development to values in India. In D. Sinha & H.S.R. Kao (Eds.), *Social values and development* (pp. 315–333). Newburg Park, CA: Sage.

Trommsdorf, G. (1985). Some comparative aspects of socialization in Japan and Germany. In I. R.

Lagunes & Y. H. Poortinga (Eds.), *From a different perspective: Studies of behavior across cultures* (pp. 231–240). Lisse: Swets & Zeitlinger.

UNESCO (1982). *Different theories and practices of development.* Paris: UNESCO.

UNESCO (1991). *World education report.* Paris: UNESCO.

UNICEF (1991). *The state of the world's children.* New York: UNICEF.

UNICEF/India (1988). *Annual Report.* New Delhi: UNICEF.

Valsiner, J. (1989). *Child development in cultural context.* Toronto: Hogrefe.

Van de Vijver, F.J.R., & Hutschemaekers, G.J.M. (Eds.). (1990). *The investigation of culture.* Netherlands: Tilburg University Press.

Van de Vijver, F.J.R., & Poortinga, Y. H. (1990). A taxonomy of cultural differences. In J. R. van de Vijver & G.J.M. Hutschemaekers (Eds.), *The investigation of culture: Current issues in cultural psychology* (pp. 91–114). Tilburg: Tilburg.

Vannoy, D. (1991). Social differentiation, contemporary marriage, and human development. *Journal of Family Issues, 12,* 251–267.

Van Oudenhoven, N. (1989). Children at risk and community response. *Notes, Comments* (No. 187). UNESCO.

Verhoeven, L., Rood, v. P., & v. d. Laan, C. (Eds.). (1991). *Attaining functional literacy: A cross-cultural perspective.* The Hague: UNESCO.

Von Bertalanffy, L. (1933). *Modern theories of development.* London: Oxford University Press.

Vygotsky, L. S. (1962). *Thought and language.* Cambridge, MA: MIT Press.

Vygotsky, L. S. (1978). *Mind in society: The development of higher psychological processes.* Cambridge, MA: Harvard University Press.

Wachs, T. D. (1987). Specificity of environmental action as manifested in environmental correlates of infant's mastery motivation. *Development Psychology, 23,* 782–790.

Wachs, T. D. (1993). Determinants of intellectual development: Single determinant research in a multideterminant universe. *Intelligence, 17,* 1–10.

Wachs, T. D., & Gruen, G. (1982). *Early experience and human development.* New York: Wiley.

Wagner, D. A. (Ed.). (1983). *Child development and international development: Research-policy interfaces.* San Francisco: Jossey-Bass.

Wagner, D. A. (Ed.). (1986). Child development research and the Third World. *American Psychologist, 41,* 298–301.

Wagner, D. A. (1988). Appropriate education and literacy in the Third World. In P. R. Dasen, J. W. Berry, & N. Sartorious (Eds.), *Health and cross-cultural psychology* (pp. 93–111). Newbury Park, CA: Sage.

Wagner, D. A., & Spratt, J. E. (1987). Cognitive consequences of contrasting pedagogies: The effects of Quranic preschooling in Morocco. *Child Development, 58,* 1207–1219.

Wagner, D. A., & Stevenson, H. W. (Eds.). (1982). *Cultural perspectives on child development.* San Francisco: Freeman.

Wallach, M. A., & Wallach, L. (1983). *Psychology's sanction for selfishness: The error of egoism in theory and therapy.* New York: Freeman.

Wallach, M. A., & Wallach, L. (1990). *Rethinking goodness.* Albany, NY: State University of New York Press.

Washington, V. (1988). Historical and contemporary linkages between black child development and social policy. In D. T. Slaughter (Ed.), *Black children and poverty: A developmental perspective* (pp. 934–108). San Francisco: Jossey-Bass.

Wassik, B. H., Ramey, C. T., Bryant, D. M., & Sparling, J. J. (1990). A longitudinal study of two early intervention strategies: Project care. *Child Development, 61,* 1682–1696.

Weber, M. (1958). *The Protestant ethic and the spirit of capitalism* (Talcott Parsons, Trans.). New York: Charles Scribner's Sons.

Weil, S. (1987). Proximal households as alternatives to joint families in Israel. In L. Shamgar-

Handelman & R. Palomba (Eds.), *Alternative patterns of family life in modern societies*. Rome: Collana Monografie.

Weiss, H. B. (1988). Family support and education programs: Working through ecological theories of human development. In H. B. Weiss & F. H. Jacobs (Eds.), *Evaluating family programs* (pp. 3–36). New York: Aldine.

Weiss, H. B., & Jacobs, F. H. (1988). Family support and education programs: challenges and opportunities. In H. B. Weiss & F. H. Jacobs (Eds.), *Evaluating family programs* (pp. xix–xxix). New York: Aldine.

Weisz, J. R., Rothbaum, F. M., & Blackburn, T. C. (1984). Standing out and standing in. *American Psychologist, 39*, 955–969.

Werner, E. E. (1979). *Cross-cultural child development: A view from the planet Earth*. Monterey, CA: Brooks/Cole.

Werner, E. E., & Smith, R. S. (1982). *Vulnerable but invincible*. New York: McGraw-Hill.

Westen, D. (1985). *Self and society*. Cambridge, England: Cambridge University Press.

White, G., & Kirkpatrick, J. (Eds.). (1985). *Person, self, and experience: Exploring Pacific ethnopsychologies*. Berkeley: University of California Press.

Whiting, B. B. (Ed.). (1963). *Six cultures: Studies in child rearing*. New York: Wiley.

Whiting, B. B. (1976). The problem of the packaged variable. In K. Riegel & J. Meacham (Eds.), *The developing individual in a changing world* (Vol. 1, pp. 303–309). The Hague: Mouton.

Whiting, B. B., & Whiting J. W. (1975). *Children of six cultures: A psychocultural analysis*. Cambridge, MA: Harvard University Press.

Whiting J. W., & Child, I. (1953). *Child training and personality*. New Haven, CT: Yale University Press.

Whiting J. W. (1974). A model for psychocultural research. *Annual Report*. Washington, DC: American Anthropological Association.

Witkin, H., & Berry, J. W. (1975). Psychological differentiation in cross-cultural perspective. *Journal of Cross-Cultural Psychology, 6*, 4–87.

Wober, M. (1974). Towards an understanding of the Kiganda concept of intelligence. In J. W. Berry & P. Dasen (Eds.), *Culture and cognition* (pp. 119–128). London: Methuen.

Woodhead, M. (1985). Pre-school education has long term effects: But can they be generalized? *Oxford Review of Education, 11*(2), 133–155.

Woodhead, M. (1988). When psychology informs public policy. *American Psychologist, 43*, 443–454.

Woodhead, M. (1991). Psychology and the cultural construction of children's needs. In M. Woodhead, P., Light, & R. Carr (Eds.), *Growing up in a changing society* (pp. 37–57). London: Routledge & Kegan Paul.

Woodhead, M., Light, R. C., & Carr, R. (Eds.). (1991). *Growing up in a changing society*. London: Routledge & Kegan Paul.

World Bank (1988). *Education in Sub-Saharan Africa, policies for adjustment, revitalization, and expansion*. Washington, DC: World Bank.

World Bank (1993). *Best practices in addressing micronutrient malnutrition*. Washington, DC: World Bank Population, Health and Nutrition Department.

World Health Organization (1986). *Protocols for the development and field testing of techniques for monitoring physical growth and psychosocial development*. (WHO/MCH/MNH/86.1). Geneva, Switzerland: WHO.

World Health Organization (1990). [Progress report on the activities of physical growth and psychosocial development (September 1988-April 1990)]. Programme of Maternal and Child Health, WHO, Geneva, Switzerland.

Yamaguchi, E. (1985). *Culture and experience*. Philadelphia: University of Pennsylvania Press.

Yang, C. F. (1988). Familism and development: An examination of the role of family in contemporary China Mainland, Hong Kong, and Taiwan. In D. Sinha & H.S.R. Kao (Eds.), *Social values and development: Asian perspectives* (pp. 93–123). London: Sage.

Yang, K-S. (1986). Chinese personality and its change. In M. H. Bond (Ed.), *The psychology of the Chinese people* (pp. 106–170). New York: Oxford University Press.

Yang, K-S. (1988). Will societal modernization eventually eliminate cross-cultural psychological differences? In M. H. Bond (Ed.), *The cross-cultural challenge to social psychology* (pp. 67–85). London: Sage.

Young, M. E. (1993). *Integrated child development—Challenges and opportunities.* Report prepared for the World Bank.

Young, N. (1992). Postmodern self-psychology mirrored in science and the arts. In S. Kvale (Ed.), *Psychology and postmodernism* (pp. 135–145). London: Sage.

Yu, A-B., & Yang, K-S. (1994). The Nature of achievement motivation in collectivistic societies. In U. Kim, H. C. Triandis, Ç. Kağıtçıbaşı, S-C. Choi, & G. Yoon (Eds.), *Individualism and collectivism: Theory, method, and applications* (pp. 239–250). Newbury Park, CA: Sage.

Zeitlin, M. (1991). Nutritional resilience in a hostile environment: Positive deviance in child nutrition. *Nutrition Review, 49*(9), 259–268.

Zeitlin, M., Ghassemi, H., & Mansour, M. (1990). *Positive deviance in child nutrition, with emphasis on psychosocial and behavioral aspects and implications for development.* Tokyo: United Nations University.

Zelizer, V. A. (1981). *Pricing the priceless child.* New York: Basic Books.

Zigler, E., & Berman, W. (1983). Discerning the future of early childhood intervention. *American Psychologist, 38,* 894–906.

Zigler, E., & Styfco, S. J. (1994). Head Start: Criticism in a constructive context. *American Psychologist, 49,* 127–132.

Zigler, E., & Weiss, H. (1985). Family support systems: an ecological approach to child development. In R. Rapaport (Ed.), *Children, youth, and families: The action-research relationship* (pp. 166–205). Cambridge, England: Cambridge University Press.

Zimmerman, B. J., & Rosenthal, T. L. (1974). Observational learning of rule-governed behavior by children. *Psychological Bulletin, 81,* 29–42.

Author Index

Subject Index

P 60
63
66